# THE INSPIRE CODE

Saša Mirković

With Christin Schaaf



Published by Game Changer Publishing

Paperback ISBN: 979-8-90158-209-1

Hardcover ISBN: 979-8-90158-165-0

Digital ISBN: 979-8-90158-147-6

www.GameChangerPublishing.com

***For Laura, Oscar, Stella, and Kosta***

*The Mirković Five is the most important self-leading team*
*I will ever be part of. Everything in this book started here—*
*at our table, in our chaos, in our love.*
*I love you.*

The Nudge

My Weekly Newsletter.

Every Wednesday.
Two minute read.

**SCAN BELOW TO JOIN**

# THE INSPIRE CODE

## HOW TO BUILD SELF-LEADING TEAMS IN THE MIDST OF CHAOS

SAŠA MIRKOVIĆ

*with Christin Schaaf*

# THE INSPIRE CODE

How to Build Self-Leading Teams in the Midst of Chaos

---

SAŠA MIRKOVIĆ

with

CHRISTIN SCHAAF

# Foreword

I almost didn't sit next to him.

I was one of the first people on the bus, a luxury coach taking us from the hotel to the evening event at a work conference. I found a seat in the front row, window-side. Classic introvert move. I was settled in, looking out the window, perfectly content to ride in peace.

Then I heard it.

"Is this seat taken?"

I looked up. A big bear of a man was standing in the aisle looking down at me with what I wasn't sure was a question or a statement.

I said, "No, it's all yours." He sat down, extended his hand, and said, "Saša Mirković."

Over the next thirty minutes, he proceeded to pepper me with questions. Not small talk. Not pleasantries. Real questions. Curious, searching, substantive questions. When we finally pulled up to the venue, and he stood to get off the bus, I remember thinking two things.

First, *I really enjoyed that.*

Second, *I'm going to keep an eye on this guy's career.*

I knew nothing about Saša's story at that point. Nothing about Bosnia. Nothing about the war. Nothing about what it took for him to get on that bus, in that country, at that conference, sitting next to me. The book you're holding will fill in all of those details far better than I ever could.

What I can tell you is what I saw in those thirty minutes: energy, passion, curiosity, and courage. I was an executive at that company. He didn't know me. He just sat down, offered a compliment, and started asking questions. That kind of courage isn't common. I noticed it immediately.

What I've watched happen since that bus ride is nothing short of remarkable.

I've been an executive coach for a long time. I've worked with a lot of leaders. Most of them are good people with good intentions who get stuck in the same patterns working *in* the business instead of *on* it, developing themselves while their team stagnates, becoming the only engine on the plane. They're not failing. They're just not growing.

Saša has grown.

There's a difference between a good idea and a best practice. A good idea looks right on paper. You read it, you nod, you say, "I get this." A best practice is something people have actually used (successfully) over a long period of time. What Saša is going to share with you in this book are best practices. Hard-won ones. Forged in places most leadership books never go.

As a coach, I teach something called the "70-20-10" of adult learning and growing.

Seventy percent of how adults learn and grow is through experience. You have to go do it. Live it. Make the mistakes. Feel the weight of the decisions. Twenty percent comes from a coach or a mentor. And ten percent comes from books, classes, podcasts, and the resources you consume.

What I love about the way Saša has built this book is that he applies all three in the same space. He pulls you in with a story or an analogy; he shares his experience with you, making you feel something real. However, because it is not your experience, it is only the ten percent. A story and/or analogy that you have consumed. Then he gives you what he calls a shoulder tap, a moment where he turns to you and says, "Here's what I just taught you." And at the end of each chapter, he recaps all the shoulder taps, all the key learnings. Then he teases you into the next chapter, connecting this learning to the next one.

This is an expert coach or mentor conducting the twenty percent. He's not just writing a book. He's coaching you through one.

In the end, he gets you to go do it. Go integrate these learnings into your own business. The seventy percent.

When I was a kid, my favorite dessert was “chocolate chocolate” cake. My mom made it for my birthday every year, “chocolate chocolate” cake, and it was so rich, so good, that you could only eat one piece. She'd let me have two on my birthday because it was a special day.

That's what this book is.

It is a rich chocolate cake. You do not want to eat it all in one sitting. There is too much here. Too much good. If you try to consume it all at once and implement everything at once, you'll overwhelm yourself, and you'll miss the point.

One piece at a time.

Here's the other thing about that birthday cake: it was meant to be shared. My mom made it for the whole table. My brothers, my sister, my friends, and I all sat around and ate together. And here's what I want you to understand before you turn to page one.

This book is not just for the founder. It is not just for the person whose name is on the door. If you develop only the leader at the top, you've still got one engine on the plane. And one engine is a problem when the turbulence hits or the engine goes out.

This book is for your team. Your leaders. The people you're asking to grow with you. Share it with them. Eat the cake together.

I'll be honest with you. I've watched Saša struggle with some of the things in these pages. I watched him work through them in real time, making the mistakes, paying what he calls the "dumb tax," recalibrating, and trying again.

At some point in the last few years, something shifted. I found myself in a conversation with him where I realized I was learning more from him than he was learning from me.

That's not something I say lightly. But it's the truth. And it's the whole point.

Leaders who are doing this right, really doing it right, eventually create something that grows without them. Teams that don't need to be managed because they've learned to lead themselves. A culture that holds its shape even when the founder steps back.

That's what Saša has built. And this book is his attempt to show you how to build it too.

Enjoy the book.

Actually, enjoy the cake.

— Ray Kelly

Senior Vice President, Executive Coach, Think2Perform

# Contents

# Prologue

May 27, 1992. Sarajevo.

I was walking down Vase Miskina Street with my friend Čajo when the world exploded.

One second, I'm thinking about bread. Next, I can't see. Can't hear. The whole street is covered in fog—except it's not fog. It's dust and smoke and something else. Something that smells like what happens when a mortar round lands in a crowd of people waiting in line to buy food.

The Breadline Massacre. That's what they'd call it later. Twenty-two people were killed and more than a hundred wounded—Čajo and I were not among them.

We ran and found a doorway in a nearby building. Čajo went back toward where we'd come from. I went the other direction.

Toward the blast.

---

I DON'T KNOW why I walked toward it. I've thought about that moment a thousand times since, and I still can't give you a clean answer.

Part of me was running calculations. *I'm A-positive. They need blood. The hospital is in that direction. Cover and move—stay close to walls, minimize exposure, take an opportunity, run, take cover, run, take cover.* Military training kicked in before conscious thought could catch up. That was one part of me. The part that had trained for this. That knew cover and distance and blood type and which direction the hospital was.

But another part of me wasn't thinking at all. It just *moved.* Something below words, below reason—a current pulling me forward because standing still wasn't possible. Not after what I'd just seen. Not after smelling what a massacre smells like. Below the training. Below the thinking. That part didn't need orders.

That was a different brain entirely.

I didn't have language for this yet. That would come years later, when I discovered Ceri Evans' work with the New Zealand All Blacks and finally understood what I'd been doing my whole life without knowing it.

Blue brain. Red brain. One calculates. One feels. One maps the problem, and the other already knows the answer before the map is finished.

Two systems. Running simultaneously. Sometimes fighting each other. Sometimes, saving your life.

---

I WAS one of the first people there.

I remember the quiet more than anything. A street full of people thirty seconds ago. Now, just dust settling. There are pictures of what that looked like. I don't want to go into details here.

Total shock. Disbelief. That particular kind of rage that sits in your chest like a hot stone. *I can't fucking believe we're going to be this stupid. I need to do something about it.*

I gave blood. I learned the military was pulling out, under some agreement between Bosnian authorities and Serbian forces. I walked home covered in other people's blood. My mother had sent me out for bread. She thought I was dead.

By 8 p.m. I was at Alma's apartment—she was a painter, and her place had cover from sniper fire—and I was shit-faced. Numb. The shock and the alcohol doing what they do when your nervous system can't process what you've witnessed.

But I was scheduled for neighborhood barricade duty. So I started washing off.

That's when they started bombing my neighborhood.

---

RATKO MLADIĆ HAD BEEN NAMED commander of Serbian forces. The radio had mentioned this young general. "Pretty terrible," someone said.

The military withdrawal wasn't a retreat. It was repositioning. Clearing their own people so Mladić could, in his own words, "bomb them out of their minds."

A rocket hit the building behind mine. Two girls were killed. I didn't know them. I had not seen them before that night. I was one of the guys who went in.

It ended with me carrying a woman—maybe twenty-five, twenty-six years old—out of the rubble. She died in my hands.

I don't remember how I got home that night. I don't remember the next couple of days.

---

HERE'S what I do remember: At some point, the fog cleared. Not the smoke in the streets—that would hang over Sarajevo for years—but the fog in my head.

And when it lifted, there was only one thought: *How do you live after something like this?*

The answer came from the same place that walked me toward the blast. Not logic. Not strategy. Something that had been there the whole time.

*I'm going to fight these fuckers for the rest of my life. And those fuckers are everywhere.*

That sounds like rage talking. And it was, partly. But rage burns out. Rage is fuel that consumes itself.

What stayed was something different. A recognition.

There are people in this world who destroy. And there are people who build. There are people who create chaos, and there are people who create order within it.

I needed to be on the side of good. Not just survive. Not just escape. *Build.* Build teams. Build systems. Build something that could hold together when everything else was falling apart.

That decision required both brains.

The blue brain. Chaos can be defeated with order. Discipline creates freedom. The unglamorous work of getting the right resources to the right place—that's what keeps people alive when the world is trying to kill them.

The red brain. This isn't about efficiency. It's about people. It's about choosing who you want to be when the worst of human nature is on full display. It's about love—unreasonable, illogical, stubborn love for strangers you'll never meet and teammates who are counting on you.

Two brains, working together. Neither one is sufficient alone.

---

I DIDN'T KNOW it then, but that day, May 27, 1992, was the beginning of everything that followed.

The teams I would build. The businesses I would grow. The leaders I would develop. The framework I would eventually call Elite Leadership.

It all traces back to a morning when I walked toward an explosion instead of away from it and discovered that the leader I would become required both the engineer and the human. The calculator and the feeler. The strategist and the servant.

You need to understand where these two brains came from.

That story starts in Zenica, a socialist experiment of a city built around a steel mill, where a boy with a practical-realist mother and a charming-salesman father learned to code-switch between logic and heart without ever knowing he was doing it.

It starts with character.

# ACT I
# The Leader

## INTRODUCTION

When I start a new book, I read the last page first.

I want to know if I like the ending before I commit to the journey.

So I'm going to do you a favor. Here's the ending.

I am a private wealth advisor and Certified Financial Planner (CFP). I lead one of the top one percent wealth teams at Ameriprise Financial, one of the best in New York state. I've been inducted into the Ameriprise Hall of Fame and sit on the Chairman's Advisory Council. Last year, I received the Ameriprise Outstanding Leader Award.

Our company has been named one of the best places to work in the Capital District. We've grown ten times (10X) in the last ten years. I went from owning one hundred percent of a business I couldn't escape to owning thirty-eight percent of a business that runs without me—and my personal stake tripled in value.

I have seven business partners who chose to be here. Team members send me random texts that just say "*Thank you.*"

That's the ending.

If you like it, keep reading. If you don't, put this book down and go find another one. No hard feelings.

But here's what you need to know: The beginning didn't look like this.

I survived a war. I rebuilt my life in a country where I knew no one. I started a business from scratch. And I almost destroyed it.

Not the market. Not the competition. Me.

---

December 2014. Four days after my first hip surgery.

I'm sitting in my recliner, surrounded by flowers and gift baskets from my coaching clients. The people who pay me to help them become better leaders are checking in. Sending cards. Texting to see how I'm doing.

My own team? The people I pay? Silence.

Then my business partner texts. He's coming over, bringing Starbucks.

He walks in with coffee, makes small talk, and then pulls out his iPad.

My stomach drops.

I know what that iPad means. I teach leaders to use the Whole Message model when they need to deliver tough love. Write it out. Read it aloud.

I've taught it hundreds of times. I've received it before. But four days after surgery, still foggy from painkillers, I didn't see it coming.

He reads, "You change things constantly. The team is frustrated. Demoralized. You're impossible to work for. It's falling apart. And it's your fault."

I'm sitting there, hip throbbing, coffee going cold, hearing that everything I built is crumbling.

Because of me.

The worst part? He was right.

The team was miserable. And if I'm honest, so was I.

First, I got angry. How dare he come into my house four days after surgery and ambush me with this? Then I got sad. The kind that sits in your chest and doesn't move. Then I blamed everyone else. The team. The market. The timing. Anyone but the guy in the recliner.

Eventually, I ran out of places to point.

I landed somewhere quiet. Somewhere honest.

I had a choice: keep defending the leader I'd been, or become the leader they needed.

If I wanted things to change, I had to change first.

So I changed.

For me, that means getting on my bike. Or getting in the car—back then I was driving between offices constantly. I don't sit with a problem. I move with it. English is my second language, so I listen to books. Reading while driving is frowned upon.

I went through everything I could find on elite teams. The New Zealand All Blacks. Navy SEALs. Championship organizations across every industry. I paid attention to what worked and what didn't. I looked for what I could pull out and try on my own team. Not a philosophy. A specific move.

And something clicked.

I realized I had been on elite teams before—Rugby. Military. Theatre ensembles where everyone breathed as one. I knew what it felt like to be part of something bigger than myself, that electricity when a group of people commits fully to each other.

I wanted that again. But this time, I couldn't just show up and be part of it. I had to build it. I had to figure out how to create the conditions for that kind of team and lead from the front.

So I built my own playbook.

Not theory. Not someone else's framework with a new label slapped on it. My own definition of leadership. My own understanding of what it actually takes to build a self-leading team.

I tested it. I failed. I adjusted. I tested again.

And something started to shift.

When I transformed, my team transformed.

Not because I told them to. Not because I pushed harder. Because I became someone worth following.

I stopped playing chess master—moving pieces, controlling outcomes, wondering why nobody cared about winning as much as I did.

I became a gardener instead.

Gardeners don't force things to grow. They create the conditions. They tend. They trust the process. They understand that the plant has its own talent and unique genius. The leaders' job is to get out of the way of it while making sure it has everything it needs.

That shift sounds simple. It wasn't. Chess masters don't give up the board easily.

And somewhere along the way, I stopped seeing my team as "the people I pay." They became the people I invest in. The people I grow with. The people who choose, every single day, to build something alongside me.

When I changed how I led, they changed how they showed up.

---

What you're holding is the playbook.

In the pages that follow, I'll show you where I came from and what forged me. You'll see the transformation—mine and my team's—up close.

And in the final act, I'll hand you the tools, the frameworks, the practical steps—everything I learned so you can build your own self-leading team without paying the "dumb tax" I paid.

I did the work, so you don't have to start from scratch.

People have been telling me to write this book for years. They found my story fascinating. Inspirational, even.

But I kept putting it off. I didn't know if I had the right to write it.

I was looking at it all wrong.

I don't have the right. I have the duty.

I reject scarcity. I embrace abundance. I believe we are here to make each other better. And I know I'm not the only one who's been stuck in what I call the "Founder's Foxhole."

You built this thing. Poured your life into it. You succeeded more than you failed. You're still here.

And I know something else about you.

You're not the founder who takes the private equity check and walks away, leaving the business in shambles. That's not who you are. You made promises. You have integrity. You want to leave things better than you found them.

So you keep solving problems. Keep growing. Keep making an impact. Because this thing has your fingerprints all over it, and it matters to you that it matters.

But here's the trap.

I'm a financial planner. I run these numbers for clients. How much wealth is locked inside the business? What would it take to close the gap? What does exit actually look like when you strip away the rose-colored glasses?

I ran the numbers on my own business to get my own answers...

The answers weren't comfortable.

Most of my wealth was sitting inside a business that couldn't run without me. If anything happened—if I burned out, if the market turned, if I just wanted out—I had little to show for it. The business was valuable. I was trapped inside it.

I had to de-risk the business. To do that, two things had to happen.

I had to build a team that clients would trust—not as a replacement for me, but as an upgrade. And I had to get out of the way enough for my team to actually function without me holding everything together. Me.

That meant my leadership had to take a new shape.

I had to become a leader who develops leaders. A leader who empowers people to show up in their own genius. A leader who helps the garden grow even when I'm not in it.

---

I wrote this book for three kinds of people.

**The founder who's stuck where I was stuck**. You've hit real milestones, but you're realizing the habits that built this business are now the chains keeping you from the next level. There's a path through. I walked it. These pages will show you how.

**The next-gen owner**. Your job is not to become a copy of the founder. Your job is to help your founder cross the chasm. She will have doubts. He will have fears. Your words and actions should be building trust and deepening it so the founder can hand over control, knowing the mission is safe. You're not just there to receive. You're there to make the founder and the team better.

**A team member who isn't an owner yet**. You define the limits of your own potential. Not the company. You. This book will show you how to add so much value that the owners find themselves in an uncomfortable position where they have to keep paying you more because the business with you is significantly better than without you. Be coachable. Act like an owner before anyone gives you the title.

---

I didn't build this alone. Every principle in this book was tested, broken, rebuilt, and proven by real people on real teams who chose to show up every day and build something bigger than themselves.

The Inspire Code is what I call everything that follows. Not a formula. It's the operating system I built from thirty years of leading under pressure—in war, in business, and in every hard room in between. Blue brain and red brain. Engineering and heart. The discipline to build systems and the humanity to make people want to be part of them. That's the Code.

The Code is not a checklist. It's not a sequence you complete and move on from. It's a system you run all at once—working on yourself, building your team, and growing the business at the same time. This book organizes that work into three acts to make it readable. But in real life, all three are always happening.

That's what the Inspire Network is. Not a program. Not a course. A tribe of people who believe that elite leadership is learnable, that self-leading teams are buildable, and that the best investment you'll ever make is in the people around you.

If you're ready to stop playing chess master and start building your garden, we're here.

Come find your tribe.

Godspeed.

Now let me show you where it all started.

# ONE

# Character

## THE OPERATING SYSTEM YOU DIDN'T CHOOSE

My mother vacuumed like she was punishing the carpet.

I was maybe ten years old, trying to help. Running the vacuum across the living room floor of our apartment in Zenica, feeling pretty good about myself. Contributing. Being useful.

She followed behind me. Arms crossed. Eyes on the floor.

"You missed a spot."

I went back over it.

"There. You missed another one."

I got that one too.

"And there."

This is how it went. Every time. It didn't matter if it was vacuuming or homework or how I set the table. Nothing was ever finished. Nothing was ever good enough. There was always a spot I missed.

She was what Dan Sullivan would later call an "in-the-gap" person, always pointing to the distance between where you were and where you should be and never letting you rest in what you'd accomplished.

She was installing something in me. Writing code that would run underneath everything I did for the rest of my life.

I didn't know it then. I didn't have language for any of it. I just knew that nothing I did was ever quite finished.

That's the thing about character. It doesn't announce itself. It just runs.

**Shoulder Tap:** Standards matter. The gap between where you are and where you could be is where growth lives. She wasn't punishing me. She was teaching me to see potential—mine and everyone else's.

My father worked a room like he was born in it.

He'd walk into a gathering, any gathering, and within ten minutes, he was everybody's friend. Handshakes. Laughter. The kind of charm that made people feel like they were the only person in the world.

He was a salesman, then a politician. Two jobs that reward the same skill: making people like you fast.

I watched him do it hundreds of times. The way he'd lean in when someone talked. The way he remembered names, details, the things you mentioned last time. The way he made connection look effortless.

He was the youngest son in his family. His mother and youngest sister looked up to him like the second coming. When you combine that with political success—people removing obstacles for you, telling you yes, treating you like you matter—something happens to a person. His unreasonable self-confidence, which I inherited, could tip into ego when left unchecked.

That's where Mom came in. She was his counterbalance. The one who kept him grounded when the political world tried to convince him he was more important than he was. She'd push back on the hoopla and remind him what was real. They needed each other for that.

He was installing something in me, too. A different kind of code.

**Shoulder Tap:** Connection is gravity. It pulls people toward you. But gravity without grounding becomes performance. You need someone who will tell you the truth.

## TWO BRAINS, ONE TABLE

Two parents. Two operating systems.

Mom was the engineer. Logical. Blue brain. Relentless. Standards that never lowered. She saw the world in terms of problems to solve and gaps to close. If it wasn't a hundred percent, it wasn't done.

Dad was the connector. Emotional. Red brain. Magnetic. He saw the world in terms of people to meet and relationships to build. He never forgot his roots, even as his career climbed. People who worked for him respected him. People who knew him loved him.

Decades later, I'd read Ceri Evans' *Perform Under Pressure*—the book that helped transform the New Zealand All Blacks into the most dominant team in rugby history—and finally found the words: "blue brain" and "red brain." The logical mind and the emotional mind. The engineering brain and the relationship brain.

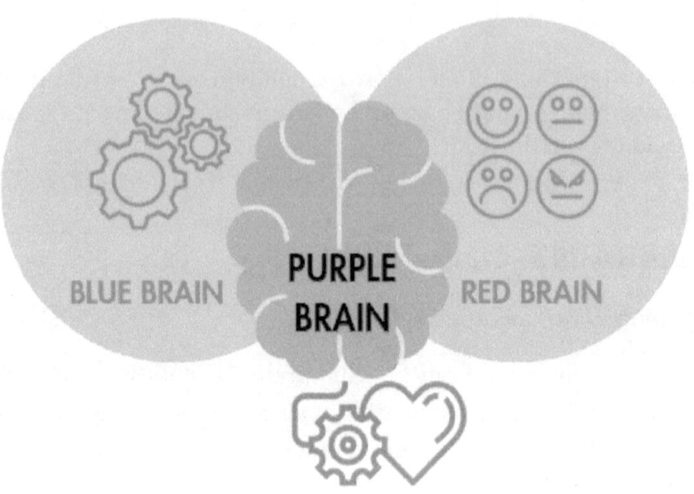


But the words came later. The education came first. I learned it at the dinner table. I learned it by watching two people who loved each other install completely different software into the same kid.

Here's what I've come to understand, looking back from forty years of distance: they were yin and yang. Perfectly suited for each other. My mom's side of the family loved my dad. My dad's side of the family adored my mother. They complemented each other in ways that made both of them better.

They just had a terrible time expressing it.

**Shoulder Tap:** You inherit more than you realize. The question isn't whether your parents shaped you—they did. The question is whether you'll examine what they gave you and decide what serves you and what doesn't.

## THE CONTRADICTION

My parents provided unconditional love and support for my sister and me. There was never a question about that. But their communication with each other was a disaster.

They would spend months without talking to each other. Sleeping in the same bed. Walking past each other in the apartment. Silence thick enough to choke on.

We didn't live in a house. We lived in an apartment building. When you have two parents who aren't speaking to each other, and they're both home, there's a pressure that fills every room. No escape. No space to breathe.

I was the oldest and understood this first, so I became the one they both talked to. Their grievances, their frustrations, their side of the story, aired to me as their child. I was stuck in between, translating one brain to the other without knowing that's what I was doing.

I got to a point where I said to each of them, separately, "You two should get a divorce."

They both had the same answer. Word for word.

"We can't do that."

"Why not?"

"Because of you and your sister. We have a duty and a mission to help you become the best people you can be."

At the time, I didn't understand what I understand now. When you are a parent, there is no greater mission than raising your children. They stayed together not out of weakness but out of commitment to something bigger than their own frustrations.

I remember a Saturday brunch in Zagreb in 1994. I was about to fly to Paris on a business trip for Catholic Relief Services, fundraising across France. I was also in the middle of a relationship that wasn't working, and I wanted my dad's perspective.

I described the relationship to him. Asked him to please not interrupt until I finished. I wanted someone else's confirmation on what I was already suspecting.

When I finished, his first words were: "Wow. You know, your mother and I loved each other."

That opened something. I asked him why they were the way they were—the silence, the months of not talking.

"I don't know," he said. "I just didn't know how to respond to things. I loved your mother. She was the love of my life."

And I knew she loved him. But the way they expressed it was just different. Strange. Hard to read from the outside.

No family unit is perfect. But looking back, I was one of the lucky ones. Two parents. A product of both of them. They could judge each other behind closed doors, but they were always united when it came to us.

**Shoulder Tap:** Mission holds people together when communication fails. My parents couldn't figure out how to talk to each other, but they never lost sight of why they were there. Leaders who anchor a mission can survive almost anything.

## THE CITY THAT BUILT US

Zenica wasn't a normal city. It was an experiment.

Yugoslavia, after World War II, needed steel. Lots of it. So they built a city around a mill. *Željezara*—the ironworks—and everything that fed it. Jobs, housing, schools, hospitals. People poured in from everywhere. The whole place was one giant construction site for decades.

My father rode that wave. The city was growing, and he grew with it. By the time I was twelve, he was mayor.

We moved from our old five-story building to a new fifteen-story high-rise. Bigger apartment. Bigger playground. Ten buildings in the complex—people constantly moving in, moving up, moving out.

The difference hit me on the soccer field. In the old building, we barely had enough kids to fill a team. In the new complex, we had enough for multiple teams. We ran tournaments. The scale of everything changed overnight.

The whole city was one big sociological experiment. And I was growing up in the middle of it, absorbing everything. Watching how systems worked. Watching how people navigated them.

> **Shoulder Tap:** Environment shapes opportunity. The same kid in a different context becomes a different person. Leaders pay attention to the environments they create because those environments are writing code into everyone who works there.

## A BRAND OF SOCIALISM

I should explain something about where I came from.

I grew up in a socialist community. Not communism—we knew that was utopia, an idea that couldn't survive contact with actual humans. In our version of socialism, everyone was treated equally, at least on paper. The state provided. The collective mattered.

My parents had more than the average person. Both worked. Both achieved. We didn't starve. We had everything we needed, within reason.

But that came with expectations. It was built into us to be responsible with money. You could lose it. And it was irresponsible—bad taste—to show off or shove your material possessions in other people's faces.

Humility was a brand of character my parents instilled in my sister and me. Not automatic. Not natural. Learned. Developed. Practiced until it became reflex.

I remember wanting a bicycle. Other kids in the neighborhood had them. I asked my parents.

"We don't have the money for a bicycle right now."

"How do they have money for a bicycle?"

It wasn't really about money. It was delayed gratification. You have to earn it.

I eventually got a bicycle. Not the top-of-the-line model, but a good one. Because when my dad wanted to buy the cheapest option, my mom would push back: "You can't afford to buy cheap stuff." And he would agree.

> **Shoulder Tap:** Humility isn't weakness. Not being too big to get small things done. Not shoving your success in other people's faces. It's developed. Learned through repetition. Practice until it becomes who you are.

## THE TWENTY PERCENT RULE

I'd been making money since I was twelve. Not a lot, but enough. Acting in movies. Performing in the National Theatre. Radio shows. Commercials. I had earnings before most kids had chores.

But my mom didn't take a serious interest in any of those earnings. That was play money. Entertainment money. Not real.

Real came after college, when I got my first job in what she considered a legitimate profession.

I came home with my paycheck, feeling like a man. Independent. Earning.

Mom and I had a ritual—coffee together after I got home from work. That day, she asked to see my paycheck. I showed her.

She studied the numbers. Nodded.

"Good. You're making good money." She handed it back. "Now take twenty percent and put it in a bank."

"Why?"

"Because I said so."

I argued. Of course, I argued. But I also did it—sort of.

I saved the money, but I didn't put it in a bank. Instead, I walked to what we called the "Wall Street of Sarajevo"—a street near Hotel Europa where the black market for currencies operated in plain sight.

Every paycheck, I played currency arbitrage. Twenty percent. Sometimes thirty. Sometimes eighty, if I had a feeling. Converting Yugoslav dinars into currencies that actually meant something: U.S. dollars, German Deutsche marks, Swiss francs.

When the war came, the economy collapsed overnight. The dinar became worthless—it wasn't even the currency of our country anymore. Prices were listed in Deutsch marks or U.S. dollars by the next morning.

The people who hadn't saved had nothing. The people who had saved in Yugoslav dinars had a little more than nothing. The few of us with hard foreign currency could get whatever was available.

Here's the part nobody talks about. As the banks collapsed, the prices immediately—overnight—changed from Yugoslav dinars to Deutsch marks or U.S. dollars. Exact change became the problem. If you wanted to buy a loaf of bread and the price was twenty Deutsch marks but all you had was a fifty Deutsch mark note, you paid fifty. Nobody could make change.

The lesson wasn't just "Save money." The lesson was "Prepare for the world to break." Because it will.

Twenty years later, one of the ten principles we teach clients is to save twenty percent. Not because it's clever. Because my mother burned it into me before I knew why.

**Shoulder Tap:** Discipline creates options. When everything breaks, and eventually it does, the people who prepared have choices. The people who didn't have any.

## THE IRONING LESSON

Mom ironed Dad's shirts.

She did it well—she did everything well—but she grumbled. She was an independent-minded woman, and she did not like the role that society had carved out for women. The expectation that this was her job. That this was what wives did.

She never said it was beneath her. It wasn't that simple. She just refused to accept that the world had to work this way.

I watched this ritual for years. The iron hissing. The muttering under her breath. The quiet resistance that never quite became rebellion.

Somewhere in there, I made a decision. A vow, written deep:

*I will always make enough money to dry clean my shirts.*

But more important than the vow about shirts was the manifesto that came with it. Watching my mother—brilliant, capable, independent—grumble her way through a task that society assigned her simply because she was a woman changed something in me.

This is when I became a feminist.

Not the word. The commitment. I made a decision about the kind of man I would be. I would be a great husband. I would be a great brother to my sister. I would support, elevate, and champion every woman in my life—not because they need saving, but because they deserve a man who sees them as equals and acts like it.

That code has shaped every team I've built. Every person I've selected. Every room I've walked into.

**Shoulder Tap:** Support the women around you. Elite teams are diverse. The best leaders don't sort people by gender before they sort them by talent and unique genius. Natural ability doesn't have a gender. This isn't politics. This is character. And if you're not building with that in mind, you're leaving talent on the table and integrity on the floor.

## NATAŠA

I remember vividly the day Nataša came to our house.

I remember watching from the stairs as my mom and dad carried her in from the hospital. This tiny thing, wrapped in blankets. The world changed at that moment. I became a big brother.

My mom and dad made it clear: Being the big brother was the coolest thing in the world. I had a responsibility to protect her. She was the one person who would always be in my corner. And I was the one person who always needed to be in hers.

That message came through in everything they said and did. It was one of the things they agreed on completely.

But we were very different people, my sister and I.

She was more like my dad—galvanizing, working the room, magnetic. And music became her tool. I played the violin. She played piano, partially because I told her, "Don't play violin." (More on that later.)

When she came home from class one day, she told my parents that her teacher said they should buy her a piano.

Mom and Dad exchanged looks. "That's kind of expensive. We need to know you're really going to stick with it."

She nodded, very serious. "I understand. If you don't have money this week, maybe you can buy it next week."

Two weeks later, a Petrov upright piano appeared in our apartment. I don't know if we had the money or not. It just showed up.

She played constantly. That piano led to a career in the arts and singing. She found her genius and built a life around it.

Here's what you need to know: To my parents, the arts were hobbies, not professions. Because of that, I went into business and engineering because that's what serious people did.

I made a vow to myself about Nataša. I would do everything in my power to let her pursue what she had genius and talent for. Because I wasn't given that freedom, I would make sure she never faced the same wall.

This was servant leadership before I had a language for it. Not leading because I had a title—in this case, "big brother" was the only title I held. Leading because I saw what was needed and chose to provide it. Choosing to give someone else what I didn't receive.

**Shoulder Tap:** Become aware of what you inherited. Then make a conscious, empowered choice to keep it or change it. Give someone else what you didn't get. That's where character begins.

## THE TRAP

Here's what I couldn't see yet: The same code that makes you capable can make you difficult to work with.

Mom's relentless standards? They built discipline. Work ethic. A refusal to settle. She loved her children fiercely—every "you missed a spot" was her way of pushing us toward our potential. But that same instinct, pointed at people who didn't sign up for it, can crush instead of develop. The gap between excellence and exhaustion is smaller than you think.

Dad's effortless charm? It built connection. Warmth. The ability to make anyone feel valued. But ego unchecked becomes blindness. You start believing the room loves you because you deserve it, not because you earned it.

I inherited both programs. And for years, I didn't see how they were shaping my leadership.

December 2014. Four days after hip surgery. My business partner walks in with a Starbucks and an iPad.

*You change things constantly. The team is frustrated. Demoralized. You're impossible to work for.*

That was Mom's code running unchecked. "You missed a spot" applied to a team that needed encouragement, not endless correction. Standards so high that nobody could breathe. The in-the-gap mentality pushing people away instead of pulling them forward.

I'd inherited her code. And I was running it on people who hadn't asked for it.

**Shoulder Tap:** Your greatest strengths, overused, become your greatest weaknesses. Character means knowing where your lines are and building systems to catch yourself before you cross them.

## THE GIFT I DIDN'T WANT

Mom's constant pushing made me want to resist.

Even though I recognized the power of systems and standards and discipline, I never missed a single opportunity to argue, to find the exception, to prove she wasn't always right. That's the connection between sons and mothers—at least this son and this mother.

My resistance led me somewhere unexpected. I started studying psychology. Philosophy. Human behavior. Not because it was cool or fashionable. But because I needed help.

I wanted to understand why the hell my parents were the way they were. Why two people who clearly loved each other could spend months in silence. Why communication broke down so completely between people who shared a bed, shared children, shared a life.

Carl Jung said thinking is hard—that's why everybody's judging. And the judging my parents did of each other was constant. But so was their love. They just couldn't figure out how to hold both at the same time.

I recognized early that ninety-five percent of all problems between people are poor communication. Judging instead of giving grace and space to express. Assuming instead of asking.

This natural, stuck-in-between existence—having to switch between two brains, translate one parent to the other, hold contradictions without resolving them—became one of my unique gifts.

I hated it at the time.

But it saved my life, literally and multiple times, during the Siege of Sarajevo. And it became the foundation of everything I brought to America, to entrepreneurship, and to building teams.

**Shoulder Tap:** The thing you hate about your upbringing might be the thing that saves you. Don't be too quick to reject what shaped you. Examine it first.

## LIVING IN PURPLE

Blue brain. Red brain. Logic and emotion. Engineering and connection.

Most people lean in one direction. Engineers who can't read a room. Connectors who can't build a system. Leaders who are brilliant at strategy but terrible with people. Leaders who are loved by everyone but can't execute.

Here's what I've come to understand: Elite leaders don't choose one brain over the other. They learn to operate in purple.

Purple is the integration. Both systems running simultaneously. Logic informing emotion. Emotion informing logic. The engineer who knows when to stop optimizing and start listening. The connector who knows when to stop talking and start building.

My parents each operated in one color. Mom was blue. Dad was red. They never figured out how to meet in the middle—at least not in how they communicated with each other.

But by forcing me to live between them, they gave me something neither of them had alone: the capacity to hold both. To code-switch. To read a room *and* build a system. To connect with people *and* hold them to standards.

Purple isn't a personality type. It's a practice. The best teams I've ever built—and the best teams I've ever studied—operate in purple. They have the systems and the soul. The engineering and the heart. The standards and the grace.

## WHAT CHARACTER ACTUALLY MEANS

When I think about character now, I think about what my parents had in common—not where they differed.

They were both leaders in their organizations. Mom in accounting. Dad in politics and sales. Different worlds, different skills. But what people recognized in both of them was the same thing: their character.

Here's how I define it: Character is not being too big to get the small things done. Nothing is beneath you. How you treat a janitor—or anyone who has no transactional value to offer you, no opportunity to advance your career, no reason to matter to you except that they're human—determines the quality of your character.

My grandfather understood this. He was a bit of a celebrity in his time, successful enough that he could have lived a very different life. He chose instead to do honest work. Stay out of politics and hoopla after WWII. Focus on what actually puts food on the table.

My mom idolized him. And I happened to have a birthday the day after his. So of course, I thought I was "chosen." My mom made sure I knew that.

But what I actually inherited wasn't specialness. It was the power of personal example. Watching someone live with integrity, day after day, when no one was keeping score.

**Shoulder Tap:** Character is what you do when no one's watching. It's how you treat people who can't help you. It's the small things, done consistently, that reveal who you actually are.

## WHERE YOU COME FROM SHAPES HOW YOU SEE

I grew up code-switching between two brains.

I recognized the power of Mom's systems—I just refused to give her the satisfaction of admitting it. Outside the house, I leaned into Dad's warmth—connection, charm, making people feel seen. I learned to run both programs. To hold contradiction. To translate between worlds.

Most kids pick one parent to emulate. I learned to carry both. To see the world through the engineer's eyes and the connector's eyes at the same time.

I didn't know this was unusual. I didn't know it would save my life. I didn't know it would become the foundation of everything I'd later teach about leadership.

As leaders, we have a responsibility to communicate. To facilitate communication. To suspend judgment and focus on building on what is strong—not ignoring what needs work, but leading with strength.

I just knew that where I came from—Zenica, the steel city; Mom, the gap-hunter; Dad, the room-worker; Nataša, the first person I chose to protect differently—shaped how I saw everything.

Character is the foundation. It's what's running underneath before you're aware that anything is running at all.

But character alone isn't enough. The two brains needed arenas. Places to develop. Things that came naturally—and things that didn't.

That's where I discovered what I was actually built for.

## BEFORE YOU MOVE ON → SHOULDER TAPS FROM THIS CHAPTER

- Standards matter. The gap between where you are and where you could be is where growth lives. She wasn't punishing me. She was teaching me to see potential—mine and everyone else's.

- Connection is gravity. It pulls people toward you. But gravity without grounding becomes performance. You need someone who will tell you the truth.
- You inherit more than you realize. The question isn't whether your parents shaped you—they did. The question is whether you'll examine what they gave you and decide what serves you and what doesn't.
- Mission holds people together when communication fails. My parents couldn't figure out how to talk to each other, but they never lost sight of why they were there. Leaders who anchor to the mission can survive almost anything.
- Environment shapes opportunity. The same kid in a different context becomes a different person. Leaders pay attention to the environments they create—because those environments are writing code into everyone who works there.
- Humility isn't weakness. Not being too big to get small things done. Not shoving your success in other people's faces. It's developed. Learned through repetition. Practice until it becomes who you are.
- Discipline creates options. When everything breaks—and eventually it does—the people who prepared have choices. The people who didn't have any.
- Support the women around you. Elite teams are diverse. The best leaders don't sort people by gender before they sort them by talent and unique genius. Natural ability doesn't have a gender. This isn't politics. This is character. And if you're not building with that in mind, you're leaving talent on the table and integrity on the floor.
- Become aware of what you inherited. Then make a conscious, empowered choice: keep it or change it. Give someone else what you didn't get. That's where character begins.
- Your greatest strengths, overused, become your greatest weaknesses. Character means knowing where your lines are—and building systems to catch yourself before you cross them.
- The thing you hate about your upbringing might be the thing that saves you. Don't be too quick to reject what shaped you. Examine it first.

- Character is what you do when no one's watching. It's how you treat people who can't help you. It's the small things, done consistently, that reveal who you actually are.

Knowing where you come from is one thing. Knowing what you're built for—that's a different discovery entirely. And it doesn't come the way you'd expect.

TWO

# Natural Ability

## THE PICTURE NOBODY ELSE CAN SEE

In my head, I look like Bradley Cooper. When I tell people this, they laugh.

We all carry a picture of ourselves. What we look like. What we're capable of. What we bring to the room.

The problem is nobody else can see that picture. They're carrying their own.

And underneath both pictures—yours and theirs—are systems running in the background. Natural ability. Talent. Unique genius. God-given gifts that don't come with a label. Nobody knows what yours are unless you show them. And you can't show them what you haven't found yet.

I was nine years old. Second grade.

I wanted to play violin because my cousin Cune played violin. He was cool. He looked good doing it. The way he held the instrument, the sounds that came out—I wanted to be like him. So I told my parents I wanted to play violin.

They said buying a violin was expensive. It was a commitment. If they bought me a violin, I would go to music school. I agreed.

What I didn't understand then: In Yugoslavia, music school was completely separate from regular school. A separate building. A separate schedule. A half-hour walk across town to a different world. Music school lasted seven years. And nobody switched instruments. Once you're in with a violin, you're in. Hook, line, and sinker.

My parents bought me a violin. I was committed for the next seven years.

The newness wore off fast. In order to be good at the violin, you have to practice. If you don't, it sounds awful. Squeaky. Painful to listen to.

I did not want to practice. It cut my fingers. No one told me about that part. And I had so many other parts of life that were way more important—soccer, basketball, tennis, acting. Anything but violin.

It did not make me cool like my cousin.

To add insult to injury, I was in a school with people playing different instruments. I was one of maybe four or five kids playing violin, but there were people playing accordion, guitar, piano—all kinds of instruments. We'd have classes together once a week and listen to each other play in recitals. They all sounded way better on their instruments than I did on mine.

I thought if I played guitar or piano or drums, I'd probably sound better than them. But I couldn't switch. Nobody switched.

I wanted to play guitar. *No, we bought you a violin.*

I wanted to play piano. *No, we bought you a violin.*

I wanted to quit. *We don't quit.*

For years, the violin was my frustration. I had some talent. Just not enough interest to do anything with it. The other kids practiced. They advanced. They became really good. Natural talent surrounded me from the beginning, and they put in the work.

I didn't.

The picture in my head didn't match reality. No amount of wanting could close that gap without work I wasn't willing to do.

**Shoulder Tap:** Talent is worth nothing if you're not willing to put in the work.

## YOU CAN'T JUMP

Zenica was an experimental city where I could try anything. I wanted to play volleyball. Watching it on TV, I thought it was a really cool sport. So I went to try it out.

And I really enjoyed it.

Teamwork. The intricacy of setting plays up. The flow. Six people reading each other without speaking. Everyone giving something up for the point… There's a beauty in volleyball that I was attracted to.

Unlike violin, where I didn't work hard because I didn't like it, volleyball was something I really enjoyed. I worked hard. Threw myself on the ground. Did all the things I thought you were supposed to do.

But even though I never missed practice, I was never put in a real game. Not once.

I thought the coach didn't like me.

After God knows how many weeks of practice and not being put in the game, I finally mustered up the courage to ask, "Coach, why don't you ever put me in the game?"

He looked at me like I'd asked why the sky was blue.

"Saša, you can't jump."

"Why does that matter?"

"Well, you've got to be able to jump if you want to play volleyball."

"But I want to play."

"I know you do. You do cool things in practice; you're just not good enough to play in the game."

I was twelve years old.

Tennis was the same. I'd watched tennis since I was a kid—Roland Garros and Wimbledon every year. Two and a half weeks of tournaments, broadcast on our local channels. Yugoslavia had players who were pretty good. This is where I fell in love with elite performance.

I loved the flow of it so much that I would go practice against a wall for hours. That's where I learned what flow felt like—that transcendent state where things just come at you, and you respond without thinking.

When I stepped on the court, it was different than playing against a wall. I had real opponents. I had to run. I had to be fast. And I wasn't made to be fast or to run. I played matches, but I didn't win.

Too big. Too slow. Couldn't jump. I could not connect the dots. I thought I was working hard and trying but not getting the results. This wasn't the violin—I wanted to be good, and I enjoyed both sports. But this wasn't about effort. This was biology. My body wasn't built for what those sports require to be elite.

> **Shoulder Tap:** Sometimes the obstacle isn't effort. It's fit. You can want something desperately and still be wrong for it. That's information, not failure.

## THE REAL SPORT

My cousin Dijana asked me to help move furniture out of her parents' apartment on the eighth floor to a different apartment building on the fifth floor.

The floors matter because those elevators weren't designed for freight—they were designed for humans. So we're carrying heavy furniture down eight flights of stairs, over to a new apartment, and then up to the fifth floor.

Dijana's mother was my babysitter. I basically grew up in their house. They were my favorite people. And I was the cousin who was big and strong. So I showed up to help.

On the way down, carrying a big sofa with two other guys, there's banter going on. We're talking. And Miki—who would later become the skipper of my rugby team—says to me: "Saša, what sport do you play?"

I said, proud of myself, "Tennis and volleyball."

They dropped the sofa. Right there in the stairwell. They started laughing hysterically.

"What is wrong with you people?"

"Tennis? And volleyball? *You?*"

"Yeah, what's wrong?"

"Dude, you need to play a real sport."

First, I was offended. Then I was curious.

"What's a real sport?"

"Rugby."

I didn't know anything about rugby. It sounded aggressive. But I was always a big, chunky guy. Not very fast. Couldn't really jump, as I had recently been informed.

Monday after that weekend, I went to my volleyball practice, where Miki and one of the other guys were waiting.

"You. Come with us."

"What?"

"We're going to real practice."

In Zenica, there's a big park where all the sports clubs practice every afternoon. I was on one side of the park. They came, picked me up, and dragged me to the other side.

That's where I walked into the rugby sheds.

And everything was different.

I walked in, and people looked up. Heads turned. The room shifted. "Whoa. *This is the guy.*"

I had been in the wrong tribe. This was my athletic tribe. People were excited to see me. Not tolerating me. Not wondering what I was doing there, but excited about what I might become.

The same body that had made me a joke on the volleyball court was now celebrated in the rugby sheds.

We went to practice and training. Within weeks, I was put in a game. I didn't even know the rules.

They said, "You don't need to know the rules. Just do what we tell you. Your job is to go tackle people."

They trained me how to tackle and how to be tackled without breaking my neck. And all of a sudden, my need for purpose, for meaningful relationships, and for belonging started clicking.

I was about fifteen years old. Within eighteen months, I was on the U18 team that won the national championship with a thirty-point blowout in the final. Elite level.

> **Shoulder Tap:** Find where you're celebrated, not just tolerated. The same traits that make you wrong for one context make you essential in another.

## THE TEACHER WHO CHANGES EVERYTHING

I should have quit violin—D student, minimum effort. My teacher agreed.

"Saša, you're good at math. Why don't you go do math? This is not for you."

My parents disagreed. "We bought you a violin. We don't quit."

So I kept showing up. Going through the motions. My classmates were the real thing. Some of them are professional musicians today. I watched them then, and I knew exactly where I stood. Not close.

Then my violin teacher went on maternity leave. New teacher. Ramiz Tahiri. Twenty-something Albanian from Kosovo. A firecracker.

In our first lesson, I expected the usual: "Here's what you're behind on," "Here's what the other students are doing," "Here's why you're failing." I'd heard it all before.

He didn't mention my grades. Didn't lecture me about commitment. Didn't talk about all the ways I was falling short. He picked up his violin and looked at me.

"Let's have fun."

He took my violin. Tuned it. Handed it back. Took his own.

"Let's play this."

We started playing. And he said, "Again." We played it again. And somewhere in the third or fourth time through, something happened. I wasn't thinking about whether I was doing it right. I wasn't thinking about the other kids who were better. I wasn't watching the clock.

I was having fun. I didn't know that was allowed.

He didn't lower the standard. He just changed what it felt like to reach for it. He found what I could do and built from there instead of starting from everything I couldn't. He made me feel like a musician before I played like one.

I went from a D student to a B+ student. After graduation, I volunteered for the orchestra and played for two more years.

Nobody made me. I chose it.

Through his leadership, Ramiz Tahiri turned me from a hater of music to a lover of it. From a person who could not give two shits to a person who actually practiced.

Same instrument. Same hands. Same notes. Different leader.

The work doesn't change. The leader changes what the work feels like to do.

**Shoulder Tap:** The work doesn't change. The leader changes how the work feels.

## LIFE IS A THEATER

I found theater in fourth grade.

I was selected to play the lead role in a school production, and I had a blast. At the end of the performance—in front of students and parents, while we were celebrating—my drama teacher pulled my mom aside.

"He has real talent. You should take him to audition at the Children's Studio at the National Theater in Zenica."

Auditioning and being selected for a show were special. Going to rehearsals and classes, learning how to become another person, all the things that acting is made of—it was transformational. Theater became my outlet for everything.

I found myself looking forward to rehearsals. First one in, last one out. Always looking for more, trying extra.

In the summer of 1978, I was cast for my first TV movie. Within a year and a half, I had the experience of a professional theater production.

I was thirteen years old. I was on top of the world. I didn't even care what role I was playing. I just wanted to be part of it.

From age thirteen to eighteen, my life was this: I hated violin. I loved going to theater rehearsals. And rugby was cool.

All three were working at the same time, but the contrast between what felt like work and what didn't feel like work was constantly in my face.

Then, starting in my junior year of high school, I learned that a special production was being cast. *Crveni Krovovi.*

That show changed everything.

The experience of being cast in that show was all-encompassing. Forty-five of us on stage from the opening. No scenery except bodies in motion. The whole narrative acted out through stage movement. Completely revolutionary.

And it was there that I learned I was not Bradley Cooper.

My acting and dancing coach would give me feedback on my performances because what was required was for me to portray the person *he* wanted the audience to see on stage.

I was cast in comedic, lighthearted roles. Roles that got lots of laughs. And because of the seriousness with which I took each role, I was recognized as a good actor. But I wasn't the leading man. I wasn't the dramatic hero. I was the one who made people laugh before I even opened my mouth.

I leaned in.

In my senior year, I was cast in every production of the Children's Studio and several professional productions. I was on stage seven days a week.

Oh yeah, I went to school too. But school was not as important as being on stage.

Theater became my life, and I thought I was going to be an actor, a director, or anything related to theater.

> **Shoulder Tap:** When something doesn't feel like work, pay attention. That's data about where you belong.

## THE RIGHT PERSON, WRONG SEAT

When I graduated from high school, I wanted to pursue acting and theater. I had talent. I was good at it. I enjoyed it. I thought I could be elite.

My mother did not want to have anything to do with it. And since my parents' only unifying position was about their kids, my father supported her and pulled out all the stops to keep me from going there.

That decision, his decision—being blocked from expressing my own talent—probably made the biggest impact on how I see talent in other people.

Because I wasn't allowed to express my own talent, I vowed that I would help others live in theirs.

It started with my sister. She was six years younger, coming up behind me. When the time came for her to pick a college, I did everything in my power to influence my parents to allow her to study music.

She did.

Years later, I caught myself doing to someone else exactly what had been done to me. Deciding what they should be. Blocking the door to what they actually were. I was so convinced I could see their genius that I stopped listening to what they were telling me about it.

I forgot that everyone carries their own picture. They get to decide. Their picture. Their timeline. Their Bradley Cooper moment. My job isn't to replace theirs with mine. I almost lost one of the best people I ever worked with because I couldn't see past what I thought she should be.

When we met, she was a young advisor in our Syracuse office. Smart. Energetic. On the leadership team. All the outside signals told me she was a great advisor—and that she wanted to be one.

Years later, when we were building our business in Albany, I reached out. I needed an integrator. She moved to Albany for the job.

And things started to stall.

Tasks weren't getting done. But other things—things not even in her job description—she was fantastic at. She single-handedly saved another advisor's career because she saw things I was blind to.

But I needed execution. Tenacity. Things moving on time.

So I pushed. Hard. Tasks. Action plans. Deadlines. All the things that had worked before. I got movement. But she became less and less the person everybody loved. Something was going out of her eyes.

I kept thinking more clarity would fix it. More direction. More defined expectations. Instead, I was watching someone I cared about become a shadow of herself.

So I resorted to what I thought was the answer. "This is the need of the company. This is the need of our organization. I think you have the skills and experience for it. I'd like you to do it."

I thought she'd be much more effective returning to an advisor role. When I suggested it, I thought she'd be relieved.

What she said stunned me.

"I do *not* want to be an advisor."

"But you're good at it."

"I. Do. *Not.* Want. To. Be. An. Advisor."

I didn't have a spot for someone who wouldn't be what I needed them to be. But I cared for her as a person and a talent. And as often happens, a different opportunity presented itself—a chance to work in the home office, a big transformation project. I was happy to support her however I could to get that role.

She left to do work that was actually hers.

It was fantastic for her. And it saved our relationship.

She was absolutely the right person. Wrong seat. I was so convinced I knew what she should be that I couldn't see what she actually was. All the pushing, the pressure, the structure, the deadlines, none of it worked. I was trying to force her into a role that didn't fit her natural ability.

Years later, the thing that brought us back together was the very thing I'd gotten wrong—seeing her for who she actually was instead of who I needed her to be.

We are now writing this book together.

**Shoulder Tap:** You can be right about someone's talent and completely wrong about where it belongs. The job isn't to tell people what they should be. It's to see what they already are.

## PRESSURE

Talent without interest is nothing. You can have every gift in the world, but if you're not interested and willing to put in the hard work, those gifts just sit there collecting dust.

And hard work doesn't happen without pressure.

Pressure comes from two places: inside you or outside you.

External pressure is the deadline. The coach who won't put you in the game. The critic in the audience. The score tied with ten seconds left, and everyone watching to see if you can make the kick. External pressure doesn't ask permission. It shows up and demands a response.

Internal pressure is the voice that won't let you settle. The standard you hold yourself to when no one is watching. The refusal to be mediocre even when mediocre would be acceptable. Internal pressure is a choice—you put it on yourself because something in you won't accept less.

Both work. Both activate hard work. The difference is who's in charge.

My mother's "you missed a spot" was external pressure. It drove me crazy, but it built standards. Ramiz Tahiri's "Let's have fun" removed external pressure and helped me find internal motivation. The casting decisions were external pressure. My decision to outwork everyone else was internal.

The best performers I've known—in sports, in theater, in business—learn to generate internal pressure so they're not dependent on external deadlines and critics to make them show up. They hold themselves accountable before anyone else has to.

I grew up with elite-level expectations. No participation trophies. You were either good or you sucked. Even though it was socialism, an environment in which you might think mediocrity was rewarded, it wasn't. Everybody wanted to win. If you sucked, you didn't play. Period.

That external pressure was constant. But at some point, it became internal. I stopped needing someone else to push. I pushed myself.

I am great at acting. I love it. But I'm not pursuing an acting career. That window closed. My time to be Robert De Niro or Daniel Day-Lewis on the stage or screen has passed.

But here's what I decided: I *will* be Robert De Niro, Daniel Day-Lewis, and Bradley Cooper in what I *do* pursue.

The same intensity and refusal to be mediocre, but applied to building businesses, developing leaders, and creating teams that lead themselves.

That's internal pressure. No one is making me hold that standard. I chose it.

> **Shoulder Tap:** Talent is potential. Hard work makes it real. Pressure activates hard work. External pressure shows up uninvited. Internal pressure is a choice. Build the internal kind—so you're not waiting for someone or something to push you.

## BEFORE YOU MOVE ON → SHOULDER TAPS FROM THIS CHAPTER

- Talent is worth nothing if you're not willing to put in the work.
- Sometimes the obstacle isn't effort. It's fit. You can want something desperately and still be wrong for it. That's information, not failure.
- Find where you're celebrated, not just tolerated. The same traits that make you wrong for one context make you essential in another.
- The work doesn't change. The leader changes how the work feels.
- When something doesn't feel like work, pay attention. That's data about where you belong.

- You can be right about someone's talent and completely wrong about where it belongs. The job isn't to tell people what they should be. It's to see what they already are.
- Talent is potential. Hard work makes it real. Pressure activates hard work. External pressure shows up uninvited. Internal pressure is a choice. Build the internal kind—so you're not waiting for someone or something to push you.

Natural ability tells you what's possible. Fit tells you where you belong. Pressure—whether you create it or it finds you—turns potential into performance.

But none of that prepares you for when effort isn't optional. When the arena is assigned. When there's no finding your fit, only surviving what you're given.

That's where discipline gets forged.

That's where I learned to embrace the suck.s

THREE

# Embrace the Suck

## THE SECOND HAND

Before I left for the military, there were parties.

In Yugoslavia, more people came to military send-offs than to weddings or funerals. It's that kind of moment, the whole community showing up to acknowledge that a boy is about to become something else. Everyone you know crowds into someone's apartment. There's food. There's rakija. There's advice—some useful, most not.

At one of these parties, a friend of my cousin's pulled me aside. Zoran Pokaz. A musician. Life of the party type—the guy who always had a story, always had a crowd around him. But at this moment, he was serious.

"What kind of watch do you have?"

I showed him. A Raketa. Russian-made. Analog. Simple.

"Good. Make sure you keep a watch with a second hand when you're in the military. The second hand is very important."

I didn't understand. "Why?"

"When you think that things cannot get worse, look at your watch and look at that second hand. You see how it moves. That means that however bad it is, it's going to pass."

I nodded like I understood.

I didn't. Not yet.

## THE MACHINE

Military service was mandatory. Every Yugoslav male served. The only choice was timing, and I chose early, right after being blocked from pursuing theater. If I couldn't do what I loved, I might as well get the mandatory thing out of the way.

Osijek. Northern Croatia. Forty miles from Hungary. The height of the Cold War. I was part of the brigade that would be first to face the Russians if they came through.

When I stepped off the truck at the training facility, I walked into what looked like the set of a military movie. Soldiers everywhere. Everybody running. Chaos with structure underneath it.

Strip. Bag your civilian clothes. Medical exam. Get sprayed. Haircut. Shower with fifty other guys. Walk to the counter.

"What's your number?"

There's no name anymore. Just a number.

They give you a tarp, a ten-by-ten square, and tell you to start throwing shit into it. Pants. Boots. Socks. Toothbrush. Complete winter gear, even though it was August. Everything you'll own for the next year.

They show you your cubby—a blue box. Small. Everything has to fit.

"Now I'm going to show you how to fold everything."

One hour later, I get it right. Everything folded. Everything in place.

The sergeant walks behind my box and knocks everything out onto the floor.

"Do it again."

"Why?"

"Do it again."

Four hours of folding clothes. The same clothes. The same box. Over and over until my hands know the movements without my brain involved.

When you're not training, you're cleaning—your section, your floor, the bathrooms. Morning, afternoon, whenever there's nothing else scheduled.

I'm on my hands and knees scrubbing tile, and I hear my mother's voice in my head.

*You missed that. You missed that. You missed that.*

I was eighteen years old. Eighteen years of "you missed a spot" had prepared me for this moment. Her relentless standards—the ones that drove me crazy growing up—were keeping me out of trouble. I knew how to clean. I knew what "done" actually looked like.

The guys who struggled were the ones who'd never had someone inspect their work before. They were learning at nineteen what I'd learned at nine.

**Shoulder Tap:** The standards that annoyed you growing up might be the standards that save you later. You don't always know what you're being prepared for.

## THE WINDOW

That first week breaks something open.

Not my spirit. Something else. The illusion that I'm in control. The belief that I can find an angle, work the system, maintain some version of myself that exists outside these walls.

One night—I don't remember which night; they all blur together—I collapsed onto my bunk. Bottom rack. Two guys sleeping above me. I'm exhausted in a way I've never been exhausted. My body aches. My mind is foggy. I'm not Saša anymore. I'm a number. I'm a cog.

And I'm thinking, *This cannot get any worse.*

Then I remember Zoran at my farewell party. I look down at my Raketa and watch the second hand move.

*Tick. Tick. Tick.*

Each tick is a second passing. Each second is time moving forward. And if time is moving forward, that means this moment—however bad it is—is already becoming the past.

The second hand doesn't stop. It can't. Physics won't let it.

Which means this will pass.

Something shifts in me. Not peace exactly. Maybe just the smallest release of tension as I realize I don't have to carry this moment as if it will last forever. It won't. The second hand proves it.

I've had watches with second hands ever since. Even now, my Apple Watch has one.

I can't tell you how many times during the siege of Sarajevo I looked at my watch. Specific moments. Specific stories. Looking at that second hand and thinking: *It's still going. This will pass.*

It doesn't make the hard things easy. But it makes them survivable.

But that night in the barracks, there's something else. Above my head, there's a window.

I look up from my pillow. Through the glass, I can see the sky. Stars. The same stars that exist outside these walls. The same sky that's over Zenica, over Sarajevo, over the theater where I should be rehearsing right now.

*There's life beyond this.*

And something clicks.

The guys who are struggling—the ones getting extra punishment, extra duties, extra misery—they're fighting. Resisting. Trying to hold onto who they were before they got here.

I'm not going to do that.

I'd figured this out in high school already. If I could keep my grades between eighty-five and ninety, at what I called "the stealth level," nobody touched me. Teachers left me alone. Parents left me alone. I had the freedom to do whatever I wanted because I'd done just enough to stay off the radar.

Same principle. Different arena.

*If you're going to be in class, pay attention. If you pay attention, you will get enough to get between eighty-five and ninety, and when you get between eighty-five and ninety, you're going to be free to do whatever you want to do.*

If I give my body to this place—if I follow the rules, hit the marks, do what's required—then my mind stays free. The sky is still there. The world I came from is still there. The person I'm going to become is still there, waiting on the other side of this.

I stopped fighting that night.

> **Shoulder Tap:** When you think things can't get worse, look at the second hand. It's still moving. That means this moment—however bad—is already becoming the past. You don't have to carry it like it will last forever. It won't.

## THE REALITY DISTORTION FIELD

Here's how I survived the military without losing my mind: I stopped being in the military.

Not literally. My body was there. I showed up, followed orders, and did everything required. But in my head, I was somewhere else entirely.

*I'm living the life of a movie. I'm not in the military. In my mind, I'm in the movie. I've converted my current reality into a movie, and I am living in a movie that happens to be in the Yugoslavian army.*

Every formation, every drill, every ridiculous rule—it wasn't happening *to* me. It was happening in the story I was living.

*I have a world that is in my head. I just happen to have a body in a different world. And if the body activates according to the rules and does what needs to be done, my imagination is free to roam and do whatever the fuck it wants.*

My theater training had given me the ability to become someone else. So I stepped into the role of a soldier in a movie about soldiers. The discomfort was part of the plot. The challenges were character development.

Because I did well in basic training—radio work, physical fitness, following orders without friction—I got pulled into the recon unit. Not full special forces—my glasses disqualified me from that—but freelance, called in when they needed someone who could handle classified information and be trusted under pressure.

*I had the best of both worlds. I was there with them and doing cool shit.*

Then came Secure Compartmented Information Facility duty, handling communications that couldn't leave the room, walking through the stunning alleys of Osijek in my dress uniform. *I'm in a spy movie situation.*

The movie in my head and the reality in my body were starting to merge. I wasn't just playing a character anymore. I was becoming someone who could operate at an elite level.

> **Shoulder Tap:** You are the writer, director, and the lead role in the movie of your life. The narrative you run in your head shapes what you can endure and who you become.

## GOOD MORNING, VIETNAM

Sunday morning.

I'm alone in the radio station. Night shift. The city of Osijek is sleeping. It's quiet, that particular military quiet where everything runs on schedule, and nothing happens unless something goes wrong.

I'd just watched *Good Morning, Vietnam* a few days before. Robin Williams as an Armed Forces Radio DJ in Saigon, breaking every rule, making everyone laugh, and being absolutely uncontrollable and absolutely brilliant.

It's 6:30 a.m. The sun is coming up. I'm tired and a little punchy, and I have access to a very powerful radio transmitter.

I grab the microphone and shout, "GOOD MORNING, VIETNAM!"

Full Robin Williams energy. Top of my lungs. The words blasting out across the city.

For about thirty seconds, I am the DJ in the movie. I am alive and free and funny and doing something completely, magnificently stupid.

Military police arrive within the hour. Handcuffs.

"Dude, do you know where your barracks are? You are in downtown Osijek, and you are yelling at the top of your lungs at 6:30 in the morning on a Sunday. And all of our officers live in apartment buildings around here."

Severely reprimanded. Not court-martialed. Fortunately, someone above me had enough connections that I didn't face the full weight of my stupidity.

But I learned something important: There's a difference between working the system and forgetting the system exists. I'd gotten so comfortable, so confident, that I'd confused freedom-within-the-rules with freedom-from-the-rules.

They're not the same thing. The first one you earn. The second one, you never have.

**Shoulder Tap:** Confidence earned inside the system is not permission to ignore the system. Know which rules bend and which ones break you.

## LAZY AND STUPID

Military service ends. College begins.

I thought the rules would be different. They were, just not the way I was hoping.

My first year, I was failing financial math.

Not struggling. Failing. The same approach that got me through high school—minimum effort, maximum charm, just enough to stay invisible—was not working. The professors didn't care if I showed up. They didn't care if I passed. They had no investment in whether I figured it out or flamed out.

My father arranged a meeting.

His friend was a financial math professor. He'd known me since I was a kid. He'd watched me coast through school on natural ability and strategic laziness.

We met at a café. My father, his professor friend, and I.

The professor asked to see my notes.

I didn't have notes. Not real ones. Not for a class I barely attended.

The humiliation of that moment—being asked to produce evidence of work I hadn't done, in front of my father—burned.

But the professor didn't grill me. He taught me.

"How do you study?" he asked.

"I read the notes."

"Read them how?"

"I... look at them," I said.

He stared at me like I'd just explained that I prepare for swimming by thinking about water.

"You need to rewrite your notes."

"What?"

He continued, "After every class, take your notes and rewrite them. Not copy, rewrite. Put them in different words. Reorganize them. Make them make sense to you."

It sounded like a lot of work. It was a lot of work. But I was failing, and failing had consequences I wasn't willing to accept.

So I tried it.

Rewriting forced me to actually process what I'd heard in class. I couldn't just transcribe words I didn't understand—I had to wrestle with them until they made sense. The act of rewriting was the act of learning.

And because of that, I passed financial math.

More importantly, I had a method. For the first time in my life, I knew *how* to study. Not just show up and hope for the best, but actually study.

> **Shoulder Tap:** Sometimes the lesson isn't the content—it's the method. Learning how to learn is the skill that unlocks everything else.

## THE PROFESSOR WHO WOULDN'T LET ME SLIDE

I've been learning English since the fifth grade.

In socialist Yugoslavia, even in the elementary school I went to, I had an option to choose among five foreign languages: English, German, French, Russian, or Italian.

I picked English, and not because I cared about English. I picked English because I liked American movies.

For the next seven years, I was at best a "B" student. Good enough that nobody bothered me, not so good that anyone expected more.

Then I got to college.

Second year. English.

I'd survived financial math. I had a study method now. But old habits die hard, and English felt easier than numbers. I slipped back into coasting.

My English professor was not interested in my coasting.

He was older. Experienced. Zero tolerance for bullshit.

The first time he catches me unprepared—sliding through on minimal effort—he doesn't yell. He doesn't lecture. He just looks at me with disappointed recognition.

"You don't come to classes. You somehow have enough balls to not be prepared and somehow give me answers that are just barely passing."

I wait for the part where he lets me off with a warning.

"So, until I get 'A' effort, you're going to have a failing grade."

Here's what that meant in Yugoslavia: you sat a final at the end of the term. Fail it, and you get another shot. Then another. Four chances total. Fail all four, and the year doesn't count. You sit back down and do it again.

He fails me in June.

Okay, I think. I'll try a little harder in July.

He fails me in July.

September comes. I prepare. Not "A" effort, but definitely more than before.

He fails me in September.

When he failed me in September, I felt confused and unsure about what to do.

But deep down, I did know what to do. The financial math professor had already taught me. Rewrite the notes. Do the actual work. Stop trying to game the system.

I started actually studying, and sure enough, the same method that saved me in financial math saved me in English.

Pain plus perspective equals progress. Pain is the key ingredient. I had to actually feel it before I was willing to do anything about it. But here's the thing about pain—it has a way of burning through excuses. You can coast on charm when the consequences are manageable. When they're not, charm runs out fast. You can't think your way to that lesson. You have to live it.

**Shoulder Tap:** Pain is a teacher. Sometimes it's the only one you'll listen to. But pain alone doesn't teach you anything—it's the perspective you choose to take regarding that pain that determines whether you grow or just suffer.

## VIENNA

Here's how English stopped being something I resented and became something I owned.

My tutor, the person my parents hired to help me pass my English exams after the professor broke me down, said something to my father that I overheard.

"Saša could be your translator."

At the time, my father was vice president of the Yugoslav Chamber of Commerce. He was going to Austria on a trip promoting and building trade relations between Yugoslavia and our neighbors.

He brought me.

At the first meeting, I had no plan. No script. No idea how I was going to render complex business concepts from Serbo-Croatian into English and back again. My grammar was shaky. My vocabulary was limited. My confidence was somewhere around zero.

I just started talking.

It wasn't grammatically correct, but nobody made fun of me. They heard what I said and responded in the way that I understood. That bridge started working.

Something shifted in that room. Not in my grammar—that was still a mess. But in my relationship to the language. I wasn't fighting it anymore. I was using it. Imperfectly, but functionally.

The second day went better. The third, better still.

Getting "gooder and gooder" every day.

I know that's not grammatically correct. That's the point. I wasn't speaking textbook English. I was speaking survival English. Communication English. Get-the-deal-done English.

Two weeks of translating. Two weeks of being thrown into situations I wasn't ready for and figuring it out anyway. Two weeks of my brain rewiring itself because it had to.

When I came back, I became a regular visitor at the American Cultural Center in Sarajevo. I got *Newsweek*, *Time*, and *Business Week* and walked around with those magazines under my arm like I was somebody important.

The language I picked because I liked American movies, and the subject had to be beaten into me through pain and failure, skills I never would have developed if I hadn't been forced to embrace the suck.

**Shoulder Tap:** You don't learn things in classrooms. You learn them in rooms where you have no choice but to perform.

## THE DAY ENGLISH SAVED ME FROM THE FRONT LINES

Late June 1992. Sarajevo.

We'd been under siege and in the headlines of the world for over two months. My mother's cancer was worsening. My sister and I were the only ones with her—my father had gone on a business trip the day the siege began and wasn't able to come back.

Like many others, I continued to go to work at my pre-war job. I was a research fellow at the University of Sarajevo in the Institute for Organization and Economics, a business think tank owned by the university. I was also a teaching assistant in the department of marketing, working under Professor Tihi. One of my projects there had been translating a logistics textbook. I'd even taught a semester on it.

I was twenty-six years old, and I was starting to realize this war was not going to end anytime soon.

The pressure to find a more active role in defense was mounting. Every time the militia ransacked our apartment looking for guns, the pressure grew. And it wasn't just pressure I was putting on myself—the army was going to come for me. It was only a matter of when.

I wanted to find a way to contribute, but I wasn't keen on picking up a gun and going to the front lines.

My name complicated things. Mirković has Christian Orthodox roots. I never considered myself a Serb, but it didn't matter what I considered myself. People see what they see, and they make judgments based on what they see. In the spring of 1992, a Serbian name in Sarajevo was enough for people to arrest you, maybe kill you. People with names like mine were bombing us.

I knew I wanted to leave Sarajevo eventually. But I did not want to leave during the war. For me, that would have been an act of treason.

So I was looking for a way to take an active role—to contribute, to fight—but as a civilian warrior. Not carrying a gun.

One Friday morning, I had an appointment at the Ministry of Defense. They offered me a role building logistics for the Bosnian Army. I was considered an "expert" because of my university work—the translated textbook, the semester I'd taught, the projects I'd worked on.

My "qualifications," in other words, were that I had read and translated a book about logistics.

When they asked for my response, I said, "I'm very interested, but I would like to talk to my mother before I give you an answer."

They looked at me like I had five heads.

"She's dying of cancer. I'm her primary caregiver. I at least need to talk to her."

They said okay.

## THE STREET

On the way back, I ran into two colleagues from the university.

Darko and Aziz.

"Where have you been? We've been looking all over for you."

"What's going on?"

"We have a meeting with Martin Raguž, the secretary in the Bosnian government for Humanitarian Affairs and Refugees. He wants to start an agency for humanitarian aid."

Darko and Aziz were going to be co-directors. One was Muslim, the other Croat. They needed someone to build logistics.

Someone with my "qualifications."

## THE MEETING

Martin Raguž laid out his vision. The city was under siege. People were starving. International aid was trying to come in, but there was no infrastructure to receive it, store it, or distribute it. No system. No organization. Just chaos and need, and they wanted to build that system from nothing.

I said, "I'm in. But you need to get me out of the job I was offered this morning."

I explained what had happened at the Ministry of Defense.

Martin laughed. "No problem."

He picked up the phone and called the secretary of defense. I could hear Martin explaining that I should work for his department, not defense.

Then Martin paused, covered the microphone, and looked at me.

"What should I tell him? Why should you work for me?"

I was stunned. My mind raced. Within a second, I said, "I speak English. And I would need to be able to communicate with the United Nations."

Martin's face lit up. "Brilliant."

He went back to the phone. "He speaks English. I need him to be able to communicate with international organizations. Thank you so much. I owe you one."

He hung up.

"Done."

My mind blew up.

"When do we start?"

"Half an hour ago."

"When do you need logistics built by?"

"The first plane is landing at the airport tomorrow at noon."

That's how I became one of the co-founders of the Agency for Humanitarian Aid. By the time I left, we had distributed almost two million tons of food to 500,000 citizens of Sarajevo every other week during the siege.

The language I picked because I liked American movies—the subject I nearly failed twice—saved my life.

Here I am now, decades later, living in America, speaking English, and making a living as a financial advisor. And writing a book—in English, no less.

**Shoulder Tap:** You don't need to know how. You need to start. The skills you dismiss today might be the ones that save you tomorrow.

## THE SUCK

Here's what the military taught me. What English taught me. What financial math taught me. What every hard thing I didn't choose but had to survive taught me: Discipline is freedom.

Not the greeting-card version. Not the poster on the gym wall. The real version—the one Jocko Willink made famous, and that I nodded along to when I finally read his book years later, because I'd already lived it.

When the arena is assigned, you don't get to find your fit. You don't get to discover your natural ability and align yourself with it. You get whatever you get, and the only question is what you will do inside these constraints.

Fighting the constraints wastes energy. Resenting the constraints poisons your mind. Wishing for different constraints changes nothing.

But discipline—actual discipline, the kind that shows up whether you feel like it or not—creates space. It earns trust. It opens doors. It gives you options that resistance and resentment never will.

The professors who failed me didn't ask what I wanted. Neither did the military. Neither did the war.

But inside each of those arenas, I found something. The rewriting method that taught me how to learn. The language that became my ticket to different work. The second hand that reminded me that things pass. The reality distortion field that made unbearable things bearable.

I didn't choose any of it. But I embraced it.

That's the suck. You embrace what you didn't choose. You find the meaning in the mandatory. You stop waiting for circumstances to improve and start extracting value from the circumstances you have.

**Shoulder Tap:** The suck is not the obstacle to your growth. It is your growth. Embrace it.

It doesn't feel noble while you're doing it. It feels like survival. It feels like gritting your teeth and getting through another day.

But on the other side, when discipline has become a habit and the hard thing has become part of you, you realize what it built.

It built someone who can handle pressure. Someone who doesn't need perfect conditions to perform. Someone who knows the worst moments pass, and the skills you didn't choose might be the ones that matter most.

## BEFORE YOU MOVE ON → SHOULDER TAPS FROM THIS CHAPTER

- The standards that annoyed you growing up might be the standards that save you later. You don't always know what you're being prepared for.
- When you think things can't get worse, look at the second hand. It's still moving. That means this moment—however bad—is already becoming the past. You don't have to carry it like it will last forever. It won't.
- You are the writer, director and the lead role in the movie of your life. The narrative you run in your head shapes what you can endure and who you become.
- Confidence earned inside the system is not permission to ignore the system. Know which rules bend and which ones break you.
- Sometimes the lesson isn't the content—it's the method. Learning how to learn is the skill that unlocks everything else.
- Pain is a teacher. Sometimes it's the only one you'll listen to. But pain alone doesn't teach you anything—it's the perspective you choose to take regarding that pain that determines whether you grow or just suffer.

- You don't learn things in classrooms. You learn them in rooms where you have no choice but to perform.
- You don't need to know how. You need to start. The skills you dismiss today might be the ones that save you tomorrow.
- The suck is not the obstacle to your growth. It *is* your growth. Embrace it.

Discipline gets you through what's assigned. It doesn't prepare you for what's chosen.

And what comes next—I chose it. Not because I had to. Because something in me refused to do anything else.

FOUR

# Finding Meaning

## INAT: THE INVISIBLE POWER OF RESILIENCE

There's a word in Serbo-Croatian: *inat*.

It doesn't translate cleanly into English. The closest approximation is stubbornness mixed with spite, but that makes it sound petty.

It's not petty. It's deeper than that.

*Inat* is woven into the tapestry of people in the Balkans. It's in our DNA. It's the refusal to be defeated by circumstance. The "fuck you" you whisper to the universe when it tries to break you. The fire that burns hotter when someone tries to put it out.

Everything I did since the day my values and my life blew up—the day of the Breadline Massacre and the bombing of my neighborhood—was in a search for meaning.

Not purpose. Purpose is a destination, something you work toward, a goal with a shape. That comes later. Meaning is different. Meaning is what you hold onto when the ground disappears beneath you. It's the answer to "why keep going?" when there's no logical reason to.

Viktor Frankl understood this. In *Man's Search for Meaning*, he wrote that when suffering is unavoidable, the suffering itself becomes the source of meaning. You can't escape it. You can only choose how you carry it.

It was *inat* that led me to make a decision that I would not leave Sarajevo until this was over. Even if it cost me my life.

I couldn't be hopeless. I couldn't be helpless. Those weren't options.

My name put me at risk.

I lived on the seventh floor. Beautiful view of the city. Which also meant a beautiful line of sight across it. The militias were hunting snipers, and a seventh-floor apartment with a Serbian name on the door was exactly the kind of place they'd look.

They came through nineteen times. Every time, I had one option. Be completely, uncomplicatedly honest. No hedging. No clever answers. Just the truth, handed over without hesitation, and hope that it landed.

It always did. I don't have a rational explanation for that. Maybe it was the way I said it. Maybe they read something in my face. Maybe it was the sight of my sister Nataša and me caring for our mother, who was dying through all of it—the siege, the snipers, the nineteen searches. Three people just trying to hold on. Maybe that was harder to suspect. Maybe it was God. Probably God. What I know is that I learned something in those moments that no classroom ever taught me. The truth doesn't just set you free philosophically. Sometimes it sets you free literally. With men holding weapons standing in your living room.

I could have left. Some did. I knew people who got out, who decided the risk wasn't worth it, who made the reasonable choice.

But here's what I saw in the refugees, including my father, and later my sister and mother, who were outside the city when the siege closed: their lives were arguably even more miserable than ours. They spent every waking moment worrying about us, about their loved ones, and feeling enormous guilt for leaving. Their personalities were falling apart. Marriages were falling apart. Relationships were falling apart. The letters and conversations I had with my sister and father were heartbreaking.

I was a beacon of light and hope. I was the guy who stayed.

I chose not to surrender. I chose not to give in. I chose not to break down.

That is *inat.*

> **Shoulder Tap:** *When everything breaks, you discover what actually matters.* When suffering is unavoidable, the suffering itself becomes the source of meaning. You can't escape it. You can only choose how you carry it.

## ORDER DEFEATS CHAOS

The morbidity of our situation during the siege has been well documented. Televised in real time. And there was something both cool and crazy about living in a siege that the whole world was watching. We felt like protagonists in a war movie, yet we were being bombed and killed and starved to death.

The reality distortion field became reality.

I wanted to get the fuck out of there as badly as I could. But I knew the life I wanted tomorrow would be impacted by what I did today. So I maintained dual focus. Survive the present. Build the future.

I poured my energy, my talents, my genius—everything—into the agency for humanitarian aid. Even though I hadn't done any of this before the war, I decided I was going to be the best logistics leader I could possibly be. There would be no obstacle too big and no problem too complex.

Fighting evil by doing good became the meaning of my life.

As they were bombing us and killing us, we were rebuilding stronger, more resilient. That became a way of life—not just for me, but for every one of us in Sarajevo.

I spent the entire war doing civilian work, not carrying a gun. I felt I could make a bigger impact by making sure that the things they were trying to destroy during the war not only survived but became better and stronger.

---

THE CRISIS COMMITTEE met regularly in those months. Head of hospital. Head of logistics (me). Nutritionists. City officials. And, for reasons I never fully understood, the head of the philosophy department of the University of Sarajevo.

He was an older man. Well-known and respected in his field. A bit of a celebrity. Quiet in the meetings. He listened more than he spoke, which in wartime made him unusual.

After one meeting, he pulled me aside.

"You know what you're doing?"

I looked at him. Was this a challenge? An accusation? He didn't seem angry.

"I think I do," I said. "But why don't you tell me what I'm doing?"

"You're trying to create order in a world of chaos. You're the only one who is building order in a world of chaos. You know how absurd that is?"

I didn't hesitate.

"With all due respect, I believe that by building order, we can defeat chaos."

The professor smiled. Something between admiration and bewilderment.

"God bless you. I think you're completely insane. And I thank God for people like you. Because people like me would not survive without people like you."

**Shoulder Tap:** By building order, we can defeat chaos. Someone has to believe that. It might as well be you.

## JOURNALING HELPS US STAY SANE IN AN INSANE WORLD

When I went home to get ready to start the agency for humanitarian aid, I brought a box of pens, the logistics textbook I had translated, and a notebook—the kind with dates on the pages, where every day has its own space. A daily journal.

I wrote every day. What happened. Who said what. What we decided.

Writing notes helped me remember. I needed to remember better than anybody else, because I wanted to be able to go back and say, "In that meeting, on that day, you said this." To me, that was self-preservation. I believed in the power of logic and argument, and I needed the data and evidence.

But I later realized that writing things down was also a way to channel extreme stress. By putting it on paper, I was detaching emotionally from the situation I was in. That detachment helped me see things more objectively. Make adjustments. Live another day.

We did not plan parties. We did not know if we were going to live. But we lived for that day.

That's where I landed. Not as a philosophy. As a survival strategy.

I don't worry about anything. I plan for the future, I learn from the past, and I live in the present.

**Shoulder Tap:** Write it down. Detaching emotionally from what you're experiencing helps you see it more objectively. Plan for the future, learn from the past, and live in the present.

## OPTIMIST BY CHOICE

In every room I was in, I chose to be the voice of optimism. The voice of inspiration.

People would joke with me about how often I said, "I've been around. I've seen things. The war is almost over."

I said the war was almost over a thousand times.

It wasn't over.

The second hand was still moving.

During the siege, I left Sarajevo for work and actually went back to the city. People thought I was crazy. Why would anyone ever want to go back?

Because I had a ten-year vision. And I also had the next-day focus.

I knew that the life I wanted to live, the person I wanted to become in ten years, would be a person who had lived through the war, survived the siege, and said "fuck you" to the forces trying to destroy us. A person who had turned *inat* into a weapon, just like 400,000 other people in Sarajevo did.

That became our calling card.

## HITTING ROCK BOTTOM

February 1993. Nine months into the siege. It was after 10 p.m.

Most of the phone lines in Sarajevo had been burned. We didn't have a connection with the outside world. The only way to communicate was through amateur radio operators—"Ham radio," they call it in America. My father was in Slovenia, on the phone with a radio amateur in Ljubljana. The Ljubljana operator was on the radio with another amateur in Sarajevo. The Sarajevo operator was on the phone with my neighbor, Knežević. And Knežević walked up seven flights of stairs to knock on my door and tell me to come to the phone.

That's how it worked. A chain of voices. Strangers passing words between a father and a son across a war zone.

And through that chain, the message came: My mother had died in Slovenia.

---

IN NOVEMBER 1992, I evacuated my mother and sister through convoys organized by the Jewish Humanitarian Agency. The siege had made everything impossible—medicine, electricity, proper care—and my mother had cancer. She needed blood transfusions. Because of my position, I was able to get them for her. But that treatment didn't exist inside a war zone at scale.

At first, she didn't want to leave. She didn't want to leave me.

Her health kept deteriorating. I finally said to her, "If we get you a blood transfusion to make you feel better, we might be taking blood from saving the lives of kids and young people. You need to go."

She relented and was evacuated in November.

Three months later, in February, she was gone.

That night, I went home to my apartment. It was curfew. I couldn't go anywhere.

And for the first time in my life, I cried uncontrollably.

The pain of losing her was unbearable. I broke down completely.

When you go through a crisis—war, pandemic, siege—everything is exacerbated. Everything happens faster. More intense. Grief that might otherwise take months to process gets compressed into hours.

That night, I went through all five stages of grief: denial, anger, bargaining, depression, acceptance.

By dawn, I was at acceptance.

I decided not to go to the funeral.

It wasn't that I couldn't. It was a decision. A purple brain decision, the hardest kind.

Everything in my body wanted me to go. My red brain, my heart, was screaming at me to be there. To say a proper goodbye to my mother. To stand at her grave and let the finality wash over me.

My blue brain ran the calculations. Getting out of Sarajevo at this time meant running across the airport runway in the middle of the night, under sniper fire. Even if I made it out, I might not be able to come back. And if I couldn't come back, everything I had built, all the meaning I had found in fighting evil by doing good, would be abandoned.

By leaving, I would be betraying the very meaning that was keeping me alive.

I double-checked my math. I measured my decision against what my mother would have said, what she would have wanted. And I was at peace. She would have demanded I stay. She was the one who taught me that duty isn't a burden—it's a choice. That the hardest thing and the right thing are usually the same thing. That you don't leave things undone.

I stayed in Sarajevo because of *inat.* Because of meaning. Because of the ten-year vision and the next-day focus.

But underneath all of that, I stayed because she raised me to stay.

> **Shoulder Tap:** Rock bottom is a foundation, not a grave. When you've hit the floor, the meaning you've built is what lifts you back up.

## TO BE A GREAT LEADER, YOU HAVE TO BE REPLACEABLE

Effective leadership is about influence. It is about getting things done through others.

Up to this point, I was not a leader. I was a manager. I was a doer.

Going through the stages of grief when my mother died made me realize something: I was trapped by my own design.

I had decided to stay. I had found meaning in fighting evil by doing good. But the way I did it was not very leaderful. Every critical system and decision related to logistics had to go through me. I was controlling everything, or at least controlling the things I felt would protect me from being called to the front lines.

Freedom is my number one value. And here I was, trying to create my own freedom, and I had trapped myself by my own doing.

This is where I learned the lesson that to be a great leader, you have to be replaceable.

---

THE FIRST PROBLEM I needed to solve was delegating authority. Too many critical things were filtered through me, things that could be done more effectively by others.

My driving force for delegation was freedom. Freedom of time. Freedom of relationships. The ability to move, to visit family, to have options.

I turned to Haris Bešlagić. He became my swim buddy in the whole process. With his counsel, his contacts, and his great sense of reality, we created a plan and started transferring critical functions of my role to others.

And as I surrendered control, something unexpected happened.

I started gaining influence.

All of a sudden, my voice was wanted. Sought after. I did not have to yell. People came to me for guidance instead of approval. They brought me problems they wanted help thinking through, not just decisions they needed me to make.

This new reality felt really good. I had the feeling I was doing the right thing.

---

AS HARIS and I worked on the plan, I delegated the things I had been doing to seven other people.

Seven.

On one hand, you could look at this as evidence that my rigid individualism was so awesome—I could do a lot of things. But on the other hand, I realized I had been the obstacle to growth for the teams I was leading.

By delegating authority, I unleashed energy. Enthusiasm. Other people taking on the mission and carrying it further. It was a beautiful thing to watch.

In nine months, I was able to transition out of the day-to-day, and the logistics arm of the agency for humanitarian aid became self-led. My team no longer needed me.

By the time I left, we had distributed almost two million tons of humanitarian aid to 500,000 citizens of Sarajevo every other week. During the siege.

That wasn't me. That was us.

As this was happening, I was able to do more things in my genius. At that time, my genius was talking to international donors and representatives of other agencies. Using my English. Using my influence as a co-founder of the agency.

For months, I had been trying to find different ways to get my hands on a UN accreditation, the pass that would give me freedom of movement in and out of the city, but without success. Then, in the summer of 1993, I met Karel Zelenka of Catholic Relief Services.

We spent a day together. I walked him through our distribution system. Our accountability measures. Our technology for tracking supplies. He was impressed.

At the end of our day together, he asked if I would be interested in helping CRS start its operations in Bosnia.

In one conversation, the UN accreditation I had been chasing for months became a serious possibility.

> **Shoulder Tap:** You can't scale yourself. You scale through systems and people. To be a great leader, you have to be replaceable.

## NEED, NOT CREED

My response to Karel was immediate. "But I'm not Catholic."

Karel smiled. "Our mission is to serve the world based on need, not creed. I believe you could be our man to get things going for us. If you're interested, we're interested."

*Need, not creed.*

That was their tagline. It was on everything—every document, every business card, every piece of letterhead with the CRS logo. Assistance given without religious discrimination.

I was looking at an organization that had already put words to what I believed. This was my first real connection to the power of a *why.* Not a slogan. A reason to exist. A reason for anyone to care.

Need, not creed. Simple. Clear. Meaningful.

These were my people.

Over the following weeks, I met Greg Hofnecht, who had just come from Cambodia to head Bosnian operations.

Greg and I hit it off right away. We had so many things in common. We clicked immediately. Shortly after, Phil Oldham and Greg Roth arrived, two project managers working on the Bosnia program out of Zagreb. They would be my counterparts. The team was taking shape.

I felt this was going to work.

Now I had to create a narrative in which the Bosnian government would allow me to leave the agency I had co-founded and run for nearly two years, an agency where I was probably the most senior member. The people I had elevated and delegated to were the ones who helped make it possible.

On October 15, 1993, I became the first employee of Catholic Relief Services in Bosnia.

---

NOTHING ABOUT WORKING in a war zone is easy. But compared to the agency for humanitarian aid, where I was building everything from scratch during an active siege—no resources, no infrastructure, and no support—CRS felt easier. Not easy. Easier.

I had freedom of movement now. UN accreditation. I could get in and out of the city. I had colleagues with international experience. Resources. A system behind me.

The work was still hard. But it was a different kind of hard. Less survival, more building.

CRS became the bridge between the meaning I had found in helping my city survive and what I wanted for myself. Not only did it help me continue doing positive work, but it helped me link meaning with what I now call "WDYWFY" (What Do You Want For Yourself), which you'll learn about in a later chapter.

The meaning needed to be practical. I needed to pay bills. I needed freedom of movement—the ability to visit my family, get out of the city, and come back in. There were a lot of people who left and never came back. I wasn't going to be one of them.

CRS gave me a bigger stage. A bigger baton. A bigger weapon.

The fuckers were everywhere. Now I could fight them in other places too.

**Shoulder Tap:** Pay attention to what energizes you when everything is falling apart. That's data about your genius.

## FREEDOM OF MOVEMENT HAS A PRICE

CRS had a mission beyond logistics: build civil society. Rebuild bridges between people on opposite sides of the front lines. Create economic ties that could outlast the war.

In order to execute those projects, Phil Oldham and I had to get in a car, drive across the front lines into enemy territory, and work with civilians on basic survival projects.

Restarting milk factories. Pasta production. The underwear project, for which we imported cotton from Egypt and employed two hundred people to make underwear for distribution on both sides.

Every time I got into one of our armored cars, I felt like my life was in other people's hands.

---

THE FIRST PART of the war, I spent trapped in Sarajevo. I knew the rules. Stay away from windows. Avoid open spaces. Don't be predictable. The fear was constant but manageable.

In the second part of the war, I was crossing checkpoints. Moving around. The fear in the second part was a hundred times bigger than the fear in the first.

The road I usually traveled was nineteen miles long. Nineteen miles. And in those nineteen miles, I had to pass through six checkpoints: the UN, the Bosnian Army, another UN, two Serbian, and one Croatian.

Six checkpoints in nineteen miles. And between each checkpoint? Frontline. No man's land.

I traveled that road many times. Sometimes several times a week. Every time I got into that armored car, every time I approached a checkpoint, the churn in my stomach was there.

It never got easier. It just became more bearable.

Because of my connections and ability to move, I became a mule. Mail. Cookies. Cash. Things that family members would send to their relatives on the other side. I would carry them through front lines and through checkpoints and learned not to think about them.

Because if I were caught with undeclared items, there would be hell to pay.

That's where a lot of my PTSD comes from.

> **Shoulder Tap:** Sometimes, the most dangerous situations look the least dramatic. The fear that accumulates in small doses can be more damaging than the fear that arrives all at once.

## FAITH WILL SET YOU FREE

What I learned during those times in Sarajevo, crossing checkpoints, is that sometimes, when things are impossible, faith gets you through.

You have to let it go and believe that things will work out. Even when you have no idea how.

I've been stopped at checkpoints more times than I can count. Most were routine.

One was not.

The checkpoint was called Sierra One. I was returning from a coordination meeting in Kiseljak.

The officer in charge decided to strip our car and search everything in it. Compare it against the manifest. He found a box of cookies and some letters that were not listed.

That was enough. He went into interrogation mode. Bullying mode. And somewhere during the questioning, he decided I was a CIA spy.

He proceeded to question me. Accuse me. Verbal abuse. Not torture, but close enough.

I was traveling with colleagues, expatriates who started advocating on my behalf. A British military vehicle stopped. Officers got out to plead for my release.

As more people got involved, the commander became more agitated. His ego was invested now. Every intervention made things worse.

I turned to my colleagues. In English, loud enough for him to hear: "Please stop saving me."

The Serbian commander understood. He started to chuckle.

That action may have turned the momentum in my favor. I don't remember exactly how, but I was able to talk my way out. About forty-five minutes to an hour after we were stopped, we were on our way again.

What I couldn't tell anyone was that I was carrying a significant amount of cash in my flak jacket. The Vatican had sent it for the Archbishop of Sarajevo, and I was the mule. I also couldn't say that I was running late for a meeting with Ambassador Holbrooke and General Wesley Clark.

---

HOW DO you survive situations like that? You can't control outcomes. You can only control your integrity.

I started believing in God during the siege of Sarajevo. Not a foxhole conversion. Not desperation dressed up as faith. Something deeper.

When you're driving through checkpoints with contraband in your jacket, meeting with people who want you dead, carrying hope between communities trying to destroy each other, you recognize limits.

If I believed I was doing things with integrity, if the meaning of the work was genuinely helping civilians, then I had to surrender the rest.

Whatever happens, happens. I accept whatever comes my way.

That's not fatalism. That's liberation.

You do your best. God does the rest.

I can't tell you how many times I should have died and didn't. Dodging grenades by walking left instead of right. Surviving checkpoints that should have ended me. Being spared when others weren't.

I started believing there is always a reason. I might not know what it is, but I learned to trust that at some point, I will figure it out.

I was spared for a reason.

Maybe writing this book is part of that reason.

**Shoulder Tap:** You can do all the planning, but having faith that things will work out will set you free. Do your best.

## BEFORE YOU MOVE ON → SHOULDER TAPS FROM THIS CHAPTER

- When everything breaks, you discover what actually matters. When suffering is unavoidable, the suffering itself becomes the source of meaning. You can't escape it. You can only choose how you carry it.
- By building order, we can defeat chaos. Someone has to believe that. It might as well be you.
- Write it down. Detaching emotionally from what you're experiencing helps you see it more objectively. Plan for the future, learn from the past, and live in the present.
- Rock bottom is a foundation, not a grave. When you've hit the floor, the meaning you've built is what lifts you back up.
- Sometimes, the most dangerous situations look the least dramatic. The fear that accumulates in small doses can be more damaging than the fear that arrives all at once.
- You can't scale yourself. You scale through systems and people. To be a great leader, you have to be replaceable.

- Pay attention to what energizes you when everything is falling apart. That's data about your genius.
- You can do all the planning, but having faith that things will work out will set you free.

There's a moment in every leader's life when the fire that forged them stops being useful. Not because the heat was wrong. Because what comes next isn't about surviving the heat. It's about learning what to grow in the soil it left behind.

Act One was about being made. Act Two is about looking at what you became—and deciding what kind of man to be next.

# ACT II
# The Team

## INTRODUCTION

### ELITE LEADERSHIP IS LIKE GARDENING– THE FRAMEWORK

I was forged in pressure. You know that now.

Surviving the fire doesn't prepare you to grow things. It just makes you really, really good at not burning.

In the years after leaving Sarajevo, I achieved things most people would call success. I built businesses. I climbed the leaderboards. I earned recognition from people I respected. I kept running into the same wall, just painted in different colors.

I was doing the work of ten people and wondering why my team couldn't do the work of one.

In February 2018, eighty percent of my team walked out the door. I want you to sit with that. Eighty percent.

I had survived a war. I had crossed front lines with contraband in my jacket. I had built an organization from nothing during an active siege. I had come to America with nothing and built a business from scratch.

And I almost lost it. Because of myself.

That story is coming. But before I tell you how it happened, I need to tell you what I couldn't see that made it inevitable.

That's when I learned the hardest lesson of my leadership journey: being a high-performing doer is not the same as being a high-performing leader.

They're not even close.

A self-leading team.

Not a team that needs a great leader to function. Not a team that performs when you're watching and coasts when you're not. Not a team that falls apart every time you take a vacation.

A team that leads itself.

You wake up one Tuesday, and your phone is quiet. No emergencies. No fires. No decisions that couldn't be made without you. You lie there for a second, waiting for the panic to set in. It doesn't. Problems got solved before they reached you. Leaders developed other leaders. The business grew in a direction nobody personally pushed it. And for a split second, you wonder—am I still needed? That's not failure. That's the whole point.

Elite teams and self-leading teams are the same thing. You cannot have one without the other. And neither is possible without the framework I'm about to walk you through.

## THE LAW THAT CHANGED EVERYTHING

In one of my early conversations with Ray Kelly, the mentor who would reshape how I thought about everything, he told me two things that changed my trajectory.

The first: "To unlock the potential of the people you lead, you need to give them purpose worthy of their best efforts."

The second: "The secret sauce in building teams that achieve transformational growth is to build them as teams of leaders."

Then he introduced me to John Maxwell's Law of the Lid.

The Law of the Lid: Your growth as an organization is determined by your leadership capacity. Period.

The bad news? Most of us have low leadership capacity. Leadership is the most underrated capability in business—and in life, too.

The good news? We can build that capacity. We can all become elite leaders.

In that same conversation, Ray introduced me to the five levels of leadership. There are several versions, including John Maxwell's, Jim Collins', and Ray's, that I now call Five Levels of Leadership in Action.

In all three versions, the Level 5 leader is described as the pinnacle. But here's how Ray defined it, and this is the definition that stuck with me: *A Level 5 leader embodies all previous levels—Be Coachable, Identify Problems, Solve Problems, Galvanize People and Drive Results—plus the ability to tie everything to the* why... *And to develop other leaders who can do the same.*

That became my mission. I wanted to become a Level 5 leader.

## BUILDING MY OWN FRAMEWORK

I needed something I could actually use. Not a list of fifty best practices. The non-negotiables. The things that, if you ignore one of them, the whole system falls apart. I went back to my own experiences. I thought about the elite leaders I'd loved and wanted to emulate. I researched others.

I'm a visual learner; I needed a picture. Something I could return to every day. Every hour. Something simple enough to keep in my head under pressure.

So imagine a beachball. Not a toy. A map.

On this beach ball are six slivers—**people, trust, conflict, rituals, adaptation, results.** And holding everything together, on both ends of the ball, is **purpose**.

Purpose is the pole that runs through the center. The axis everything else rotates around. Without purpose, the ball is just colorful rubber. With it, you have something that holds together under pressure.

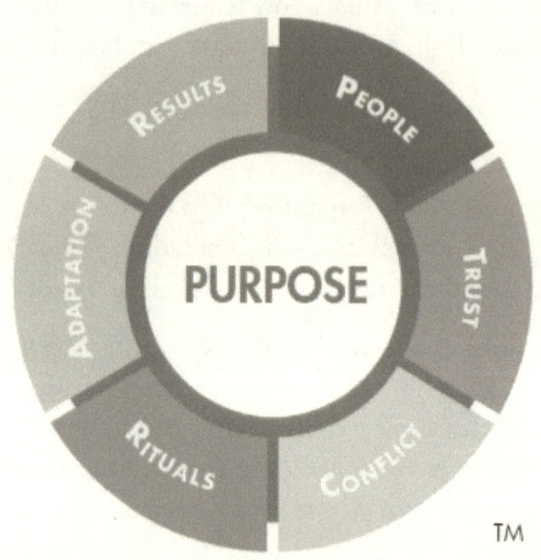


## THE SHIFT

Act One was about what the fire taught me.

Act Two is about what I learned to cultivate.

There's a difference between a leader and a gardener. A leader stands in front and says, "Follow me." A gardener creates the conditions for things to grow on their own.

You can't force a plant to grow. You can only prepare the soil. Plant the right seeds. Water them. Protect them from frost. Trust the process.

Elite leadership is the same.

The startup chaos, the survival mode, the command-and-control that built my business—those tools got me to a certain point, then they started holding me back. I hit my lid. I was at my leadership capacity.

What follows is the story of how I learned to let go. To create conditions instead of commands. To tend instead of direct.

In the chapters that follow, I'll tell you how this framework played out and how it helped me transform from a high-performing doer into a leader who builds self-leading teams.

I paid a lot of "dumb tax" learning these lessons. Dumb tax is what happens when you're too stubborn, too proud, or too green to ask for help before making the mistake. I paid a lot of it. This book exists so you don't have to.

It starts with purpose.

FIVE

# Leveling Up

## SURVIVAL IS THE VICTORY

Summer 1995. Sarajevo. My vision of becoming CRS international staff was finally coming alive.

I had been having conversations with CRS leadership for months. The promises had been made. The work had been done. I had helped with the handover between Phil Oldham and the new country director, Jim Kelly. Everything was in place.

Things were not moving fast enough. And in the back of my head, a dark thought kept swirling. Some of my family were killed in Sarajevo on the very last day of World War II. April 6, 1945. The Germans were pulling out, the war was over, and people who had survived everything else died in those final hours. *If I don't leave before this war ends,* I kept thinking, *I might meet the same fate.*

By this point, I had been living inside the siege for more than three years. Under constant fire. Snipers. Shells. The kind of daily violence that stops feeling extraordinary and starts feeling like weather.

On top of that, the last two of those years, my work with CRS had me constantly moving in and out of Sarajevo. Crossing checkpoints. Flying on planes that got shot at. Being detained long enough to wonder if this was the time it didn't work out. Every day inside the city was a risk. Every checkpoint crossing multiplied it. I was testing my luck in ways I couldn't fully account for anymore. And luck, I knew by then, has a limit.

Then Srebrenica happened. July 1995. We didn't know the full extent of what had occurred. Not yet. We knew something terrible had taken place. I had friends there who didn't make it out. The news sent my anxiety through the roof. The premonition got louder. Every day felt like borrowed time.

Then, in early August, Jim Kelly told me it was time. Move to Split, Croatia. Do the exit interviews. Be in Baltimore before Labor Day.

A few days later, Jim and I got in the car and drove.

---

THE ROAD TAKES you up and over Biokovo, a mountain range that separates the interior from the Adriatic coast. At the highest point, there's a scenic overlook. Below you, the sea stretches toward Italy. The Makarska Riviera tumbles down the mountainside like a postcard from a world that doesn't exist anymore.

I asked Jim to pull over.

He understood without me saying anything. We'd been working together for weeks. He knew what this trip meant.

I got out of the car and stood at the edge of the overlook. The wind was warm. The sky was impossibly blue. Below me, the world looked peaceful in a way that felt almost offensive.

I had been in Sarajevo for three years. Eighteen months trapped in the city during the siege. Then, another eighteen months crossing front lines and checkpoints, building programs, carrying secrets, watching friends and neighbors die while I somehow kept surviving.

Standing on that mountain, looking at that water, I had one thought: *Holy shit. I survived.*

Not relief. Not joy. Just the simple, absurd recognition that I was still alive when so many weren't. That I was leaving when so many couldn't. That the war had forged me into something I didn't fully understand yet.

Jim came over. Stood next to me. We didn't talk much.

"You want a picture?" he asked.

Yes. I wanted a picture.

He took it. Me standing at the edge of the overlook, the Adriatic spread out below, the weight of three years visible in my face even though I was smiling.

I've been back to that spot. With Laura. With our kids. Different picture. Different life. Same mountain. The man standing there with his family had become something the first man was only beginning to imagine.

But that day, I was just a guy who had made it out.

Five minutes. Maybe less. Then we got back in the car.

Work to do.

> **Shoulder Tap:** Take the moments when they come. The wins don't announce themselves. Sometimes survival is the victory, and recognizing it is the work.

## BUILD THE HABITS THAT WILL SAVE YOU BEFORE YOU NEED SAVING

CRS had a safe house apartment in Split. That's where I'd work for the next few weeks. I would organize the handoff, collaborate with colleagues, and prepare to leave the continent.

Phil Oldham was already in Baltimore. The transition was complete. Now it was my turn to move.

I should have felt triumphant. Instead, I felt like I was holding my breath.

---

THREE WEEKS after Jim and I arrived in Split, my back completely locked up.

Not metaphorically. Literally. I couldn't sit, stand, walk, or lie down without excruciating pain. Something had short-circuited in my body, and I was paralyzed by it.

No warning. No injury. Just… frozen.

That's when Dan Creson, a psychiatrist and CRS's PTSD expert, called.

He was our trauma consultant from the University of Texas. We'd brought him in to train civilians in Sarajevo on psychological first aid, building capacity for the PTSD crisis we knew was coming when the fighting stopped.

He was impossible to miss. Six foot eight. Stetson hat. Cowboy boots. He chain-smoked Marlboro Reds and was one of the top authorities on PTSD in the country. He was either fearless or crazy, but it was hard to tell which.

Before Jim and I had left Sarajevo, Dan had pulled me aside.

"You're never coming back, right?"

"Nope."

"You're not allowed to leave until we have dinner together."

I'd agreed. And now he was calling to collect.

When I told him I couldn't move, he said, "I'll be there in ten minutes."

"I can't go anywhere."

"I'll be there in ten minutes."

He showed up at the safe house apartment, looked at me barely standing, and said, "Let's go."

He made me walk. Ten blocks through Split. Every step felt impossible. By block five, I was starting to feel better. By block eight, I could almost move normally.

We found a restaurant. Sat down. Ordered wine.

And then he told me I was the luckiest son of a bitch he'd ever met.

"I've had patients where PTSD hit them, and they killed their family members. Killed their wives. Killed their kids." He took a drag of his Marlboro. "Your back hurts. You're lucky."

I didn't know what to say.

"Listen to me," he said. "I'm going to give you three things. You're going to remember them for the rest of your life."

I was listening.

"Number one. No matter what happens, no matter what symptoms show up, no matter how weird or scary or unexpected, remember, it's normal. Whatever hits you, however it manifests, it's a normal response to abnormal circumstances. Do not freak out. It's normal."

"Okay."

"Number two. Are you planning to quit smoking when you get to America?"

"Yes."

"Good. When you get there, quit. And understand this: smoking will likely become a trigger. So eliminate the trigger. If you ever start smoking again, it could trigger everything you've been holding down. Don't do it."

"What's number three?"

He leaned forward. "When everything else fails—and it will—exercise. Exercise, exercise, exercise, exercise. When you can't exercise anymore, exercise more. You need to wear yourself down. Physical exhaustion is your friend. It's the release valve."

We sat there for hours. Somewhere between the second and fourth bottles of wine, we talked about war and trauma and survival and what comes next.

By the time we finished, I could walk normally. The pain wasn't gone, but the paralysis was broken.

I've never smoked again. I've exercised through every crisis. And when the weird symptoms show up—and they still do, thirty years later—I remember: it's normal.

**Shoulder Tap:** Prepare for the invisible wounds. They don't announce themselves, and they don't follow predictable schedules. Build the habits that will save you before you need saving.

## MARRY UP

The most important decision in your life is who you marry.

On Friday, September 1, 1995, I boarded a connecting flight from Paris to New York to move to America. A new world.

There were a lot of thoughts going through my head. I had a window seat and kept my shades open for most of the flight. There's something therapeutic about being high above the clouds as you think about your life. What came before and what might happen when you land.

The most important decision I made during that flight was to suspend judgment. I knew America. Movies. News. Propaganda going both directions. The version that got exported and the version that got imported and neither one of them reliable. I had images in my head that had nothing to do with reality and everything to do with what other people had decided I should think.

I made a choice at thirty thousand feet over the Atlantic. Leave it on the plane. All of it. The assumptions, the second-hand impressions, the cultural baggage.

I was going to land and see what was actually there. Not what I'd been told was there. Not what the movies said. Not what the news said. What was actually, genuinely there—when I looked at it with my own eyes, without someone else's filter over them.

Start with a blank slate. Create my own impressions. Arrive free.

My first weekend in Baltimore was Labor Day weekend. The team at CRS headquarters set me up in a beautiful apartment downtown.

My first couple of months were amazing. I was meeting new people, learning new things. My life had meaning. We were working on preparing for the deployment of the U.S. military to Bosnia as part of the Dayton Peace Accords.

I was also a bit of a celebrity. When I got to the Baltimore headquarters, a lot of people knew my name. My situation reports from Sarajevo had been widely read. I had speaking engagements, telling people stories about Bosnia, raising awareness—raising funds—and helping the world learn the facts about the genocide and the siege.

That fall, an option was presented to me: consider going back to Bosnia as a member of the government to help rebuild the country.

That conversation triggered PTSD. I did not sleep for days.

The words of my friend from Houston came to help me way sooner than I thought: *It's normal. It's normal. It's normal.*

Something else happened that helped pull me forward.

I met Laura.

She started working in the same department. We were getting ready to activate the rapid response team. I was one of the members at headquarters, and she did admin support.

At first, I knew I liked her. A lot. And I thought she liked me.

But the fog of PTSD and everything else going on wouldn't allow me to make any moves. Then I found out I was being deployed in January of 1996 to Sierra Leone.

It was the week before my deployment that she and I became close. Curiosity turned into something more.

---

I WAS DEPLOYED to Sierra Leone with a clear mission: support the local program. If things went from bad to worse, I was ready. I had logistics experience, a crisis management background, and war experience.

Shortly after my arrival, the military government changed hands. It was not violent, but Sierra Leone was already in the middle of a civil war, and a change at the top meant nobody knew which direction things were going. The uncertainty was its own kind of pressure. Sierra Leone was back in the headlines.

Laura and I kept in touch. Letters at first. Real letters, written by hand, crossing an ocean in an envelope. Then she started sending cassette tapes—music she thought I'd like. Her handwriting on the label.

None of it was anything I would have listened to before. When 10,000 Maniacs or Depeche Mode came through the speakers, I remember thinking, *What the hell is this?*

But it was from her, so I played it anyway.

I played those tapes constantly. Driving from Georgia's Spanish restaurant on the beach outside Freetown, winding up through the hills to where my house sat above the city, the music became the soundtrack. A constant reminder of the world outside. The one I was trying to get back to.

Three years of war had taught me to keep the walls up. You stay functional by staying controlled. You don't let things in that might slow you down. And here was this woman, through music I wasn't even sure I liked, getting through anyway.

Every time I played those tapes, she came back into focus.

She had a boyfriend. In the past, that would have stopped me. But I'd crossed too many checkpoints to let fear of rejection slow me down. She had free choice. I just had to be worth choosing.

Ten months of letters and mix tapes and distance, and I was back in Baltimore for Phil Oldham and Jennifer Oldham's wedding. When Laura and I met again, curiosity turned into love.

---

A WEEK after I returned to Sierra Leone, she called. Two in the morning her time.

“That's it,” she said. “I don't want to spend the rest of my life wondering what would have happened if we'd gotten more serious.”

My response, without hesitation: "If you want to come to Sierra Leone, you have a place to stay.”

This turned into long-distance conversations. In 1996, an international call between Sierra Leone and Baltimore cost real money. We made them anyway. In the beginning, a couple of times a week. Then every day. Then a couple of times a day.

What do you talk about when you're eight thousand miles apart?

You talk about things that are important.

Values. Vision. The future. In those conversations, I started realizing we had the same values. A similar vision of the future. I was still carrying the war—the Breadline Massacre, the checkpoints, the things I'd seen that didn't have names yet. Laura was the first person who really listened. Not with pity. Not with horror. Just with full attention.

She didn't try to fix it. She didn't redirect to something lighter. She asked the next question. And the one after that.

The more I spoke, the more the open wounds started hurting less.

I knew that if I met her again in person, and she was the same person I was talking to on the phone, this would be the woman I would marry.

---

MARCH 1997. Laura and I met in Vienna.

Before Vienna, I told my sister, family, friends, anyone who would listen the same thing: If the woman I've been talking to on the phone is the same one I pick up at the airport, she's going to be your daughter-in-law.

Nataša made me promise I wouldn't propose until she checked her out.

She met all of my family. Then she drove with my dad and me to Sarajevo, through what was still an active war zone, so I could defend my master's thesis.

Everyone who met her fell in love with her instantly.

The sidebar conversations among my family—"Is this going to be our *snajka* (daughter-in-law)?"—turned into, "She *better* be our *snajka*. We've never met a woman like this before."

The night before my thesis defense, in the Sarajevo apartment of my mother, I proposed.

She said, "I'd like to say yes. But you need to ask my mom for permission first."

I looked at her. "That's cute. But I don't exactly live a mile away from your mother. That's a whole world I need to travel to have that conversation in person."

In the meantime, she said yes.

I looked up toward the sky and said, "You and I will go places."

The next morning I stood in front of my dissertation committee. Four hours. In a formal academic setting. With my future wife sitting in the back of the room.

Halfway through, my professor—also my thesis advisor—stopped the proceedings.

"Saša. Are you going to marry this woman?"

I looked at him. Looked at Laura. Looked back.

"Yes."

"Good. Because if you said no, I was going to fail you. Nobody sits through a defense in a foreign language for four hours unless they're in love. I just wanted to make sure you also know your material."

I passed.

---

JANUARY 1996 TO MARCH 1997. Fourteen months. We had been in the same country for a handful of weeks. We built the whole thing on paper and phone calls and cassette tapes. When I picked her up in Vienna, I had spent more hours talking to her on the phone than I had ever spent in the same room with her.

We were madly in love. We'd just gotten engaged. And we both needed to go back—she to Baltimore, me to Sierra Leone.

Our plan was simple: I would come home to Baltimore on leave later in the year, ask for her mother's blessing, and eventually we'd figure out how and when we were getting married.

We decided to keep it a secret until I talked to her mom.

Planning is helpful, but plans are worthless.

Six weeks later, another coup in Sierra Leone.

On May 25th, 1997, when the coup broke out, and I was trying to reach people in Baltimore to let them know what was going on, the only phone line I could get through on was Laura's. I guess my phone had her on speed dial.

I woke her up. "I need you to wake up and call Ken Hackett, our executive director. Tell him there's been a coup." I gave her all kinds of instructions. She made the call, and soon, our secret was no longer a secret.

When we told Ken Hackett we were getting married, he laughed. "Oh, now that makes sense. I was completely confused. Why did Laura call me?"

I was evacuated from Sierra Leone. In July of 1997, I moved in with Laura to start our new life.

Here's the thing about Laura: I thought we were the same.

We aren't.

What we share are values. Character. The desire to do good, to be better, and to help people. We have tremendous respect for each other.

Everything else? Opposite.

She likes punk rock. I love classical music. She falls asleep at symphony concerts. I can't understand how anyone survives a mosh pit.

Early in the marriage—Montreal, epic fight—we realized we didn't want to do any of the same things for fun.

*How the fuck did we get married?* I remember thinking. *We don't want to do anything the other person wants to do.*

The solution was simple once we stopped trying to merge into one person. One weekend, we do what she wants; one weekend, we do what I want. We get to know each other by experiencing each other's worlds instead of fighting about whose world is right.

Thirty years later, it still works.

> **Shoulder Tap:** The most important decision in your life is who you marry. Alignment isn't agreement. You don't need to want the same things to want the same future. Shared values. Mutual respect. And the humility to take turns.

## EVERY NEW ENVIRONMENT REQUIRES YOU TO PROVE YOURSELF AGAIN

Baltimore, Maryland. 1997.

CRS couldn't offer me a permanent position. The funding had shifted. My skills were needed, but "needed" doesn't always translate to "employed."

I did what every immigrant does. I sent resumes.

Three hundred eighty-five of them.

I got one letter back. One. From a company I'd never heard of, for a role that had nothing to do with my experience, offering a salary that seemed insulting compared to the responsibility I'd carried in war zones.

Three hundred eighty-four rejections. Silence. The American silence that says *you don't exist here.*

I was a logistics chief who'd built humanitarian operations from nothing. I'd managed crisis teams under fire. I'd led people through conditions that most Americans couldn't imagine.

None of that translated.

The credentials that mattered in Sarajevo meant nothing in Baltimore. My experience was too foreign, too unverifiable, too strange. Nobody knew how to read a résumé that said, *"Built emergency aid distribution network during active siege."*

Finally, a realization: *Maybe I should focus on entry-level.*

Eight applications to financial services firms. Eight callbacks. After 385 silences, eight callbacks.

I had a heartbeat. In financial services, everyone with a heartbeat gets a call. I qualified.

**Shoulder Tap:** Your past credentials don't transfer automatically. Every new environment requires you to prove yourself again. Pride will tell you that's unfair. Wisdom will tell you that's opportunity.

## MIND OF A CAPITALIST, HEART OF A SOCIAL WORKER

The Merrill Lynch interview was memorable.

The interviewer leaned back, assessed me, and asked, "How many millionaires do you know?"

Zero. The answer was zero. I knew refugees and humanitarians and people who measured wealth in survival rather than portfolios.

I didn't get that job.

American Express Financial Advisors was different. They didn't ask about my network. They asked about my values, what I believed about helping people with their finances.

I told them what I'd learned in Sarajevo: you can't help people by telling them what they need. You have to understand what they actually want, then build systems that connect the two.

Bill Morgan looked at me and said, "If you have the mind of a capitalist and the heart of a social worker, this is the place for you. And if you're smart enough to be dumb enough to do what we ask you to do, the sky is the limit."

That phrase became my operating system.

The choice between making money and making a difference is a false choice. The best businesses are the ones where profit is a byproduct of genuine service.

I was hired.

---

DURING MY FIRST year at American Express Financial Advisors (now Ameriprise Financial), I saw what it looks like when things actually work. I did what I always do. I learned the system, applied myself, built a vision. It worked. Within a year I was one of the top first-year advisors in the company. Then District Manager. Then VP. Then we moved to Albany.

On my fortieth birthday, I made the move from employee to owner, founder. We built a financial advisory practice. The same work I'd been doing, but now it was ours. From executing someone else's vision to building our own. Laura was my co-founder, my business partner. She's been in this from the start.

We weren't going to build a business for profit only. Our background—the way we met during the crises, the service that CRS had provided to millions of people—had branded us as the type of leaders who believed that running a business for profit alone is not enough of a reason to get up in the morning.

We wanted to build businesses with a positive impact. Not just on our team members and our family and our clients, but on the communities we lived in.

Mind of a capitalist. Heart of a social worker.

Both. Always.

> **Shoulder Tap:** The choice between profit and purpose is a false choice. The real skill is designing systems where they reinforce each other.

## LUCKY OR ELITE?

People ask me sometimes, "Were you lucky?"

To survive the war. To find Laura. To land in America with a job and a purpose and a path forward.

Yes. Of course. Luck is always part of the story.

But luck wasn't the whole story.

I wasn't a refugee—I had a job waiting. I spoke the language. I had purpose, a reason to get up every morning that didn't depend on external validation.

That's not luck. That's preparation meeting opportunity. That's years of discipline and skill-building and the willingness to embrace the suck before the suck became survival.

The war taught me that luck favors the prepared. Not because preparation guarantees anything—it doesn't. But because when opportunity shows up, the prepared are the only ones ready to receive it.

Americans, I discovered, are awesome people. Generous. Open. Willing to give a strange immigrant with a thick accent and a weird resume a chance.

But they weren't giving me a chance because I was lucky. They were giving me a chance because I'd done the work to be ready when the chance arrived.

I had survived the war, found my partner, and built a business rooted in something real.

But knowing what you believe and knowing how to build it into a team are two very different things.

## BEFORE YOU MOVE ON → SHOULDER TAPS FROM THIS CHAPTER

- Take the moments when they come. The wins don't announce themselves. Sometimes survival is the victory, and recognizing it is the work.
- Prepare for the invisible wounds. They don't announce themselves, and they don't follow predictable schedules. Build the habits that will save you before you need saving.
- The most important decision in your life is who you marry. Alignment isn't agreement. You don't need to want the same things to want the same future. Shared values. Mutual respect. And the humility to take turns.
- Your past credentials don't transfer automatically. Every new environment requires you to prove yourself again. Pride will tell you that's unfair. Wisdom will tell you that's opportunity.

- The choice between profit and purpose is a false choice. The real skill is designing systems where they reinforce each other.

That education would start with a question that would reshape everything I thought I understood about leadership, purpose, and why anyone should follow anyone else anywhere.

Ray Kelly asked, "Why should anyone give you their best?"

I didn't have an answer. Not yet.

SIX

# Purpose-Driven

## HIGH-PERFORMING DOER ≠ HIGH-PERFORMING LEADER

When I landed in the D.C.–Baltimore Market Group of American Express Financial Advisors (now Ameriprise Financial) in 1998, five years after leaving Sarajevo, I found something I hadn't felt since the war: a tribe.

This was the top market group in the company, and I was in one of the top offices. Elite. Somehow, I'd talked my way in.

Being a financial advisor fit me in ways I didn't expect. I was doing well by doing good. Helping people make important decisions about their lives. Watching them achieve their own freedom through the work we did together. Mind of a capitalist. Heart of a social worker.

That passion carried through everything. In my first year, I was one of the top performers in the company.

My first district meeting as a rookie district manager was fifteen or sixteen people in a conference room. Ten of them were brand new. It was their first month on the job. The rest were veterans. On the wall was a whiteboard with the leaderboard.

My name was number one.

I stood up and introduced myself. "Hi, my name is Saša. That's me."

Instant credibility. Instant expectation. And I knew that to be a great leader, I had to lead from the front. So I kept doing the work alongside them. Walking with them. Showing them how it was done.

My district started achieving extraordinary results. By every account, we were killing it.

That success opened a door to the next level: field vice president.

## THE BUS RIDE THAT PLANTED A SEED

Spring of 2002. Leadership Summit in Cabo San Lucas. The annual conference where top leadership teams gather to share lessons and celebrate wins.

Matt Carbone, a fellow leader, planted a seed that week: "You should become a field vice president."

At that conference, I met Ray Kelly.

Ray presented from the stage as the leader of one of the top teams in the company. He was where I wanted to be—a successful senior leader who had figured out how to get extraordinary results through people, not just through his own effort.

Ray and I sat together on a bus heading to an evening event. For thirty or forty minutes, we talked. His wife wasn't on the trip because she was pregnant with their daughter. Laura wasn't there because she was pregnant with Oscar. We had a lot in common personally—young families, big ambitions, a shared belief that leadership mattered.

I didn't know it then, but Ray Kelly would change my understanding of leadership. That bus ride was just the seed.

## WHEN ONLY ONE DOOR OPENS

After Cabo, Laura and I made a decision: I would pursue becoming an FVP.

I applied for five positions: Denver, Tampa, Paramus, Ann Arbor, and Albany.

I got rejected from all of them.

Except Albany.

Denver picked someone else. Tampa picked someone else. Ann Arbor picked someone else. Every single one, someone else. I wasn't the cookie-cutter guy. I was different. Weird. An immigrant with an accent and an unconventional path.

But Albany said yes.

Albany was also dead last on the scorecard. So, you know. Lucky me.

I talked to Laura. All of our family and friends were in Maryland. The only thing we had in Albany was a job, a job at the bottom of the rankings in a place where we knew no one.

Her response surprised me.

"You've lived all over the place," she said. "If we don't do this, I'll live in Maryland my whole life."

It wasn't my decision. It was hers.

We sold everything. Took a sixty percent income drop. Burned the boats. In the summer of 2002, as markets were collapsing and we were learning how to be parents, we moved to upstate New York with a newborn and nothing but a chance.

## WHEN RESULTS BECOME YOUR PURPOSE

I started my VP career in last place on the scorecard.

And through sheer force of will, I carried the Albany office toward the top. I was supposed to be recruiting and developing people. Instead, I was recruiting and doing the *work* for the people I led. Closing their deals. Running their meetings. Leading from the front the only way I knew how: outworking everyone.

As the numbers improved, I thought my leadership was getting better.

I was wrong.

Here's what happens when you get into a high-performing culture: numbers and accomplishments become your purpose. Checking things off becomes your purpose. Results become your purpose.

And for a while, that works. You hit targets. You win awards. You climb the leaderboard. From the outside, it looks like success.

But I was miserable.

By the end of my second year in Albany, I found myself back in the bottom quartile. Finish two quarters in a row below the Mendoza line, and you lose your job.

I had lost my sense of purpose beyond the numbers. And I was feeling alone again.

Eighty hours a week. Sometimes more. I'd leave before Oscar woke up and get home after he was asleep. Laura was doing everything at home—raising Oscar, keeping our life together. I was building an office that was supposed to give us freedom.

We had become two ships passing in the night.

She'd leave me notes on the kitchen counter. I'd text her between meetings. We had Oscar and Stella by then, and our conversations had shrunk to logistics: "Who's picking up the kids?" "Did you pay the electric bill?" "What time is the pediatrician?"

She was a full-time mom. I was the provider. Building an office, learning how to get results through other people, and barely succeeding.

The loneliness wasn't about being physically alone. It was about being disconnected from the person I'd chosen to build a life with. We were both working hard. We were both exhausted. And we were both lonely in the same house.

I hated it. My life was miserable. My family life barely existed.

I was a high-performing doer, not a high-performing leader.

And those are not the same thing.

## DARE TO DREAM WHEN THINGS SUCK

February 2006. Albany. Ten years since I'd left Sarajevo. Eight years married. Two kids. I hated my job, but more importantly, I hated being alone again.

Not alone in the literal sense. I had a wife I loved, kids I adored, and a team that depended on me. I felt alone in the way that matters most. Disconnected. Running so hard that I'd lost touch with why I was running in the first place.

As a leader at Ameriprise, I was having many Dream Book conversations with clients. I'd sat with clients and walked them through their futures. Their dreams. Their non-negotiables. Since I practice what I preach, I decided it was time for Laura and me to have our own conversation about the future and our dreams.

We took some time. We both filled our Dream Books. We had a nice dinner at a restaurant. And over that conversation, we made some very important decisions.

One, we both hated my job.

Two, we realized that Niskayuna, New York, is a great place to raise kids.

We didn't want to move.

Then I said something that opened a door neither of us expected: "If I quit my job, you have to quit yours."

Laura looked at me like I'd lost my mind. "How can I quit being a mom?"

"You have a master's degree in international law from American University. You're nationally recognized in marketing for your work at CRS. You took a chance on me when nobody else did. And now the only thing we talk about is poopy diapers. It's got to be more than that."

"I can't work any place where I won't have the flexibility to be a mother," she said. "So we need to work together."

Done.

## WHY DO YOU GET UP IN THE MORNING?

There was one more conversation we needed to have—not about business, but about ourselves and what we were building.

It was an Ameriprise exercise. We each went through a deck of values cards and identified our core values—the non-negotiables that would guide our decisions.

My top five: freedom, family, leadership, integrity, health.

Then came an exercise that asked a simple question: What verb would you assign to each of your core values?

I looked at freedom. And the verb that came to mind was "advancing."

Advancing freedom.

It became clear. That wasn't just a value. That was my purpose. I get up in the morning to advance freedom—my own and others'. Everything I'd done since leaving Sarajevo made sense through that lens. Helping clients achieve financial freedom. Building a business so Laura and I could have freedom. Leading teams so others could grow into their own freedom.

Over time, I refined that discovery into my personal credo: "Advance **freedom** by loving **family** and making choices that will improve physical, emotional, and financial **health** so that I can **facilitate change** for myself and others through **integrity** and l**eadership**."

That clarity changed everything. We decided the next eighteen years would be about our kids and our relationship. I reordered my values—freedom first, then family, then leadership, integrity, and health. And I realized something: If I wanted to be free, I needed to free myself from working for anyone else.

In the fall of 2006, we started a business. Ryan Lambert, who was a district manager in our office in Albany, became our first business partner.

Starting a business was the second-best decision I ever made. The first was marrying up.

## THE GAP I COULDN'T SEE

For the next four years, it felt like Laura and I were each running two full-time jobs.

Hers was home, kids, and helping with marketing one day a week. Mine was being an advisor, growing a business, and providing leadership. We poured ourselves into raising kids and building the business at the same time.

In 2009, the first acquisition opportunity came through, and we acquired Jeff Miller's business. Jeff made a point to impress on me that he'd made promises to his clients and my duty was to keep the promises he'd made.

We also brought on another partner, and we were navigating the financial crisis of 2008 and 2009 while integrating new clients into our experience.

On the surface, things were going great.

My sense of purpose was finally aligned with my core values.

**Freedom**—I was building my own business.

**Family**—Laura was my partner.

**Leadership**—I was growing a team.

**Integrity**—I was keeping promises.

**Health**—I was sustaining the journey.

I knew exactly why I got up in the morning. And I was living it.

But there I was, feeling stuck in the same pattern. But this time, I didn't have regional VPs to blame. Under the hood, something was off. I felt like I was running everything alone. My business partners and the team felt this was the "Saša Show."

I was bursting at the seams. Working hard. Getting results. And I sensed that the potential of our team wasn't even being tapped.

I couldn't blame corporate or the scoreboard or anything else. This was my business. I needed to own it. And I needed to figure out what to do with it.

Here's what I didn't understand yet: My purpose, aligned to my values, was enough to get me out of bed every morning. It wasn't enough to get everyone else on the same page.

Personal purpose is necessary. But it's not sufficient.

> **Shoulder Tap:** Your purpose as a founder doesn't automatically transfer to your team. Working harder won't fix that gap.

## WHY SHOULD ANYONE CARE?

Summer 2010. A Sunday afternoon. I was scrolling LinkedIn in my home office, frustrated in that particular way entrepreneurs get when they know something's broken but can't name it.

Then Ray Kelly's name appeared on my feed. Status change. He'd left his executive VP role at Ameriprise and was coaching with Lennick Aberman Group.

Something fired in my chest. The seed from that bus ride eight years earlier.

I sent a LinkedIn message: "*Can we talk? I need help.*"

Minutes later, my phone rang.

I told Ray everything. The frustration. The gap between what I was giving and what I was getting back. The sense that I was a good advisor and a good manager, but whatever I needed to do next was different.

"I know how to produce results myself," I said. "But how do I unlock the full potential of my team?"

Ray didn't answer with a question. He answered with the truth.

"To unlock the potential of the people that you lead, the very first thing you need to do as a leader is to give them a purpose worthy of their best efforts."

It felt like somebody turned the lights on in a dark room—a big, shiny light. I couldn't see anything other than light.

And I started looking.

I had a deep sense of purpose—being useful and helping people make their lives easier, better, and safer. But on the outside, my actions were all directed towards results and profits. There was a gap. My sense of deeper purpose did not translate to my team.

They were doing what was expected of them. Nothing more.

> **Shoulder Tap:** Personal purpose gets you out of bed. Shared purpose gets a team to follow you. They're not the same thing.

## DISCOVERING WHAT WAS ALREADY TRUE

You know how it goes when you decide to buy a yellow car. You see yellow cars everywhere.

As Ray and I were working on defining a purpose worthy of our team's best effort, I got a message from Derek with a link to Simon Sinek's TED Talk on how great leaders inspire everyone to take action. It felt as if the work I was doing with Ray got a huge boost.

I watched that TED Talk. I bought the book instantly. And the light started showing me the way.

Finding purpose worthy of everyone's best effort is really finding the answer to why anyone should care.

That "anyone" is the people on your team, your clients, and your community. It became very clear to me that we needed to get out of the boardroom and get out of our office—we needed to expand the circle. Include clients in giving us the words that would define our *why*.

I didn't know the formula, but I took a stab in the dark and wrote three questions that have now become table stakes as we lead other teams in defining their purpose:

1. Why did you choose to do business with us?
2. Why are you still here?
3. What can we do better?

The trick is in the first two questions. The third one is just logical—what can we do better?

I created a client advisory board. Twelve people who represented our ideal clients. Successful families. Responsible mindsets. People with board experience. People who would tell us the truth.

We invited them to dinner at 677 Prime in Albany. If you know the restaurant, you know it's not cheap. That was intentional. Every interaction with these people needed to signal that we took them seriously.

Over steak and wine, I asked the three questions.

I shut up. I listened. I took notes.

What came back surprised me.

Nobody talked about returns. Nobody mentioned financial planning strategies or portfolio allocation. Those things mattered, but they weren't why people stayed.

Three themes emerged. Over and over, in different words: *You inspire us to feel confident about our future. You simplify our lives by making complex things simple. You reduce stress by handling the things we don't want to deal with.*

Confidence. Simplicity. Less stress.

That's what we were actually selling. Not financial advice. Peace of mind.

Our clients had just told us our purpose. We'd been living it without naming it.

**Shoulder Tap:** Your purpose already exists. It's in the mouths of the people who love you. Your job is to ask the right questions and listen.

## FROM PURPOSE TO CREDO

The next step was creating our how.

At about the same time, we organized a team off-site to simplify our guiding principles, which, at the time, was a list of eleven. When you have eleven things on your guiding principles, nobody can remember any of them.

Part of the feedback Ray gave me was simple: I had to simplify them to four or five. It made sense. The Values Cards exercise has five values as a standard.

We brought our team to the same boardroom where we'd hosted the client advisory board, and I facilitated a guiding principles exercise.

We asked everyone to do the Values Cards exercise and then share their top five values and why they were important to them. As we went through this, something magical started to happen. The connections between people became deeper. We started to realize how many things we had in common. And the trust started building among us.

Now I know it was our first oxytocin activity.

Throughout the day, we got down to five guiding principles. We worked on wordsmithing them, and the final piece was putting them into actionable "I" statements, something we could easily describe.

Since my working genius is as an intuitive activator, I don't necessarily look for perfection in formulas. I look for something that feels right and looks good, something that other teams have used to transform themselves, and I use that as a prototype to build mine.

Mission. Vision. Values—that's MBA speak. It's the language of consultants and corporate retreats and binders that collect dust on shelves. Nobody gets out of bed inspired by a mission statement.

But a credo card? That's different. A credo is something you believe. Something you carry with you. Something that pulses with life.

It was only logical to look at the Ritz-Carlton credo card as an example —a statement that would express our *why*, incorporate our guiding principles, and give people a flavor of what it feels like to work with this team.

That credo card became a North Star. A guide. A light during times of transition and storms. It became a filter for decisions, especially during tough times. A filter to decide who's the right person for the team and who is the right client to work with.

It also became the heart of the narrative we use in telling the story of the team that inspires confidence, simplifies life, and reduces stress.

In Simon Sinek's book, he talks about taking the "Golden Circles" and rolling them up into a tube, into a megaphone. Your *why, how,* and *what* become the megaphone to attract people to your organization.

I am not very smart, but I'm smart enough to be dumb enough to do what believable people tell me works.

Nothing is truer than when you align your *what* with your *how* and with your *why*. People who believe what you believe will do business with you, not because of what you do, but because of why you're doing it.

Over the years, as I coached and worked with other teams, I was often asked if they could use *Inspire Confidence. Simplify Life. Reduce Stress.* And I said yes.

I got a lot of grief from Laura for that. "Why are you letting people use our *why*?"

My response was, and still is, if they're inspired by our *why*, they have the right to make it their own.

The words are just the words. Living it every day, in every decision—that's what matters.

So I consider it a compliment.

**Shoulder Tap:** Mission. Vision. Values. That's MBA speak. A credo card is inspiring. Create something people actually want to carry with them.

## BEFORE YOU MOVE ON → SHOULDER TAPS FROM THIS CHAPTER

- Your purpose as a founder doesn't automatically transfer to your team. Working harder won't fix that gap.
- Personal purpose gets you out of bed. Shared purpose gets a team to follow you. They're not the same thing.
- Your purpose already exists. It's in the mouths of the people who love you. Your job is to ask the right questions and listen.
- Mission. Vision. Values. That's MBA speak. A credo card is inspiring. Create something people actually want to carry with them.

Ray Kelly warned me about something. As you crystallize your credo, you should be prepared for some people who are original members of that team to not align with it. Instead of judging them, celebrate them. Celebrate their sense of integrity and empower them to align with a purpose that is theirs.

"It will be painful. You will lose people," he said.

Through that pain, we found alignment. And that alignment attracts the right people to your team.

I had my personal purpose dialed in. I had discovered our team's shared purpose. I had Ray's words tattooed on my brain.

What I didn't have yet was a way to tell the difference between people who shared the mission and people who were just along for the ride.

That lesson was coming. And it would cost me eighty percent of my team to learn it.

SEVEN

# Good People

## SELF-LEADING TEAMS ARE MADE OF LEADERS

Good people have character. I used to say it that way. Short, simple. It took me twenty years to understand what that actually meant—and who actually had it.

Character is just the starting point.

The software and tech industry in Silicon Valley has known something for a long time: A rockstar programmer is twenty to thirty times more productive than average. One brilliant coder can do what an entire team of average ones cannot.

The problem is, we're not in a business where smart programmers can make a huge difference.

Our purpose is to inspire confidence, simplify life, and reduce stress. We are in the hospitality industry. Our success is determined by how well we care for people in our charge.

The rockstars in our industry aren't the ones who can crunch numbers faster or build better spreadsheets.

The rockstars in our industry are leaders.

The leaders who actually change a team are also aligned to the mission —working because they believe in where you're going. And they're in the right seat. They do the work that feels like theirs, not just the work someone assigned them. That's where their genius lives.

Add pressure to that combination. The kind of pressure that activates instead of breaks, and something happens. The potential stops being potential, and it becomes performance.

Self-leading teams emerge when each team member assumes the role of a leader. Not in title, but in behavior, in ownership, and in the way they show up when nobody's watching.

That's what I was building toward. I just didn't know how far I still had to fall before I figured out how to get there.

## THE CULTURE SHIFT

As I was working on my transformation as a leader—trying to integrate Ray's teachings, trying to become a Level 5 leader—I was also trying to understand what defines a great culture.

One day, Ray and I were talking about it. He said two words: people and behaviors.

At the time, I thought we had great people. But our culture was not great.

The culture was a control culture. I was driving almost all decisions and micromanaging on a crazy level. I'd been talking a big game about leadership at all levels while bottlenecking everything through me.

In 2011, I asked Ray to teach a leadership class to our team once a month. Not because I didn't know the content, but because I wanted my team to have exposure to the coach I was working with. And I wanted to create a culture where the teacher of leadership principles wasn't me.

Most culture-building efforts stall at recognition. Everyone can see that something needs to change. That's the easy part. The hard part is what you actually pour into people. Because the right knowledge doesn't just inform. It shifts attitude. Shifted attitude changes behavior. Changed behavior, repeated and celebrated, becomes culture.

I use a rubber duck to explain this when I'm coaching. How do you get a rubber duck to float in a bathtub? You add water. Leadership culture works the same way. Your people's brains and capacity—that's the rubber duck. Leadership knowledge is the water. You don't force the duck to float. You just keep pouring.

Ray showed up every month. We studied principles. We traded stories. We tied the concepts back to our own lived experiences—the wins, the failures, the moments where someone showed up differently than they had the week before. And then we made one rule: you don't just learn it, you ACT on it. (More on that in Chapter 14.)

What that did was create a shift. Saša wasn't the teller anymore. Saša was the first implementer.

We created "Ray Said." We had a lot of "Ray-isms." In the beginning, I would come back and teach them to Laura. She would say to me, "Don't you give me that Ray Kelly stuff today."

Today, she's the one teaching Ray-isms to other people. It takes time.

But as time progressed, it became clear that some team members were embracing it. And some weren't. The ones who embraced it became more committed to the mission. The ones who didn't eventually left.

The turning point came when one of the rockstars I thought was a great leader resigned. During her exit interview, she said something that landed like a punch to the gut: "All this talk about how we're all leaders is nice. But at the end of the day, it's always going to be 'Do what Saša says.'"

I felt the blood drain from my face.

She was right.

I was making progress. But no cigar.

## WHAT WOULD HAPPEN IF I WERE DEAD?

In one of our leadership meetings around that time, I asked my business partner a question that had been burning in my head. "What would happen if I were dead?"

His response was very typical for most financial advisory business owners. The focus was on taking care of clients and the family of the deceased—compensation for the equity, who takes care of client relationships.

I looked him in the eye. "Okay, so let's say I'm dead. What happens? Play it out for me."

"Well, I'm going to pay your wife whatever the value of your business part is, and I will buy her out."

"I'm not really concerned about money. I know you're good for it. What happens with the team? What happens with the clients?"

He paused. "I didn't really think about that."

I can't blame him. Most people don't.

I didn't like the answer.

I had a framework in my head of what I wanted to build. I wrote white papers to think out loud about leadership, culture, what this team could become. It was how I figured a lot of this out. We had purpose clearly defined. I didn't think we could have more clarity than what we'd put in our credo.

What I saw was that behaviors were different from what I had in my head as elite leadership. So I pushed. I leveled up expectations for everyone around me.

Eventually, that came to a head.

## LOOKING DOWN THE BARREL

Spring of 2018. My then-business partner informed me that his vision of the future was different from mine, and he wanted to separate the business according to the agreement we'd made back in 2009.

That was fair. I had no problem with that.

When he told me that eighty percent of the team would go with him, my ego got the best of me.

"There's no chance," I said.

In the weeks following that conversation, I came to a very sobering realization.

John Maxwell has something called the "Law of the Picture," which says that people first believe in a leader, then the vision.

Eighty percent of the people did not believe in me as a leader. Including my business partner.

It was the moment of looking down the barrel and seeing the truth. It shook me to the core.

These weren't bad people. They were talented, skilled professionals. But as the conversations unfolded, a painful truth emerged: no matter what vision I shared, they did not believe in me as their leader.

I'm going to take full accountability. They picked the other vision, but it wasn't about the vision. It was me they weren't aligned with.

Here's the part that took me years to fully accept: It wasn't that my business partner did something to me. I made decisions and started acting in ways that weren't what he signed up for when he became my business partner. And the people who left with him didn't sign up for that either.

As business owners and leaders, we're all in this project, this purpose. We're living it; we started it. It's almost like an obsession.

What I forgot—and this is where I've paid the most dumb tax—is that while my obsession is important as a driving force to build self-leading teams, everyone needs to find themselves in that same place in their own way.

They all have their own reasons, their own aspirations, their own dreams, and their own purposes. Those may or may not be the same as mine.

When eighty percent of the team decided to leave, I had to respect their decisions. They were making choices based on what they wanted for themselves.

To be an elite leader, I cannot judge them. Even though it's human to judge.

Elite leaders deal with these things with grace and courage. I had that in Sarajevo. I had just forgotten about it.

I got stuck in the rat race of getting the numbers and forgot about the humans.

## THE BAND OF BROTHERS AND SISTERS

I knew this was going to be the last time I rebuilt.

It wasn't pleasant. It wasn't good. But to a certain degree, I was the one who had instigated it. I was prepared that this could happen. And fortunately, I had the framework in my head of what I wanted to build, even if it was just Laura and me starting from scratch.

I was blessed that we weren't going to be alone.

The people who stayed weren't just employees who happened to stick around. They were missionaries, not mercenaries. They believed in me and what we were building.

Maureen was my truth-teller. She was the one who said what needed to be said, whether I wanted to hear it or not. She was in the meeting with my then-business partner and me when he told me we were separating. I called Laura first. The very next call was to Maria, my future partner.

I told her what was happening. I told her I wanted to build the future of our business as a self-leading team, based on our character, our credo card, and everything we believed in.

She didn't hesitate to confirm she was in. She didn't ask about guarantees. She didn't negotiate terms. She didn't hedge her bets. Maria said yes because she believed in me and what we were building, not just what she was getting paid to do.

The next person was Kayla.

My former practice manager had just told me she was leaving. It was a hard decision. As she walked out, my one-on-one with Kayla was starting. Kayla had just become full-time. She was a young mom with a young kid. And she said, "I can do her job."

No background. No training. Character and willingness to step in. She believed in me.

The next one was Derek. In a conversation I will never forget, he said, "I don't know what it's going to look like, but I'm with you. And we're going to work through this no matter what happens."

The final piece was one of the biggest compliments I've ever received.

Richard. He was a great worker but not very engaged in our culture. When I talked to him about what I envisioned and asked him to stay with me, he said, "Yeah. I was planning to tell you guys that I'm leaving. But I can't leave you, Maria, and Laura. So I'm going to put my move on hold to stay and help you rebuild."

That was the band of brothers and sisters. Maria, Laura, Maureen, Derek, Kayla, Richard, and I.

Seven of us remained. We'd lost eighty percent of our team but kept eighty percent of our business.

That second number—eighty percent.

Eighty percent of clients. Seven people. Every client visit, every phone call, every piece of work that had been spread across the entire team was now ours. No handoff. No grace period. Clients who had just seen our team split needed to know they were in good hands.

I had been through this before. Teams I had built under fire. Teams I had built in this business. I had watched them break when pressure spiked or dissolve when the mission got fuzzy. I had been the reason some of them broke.

This time was going to be different. I finally understood what I was actually building.

I wanted a team that could run without me in the room. A business I could take a vacation from and come back to find it had not just survived but grown. I wanted to build something that would outlast me.

Seven years later, we refer to 2018 as "*The* Talent Density Event."

> **Shoulder Tap:** People first believe in a leader, then the vision. When your team leaves, look in the mirror before you look out the window.

## THE DIFFERENCE BETWEEN MISSIONARIES AND MERCENARIES

Here's what the breakup taught me about people.

Mercenaries work for the paycheck. When a better offer comes along, they're gone. They do what's expected—nothing more, nothing less. Their loyalty extends exactly as far as their compensation.

Missionaries work for the mission. They show up on weekends because work needs doing. They raise their hand when impossible deadlines loom. They stay when the ship takes on water because they believe in where it's headed.

Maria's journey with us almost didn't happen. In 2007, she was a college student who joined our firm part-time at her family's encouragement. Her fun-loving, laid-back attitude was real. But so was her work ethic.

One Sunday, I drove by the office and saw her car in the parking lot. No one had asked her to be there. She was there because work needed to get done, and she was going to do it.

That's when I knew Maria was different.

Our compensation system for advisors at the time was our attempt to quantify impact. Very low base salary, five or six different bonus opportunities for this, that, and the other thing. It was complex. It took a lot of time to track.

Here's what that system revealed: Advisors did what was required of them to earn the compensation. Some of them made pretty good money, yet the quality of their work wasn't at the same level as someone who really believed in *Inspire Confidence, Simplify Life, Reduce Stress.*

Maria didn't care how the compensation was structured. She just took care of clients. Her work and dedication were at the highest level.

And since I had a view of compensation, I started to see that she was making less money than other advisors. I knew the system was broken. But I also knew I needed to do whatever it took to reward people who were missionaries, not mercenaries. So I did my famous line, "I have a very important conversation to have with you. You and I need to go to Starbucks."

She looked nervous. "Oh, what did I do wrong?"

"I'd like to talk to you somewhere where we're not in the office."

When we sat down, I said, "You're putting me in a very uncomfortable situation."

"Why?"

"There's a huge discrepancy between the value you bring to our firm and your compensation."

My face was dead serious.

"What are you saying?"

"You need to get a significant pay raise. I'm giving you $20,000 more."

Her response was classic Maria.

"Are you sure? Can you afford it?"

I said yes. And no.

"No, I can't afford it. But I cannot afford not to have you. So I'm going to do whatever I need to do for you to make the money you need to make so you don't ever want to go anywhere else. Because you're the kind of person I want to build this team around."

Today, Maria is a significant equity partner in our firm. A highly respected leader. Living proof that when you find missionaries, you hold onto them.

Knowing what good people look like is one thing. Finding them, putting them in the right seat, and activating what they're capable of—that's the work.

**Shoulder Tap:** Select missionaries, not mercenaries. Mercenaries leave when the ship takes on water. Missionaries grab a bucket.

## TALENT DENSITY IS A FORCE MULTIPLIER

Talent density is the foundation of every elite team.

It means having fewer, better-aligned people in the right seats doing the right work. Scaling for fit, not for size. Choosing missionaries over mercenaries. It's the difference between a team in name only and an elite team that can achieve the impossible.

Eight years after our rebuild, we've achieved what most would consider impossible: the top one percent of our franchise peers, virtually zero turnover among our core team, and a culture where people actively refer other rockstars to join us.

None of this happened by accident.

It happened because we applied three principles and developed a tool to make them work.

## STEP ONE: SELECT, DON'T HIRE

There's a world of difference between filling a position and finding the right person. Hiring is transactional—you need a body, you find a body.

Selection is transformational—you need a mission-critical team member who will elevate everyone around them.

We select for character and natural ability. Character tells you who someone is when nobody's watching. Natural ability tells you what energizes them versus what drains them. Both matter more than credentials.

We look for character over credentials. Leadership, work ethic, community involvement, education—in that order.

- **The Guardians of the Galaxy**

  Realizing that it's tough to identify rockstars through interviews alone, we get many team members involved in the selection process. This helps us avoid mistakes and find passionate supporters of our purpose.

  At our firm, candidates who clear the resume screening meet with the Guardians of the Galaxy—three people who embody everything we stand for, regardless of title or tenure. Laura, Kayla, and Maureen are the keepers of our culture. They can spot misalignment before the interview is over.

  The Guardians go deep. One particular question, dubbed the Legacy Question, is always posed: "What traits from your parents do you most wish to pass on to yourself and your children?"

  When Phil met the Guardians, he impressed them. His answer to the Legacy Question came without hesitation: "Sacrifice." That was it. One word.

  After each Guardian interview, I ask for just one thing: their gut feeling about the candidate—not a scorecard, not a rubric. Their gut.

  Then comes the Thanksgiving Test. I ask the team, "Would you invite this person to Thanksgiving dinner?" If you wouldn't want to share a meal with someone at your family table, why would you invest forty hours a week in creating something together?

## STEP TWO: RIGHT PEOPLE, RIGHT SEATS

Maria didn't have a financial background, but she was a softball team leader and community influencer. Phil lacked financial internships, but he showed leadership in school and sports.

Character over credentials. Every time.

- **Talent and Unique Genius**

  But character alone isn't enough. You need to know where someone's natural abilities fit. That's why we developed TUG Cards™—Talent and Unique Genius—a tool that combines Values, Working Genius, Kolbe, and PrinciplesYou assessments to map each person's unique wiring. TUG Cards™ help us see not just who someone is, but where they'll thrive. When you put high-character people in seats that match their natural abilities, ordinary people become rockstars.

  (We'll give you the detailed playbook on TUG Cards™ in Act Three. For now, know that it's at the heart of how we build talent density.)

## STEP THREE: PUT THEM UNDER PRESSURE

Every elite team I was part of had a selection process that didn't stop with onboarding. It always felt like the selection process was ongoing.

Not that you're constantly trying to earn your job. But to be part of a team of leaders in a values-based culture, pressure isn't punishment. It's proof.

Good people embrace that. They have a growth mindset. The comfort zone is where things die. Good people are here to do bigger things than earn a paycheck.

- **Selection Is a Two-Way Street**

  Every day, your people come in, and they choose to be on the team. And you are choosing to have them.
  There's a responsibility that leaders have to the people and to the team.

- **The Keeper Principle**

  One question tells you where you stand: Would I be willing to mortgage my house to keep this person?

  Not metaphorically. Actually. If the answer is yes, that person deserves everything you've got. The conversations, the investment, the fight to keep them. If the answer is no, the most respectful thing you can do is to help them find somewhere the answer would be yes.

**Shoulder Tap:** Talent density is a force multiplier. Select for character and natural ability. Put the right people in the right seats. Then watch them rise under pressure.

## WHEN ROCKSTARS LEAVE

There are times when great people will decide to leave the team.

In financial services, when someone decides to leave, the response is simple: pack your stuff and go. Don't let the door hit you on the way out.

At Inspire Confidence Group, we celebrate their decision to move to the next level of the game. We don't escort people out. We celebrate that they got to a point where they want to take a path that might be different.

As sad as it is to see them leave, we're proud of their accomplishment. They're fulfilling their purpose. Getting what they want for themselves.

One Friday afternoon—I'll never forget it—Richard asked if he could talk to me.

"Oh, that's not good," I said.

"Well, it depends," he said. "As you know, I was planning to leave a year and a half ago, and I couldn't in good conscience leave you and Maria alone. Now you have Phil, Connor, and some other people around. I feel it's time for me to move on."

My heart dropped, but I was full of joy for him.

So I did what I always do now.

"Where do you want to go? Do you still want to be part of this team? Because I'm going to do whatever it takes to keep you. I'll go buy a business somewhere if you want to live in a different location."

He said, "I appreciate that, but I think it's good for me to be on a different team."

"Okay. I will do whatever I can to help you find a place. Do you want to stay with Ameriprise?"

He looked at me in disbelief that I would offer that. "Yeah, potentially."

"Where do you want to go?"

"What do you mean?"

"I have a network of people I know in the whole company. Tell me where you want to go and what location you want to be in, and I'll make some phone calls—even if it's San Diego."

I dropped San Diego because, to me, San Diego is the ultimate place.

He said, "Well, it is San Diego."

"Okay. What kind of business do you want to be part of?"

"I don't know."

"I know the VP who leads that territory. I'll call Marcus Ranger and let him know a rockstar from my team wants to go to his territory, and I'm going to ask him to make recommendations and introductions to teams that could use someone like you."

At first, Richard was completely shocked.

A few weeks later, the introduction Marcus made resulted in Richard's new position. He moved to San Diego.

Were Phil and Connor ready to be without Richard? No. But they embraced the opportunity. They stepped up. They leveled up their game. And that was a great thing for them because they didn't have to wait four years to get the promotion.

For those remaining on the team, when a rockstar leaves, it signifies one of two possibilities: "How is this going to impact me?" or "This is an opportunity to step up."

The right type of people choose to see it as an opportunity. This is how we developed so many leaders over the last ten years.

> **Shoulder Tap:** When rockstars leave, celebrate them. The people who stay will tell you everything about your culture by how they respond.

## PEOPLE BEFORE NUMBERS

As leaders of self-leading teams, your people need to come before numbers.

When you put people before numbers, the results they hit are so much more meaningful.

That's where purpose comes in. As a leader of self-leading teams, purpose is the glue that holds everything together—the way you act as a leader, the people you select, and how you build culture where behaviors align with values and credo.

But the right people in the right seats isn't enough.

Even rockstars can't perform at their best without the invisible infrastructure that holds everything together.

That infrastructure is trust.

## BEFORE YOU MOVE ON → SHOULDER TAPS FROM THIS CHAPTER

- People first believe in a leader, then the vision. When your team leaves, look in the mirror before you look out the window.
- Select missionaries, not mercenaries. Mercenaries leave when the ship takes on water. Missionaries grab a bucket.
- Talent density is a force multiplier. Select for character and natural ability. Put the right people in the right seats. Then watch them rise under pressure.
- When rockstars leave, celebrate them. The people who stay will tell you everything about your culture by how they respond.

I had the right people. What we didn't have was trust. And I had no one to blame for that but myself.

EIGHT

# Cultivate Trust

## TRUST IS THE CURRENCY OF LEADERSHIP

Maureen ran RiverSource Life Insurance Company of New York. She has an MBA. Decades of operational leadership. The kind of executive who could walk into chaos and find the signal in the noise.

In January 2015, I hired her as our chief operating officer. Her mission was simple: take us from above average to elite.

For two and a half years, she tried everything. Every management technique in the playbook. Our results? Flat. Something was stuck, and we couldn't name it.

Then came the summer of 2017. We were in one of our leadership workshops, working through Patrick Lencioni's The Five Dysfunctions of a Team, in which he puts "Trust" at the base of his pyramid, signifying that it's the foundation that everything else crumbles without.

A few days later, Maureen and I were in our weekly one-on-one. She had that look. The one where she's about to say something I don't want to hear.

"You know what your problem is?"

"Tell me."

"There is no trust between you and your partner."

The words hit like a shockwave. My chest tightened. I wanted to argue. To defend. To explain all the reasons she was wrong.

But I couldn't. Because somewhere beneath the defensiveness, I knew she was right.

Later that week, I went for a bike ride. Headphones in, Lencioni's book playing again. This time, I heard it differently. Maureen had handed me new glasses, and I could see what had been invisible.

The lack of trust wasn't some abstract team problem. It was specific. It was personal.

My business partner and I didn't trust each other.

We'd been dancing around it for years. We had different visions, different values, and a low-grade tension that infected every meeting, every decision, and every interaction with the team. People could feel it. They just couldn't name it either.

Once I saw it, I couldn't unsee it.

I kept coming back to something Simon Sinek said: "A team is not a group of people who work together. A team is a group of people who trust each other."

Once Maureen told me what she told me, that quote gave me a shoulder tap I couldn't ignore. The trust account was running low. And trust works exactly like a bank account. Every interaction is a transaction. You make deposits. You show up, you follow through, you tell the hard truth with care, you give credit where it's due. And you make withdrawals. You miss a deadline, you override a decision, you say one thing and do another. Every little thing counts. The small stuff adds up faster than you think.

Here's what I didn't fully understand at the time: the account balance determines everything. When the balance is high, you can ask people to follow you into uncomfortable territory—a big change, a hard pivot, a decision that doesn't make sense yet—and they'll go. Not blindly. But willingly. Because the account has earned it. When the balance is low? They won't budge. Doesn't matter how good your idea is. Doesn't matter how right you are. An overdrawn account can't cash a check.

That was me. I'd been making withdrawals I didn't fully see. The micromanaging, the bottlenecking, the gap between what I preached and what I practiced. And when I came in with the next initiative, the next big idea, the next push for change—the account couldn't cover it. The resistance wasn't personal. It was math.

I knew what I needed to do. I needed to build the balance back up. But first, I needed to understand how trust actually works—how it grows, how it breaks, and how you earn it back once it's gone.

> **Shoulder Tap:** The trust problem you can't name is usually the one sitting next to you.

## THE LIFECYCLE OF TRUST

Trust isn't a one-time transaction. It's a cycle.

Given first, earned next.

Someone has to go first. Someone has to extend trust before it's been fully earned. That's the leader's job. Once trust is given, it gets tested. People prove themselves through small moments, consistent follow-through, and hard conversations handled well. You build it through regular practice—through showing up, again and again.

Trust must also be continuously renewed. Trust isn't a trophy you put on a shelf. It's a living thing. It requires ongoing investment. Regular deposits. When trust is damaged, because it will be, it requires repair.

**LIFECYCLE OF TRUST**

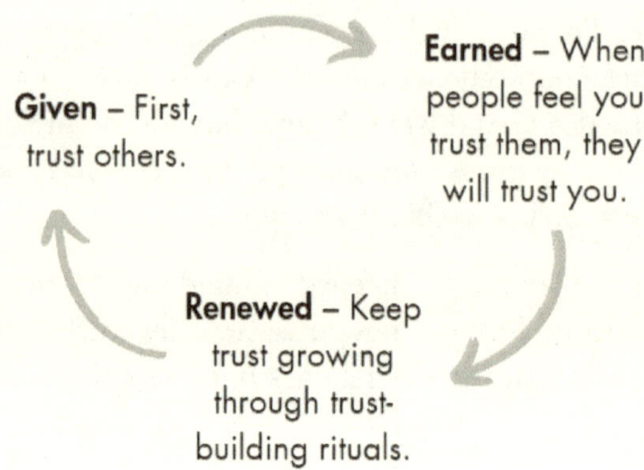


**Shoulder Tap:** Trust is the currentcy of leadership. Without it, you're bankrupt before you start.

## TRUST IS GIVEN FIRST

You don't earn trust first. You give it first.

This runs against everything we're taught. *Prove yourself. Show me you're worthy. Trust is earned, not given.*

That's backwards.

Six months after Richard left for San Diego, Phil and Connor had been supporting Maria and me. They did the behind-the-scenes work that allowed us to actually sit in front of clients and move things forward. They were learning how to become advisors themselves. Grinding through the financial planning, producing the client visits, keeping the engine running while Maria and I were the face of it. We were just starting to find our rhythm. Just getting momentum.

Then Connor announced he got another job. An opportunity he couldn't miss. He would be leaving at the end of the year.

We called Phil in and said, "This is what's going on, and we will do whatever it takes for you not to drown."

We meant it.

"We're going to hire somebody to help. We'll outsource. We'll bring stuff in. We will do the work. Don't worry. Don't leave."

Phil looked at us and said something I'll never forget: "Okay. I've got to trust you."

I had given Phil my trust first. I promised that we would take care of him. And we did whatever it took. We hired a firm to help with the work. We rearranged things. We eventually brought in new people.

You have to take care of your people.

That's where trust begins. Not with contracts or compensation. With going first. By extending trust before it's been fully earned.

> **Shoulder Tap:** Trust is given first. Someone has to go first. That's the leader's job.

## TRUST IS EARNED NEXT

When my partnership dissolved in 2018, I had to rebuild from rubble. The ones who stayed—Maria, Laura, Kayla, Maureen, Derek, Richard—became the foundation of everything that came next.

Maria and I decided to become formal partners. And I knew exactly where we had to start.

The biggest mistake I made with my previous business partner? We never worked through issues. We didn't even have a regular scheduled time to have conversations. But the conversation is the relationship.

If Maria and I were going to be real partners, we needed regular, scheduled time to stay in sync. I called it "coffee time"—Monday mornings, 9 a.m., before anything else touched our calendars. Not a status meeting. Not an agenda-driven check-in. Just coffee. Just conversation.

The purpose of coffee time is to get and stay in sync. We start with sharing our wins with each other. Personal and business. We bring each other to our side of the beach ball, which we'll talk about in the next chapter. We tackle tough issues. We make sure we're in alignment before we leave.

Eighty percent of the time, it's casual. No problems. But twenty or thirty percent of the time, there are really tough things we need to work through. Having it on the calendar makes it a ritual. Something we protect. Something that builds trust through repetition.

Within weeks, we'd stripped the busywork that used to consume us before client visits—the elaborate prep documents, the redundant checklists—and agreed to focus on what matters. Nothing else.

It felt like exhaling after holding your breath for years.

**Shoulder Tap:** The conversation is the relationship. Schedule the coffee time. Protect it.

## THE STEAMROLLER MOMENT

Because of those coffee times, we earned enough trust that when I started steamrolling her, Maria could say something about it.

And because of those weekly conversations, I'd learned to step back and listen.

Early in our partnership, I got excited about Helios, a research partner for discretionary asset management models. In my mind, this was a no-brainer. I was ready to move yesterday—Maria wasn't.

We were on a call with Chris Scuba from Helios, working through implementation details. Chris was trying to nail down logistics. I was already thinking about the rollout.

Then Maria said something that stopped me cold. "I feel like you're steamrolling me here."

Silence.

The old Saša would have overridden the dissent. Pushed through. Figured we'd work out the concerns later. That's what I'd always done.

But Maureen's diagnosis was still ringing in my ears. *There is no trust in this team.*

And Maria felt comfortable enough—because of those coffee times—to call it out.

I stopped.

"Okay," I said. "Help me see what you're seeing."

What Maria saw was everything I'd missed. The implementation load. The already-stretched team. The dozen other priorities competing for the same scarce resources. She wasn't resisting change—she was protecting the people who would have to execute it.

We "interrogated reality" together—her phrase, borrowed from Susan Scott. It means you don't just defend your position—you genuinely try to see the world from the other side of the beach ball.

Over the next couple of weeks, Maria and I built a staged plan. Who handles what. How we communicate with clients. The compliance requirements. The trading protocols.

Six weeks later, we launched. Not six days. Six weeks. Because we'd built something we both believed in.

That became our blueprint. We don't override each other's concerns. We don't steamroll. We trust the friction because the friction usually means someone sees something important.

**Shoulder Tap:** Trust is earned through regular practice. When you've built it, people tell you the truth, even when it's hard to hear.

## TRUST IS CONTINUOUSLY RENEWED

Trust isn't a trophy you put on a shelf. It requires ongoing investment. Regular deposits. Daily practice.

The basic unit of trust in an elite team is a pair.

Navy SEALs call them swim buddies. In training, you're never alone. Your swim buddy is your responsibility, and you're theirs. That bond forged in brutal conditions becomes the foundation for everything that follows.

At Inspire Confidence Group, nobody works alone. When I visit with a client, I have a second chair supporting me. When I travel to do presentations, I take a swim buddy. Every financial plan is a coordinated effort with a lead advisor, a second chair from the advice team, and a member of the client experience team. Not because we don't trust individuals. Because we trust pairs more.

The more we work together, the stronger the relationships become. The stronger the relationships, the deeper the trust. The deeper the trust, the better we perform.

SEALs have a combat tactic called "cover and move." One shooter lays down cover fire while the other advances. Then they swap, leapfrogging forward, each protecting the other, until they reach their objective.

That's elite team performance. Having each other's backs so that individuals and the team succeed together.

"Cover and move" isn't a one-time exercise. It's a daily practice. A mindset that embeds and deepens trust over time.

## DELEGATE AUTHORITY TO ELEVATE PERFORMANCE

Nobody told me that control and trust can't live in the same house. I had to figure that out the hard way.

Here's the trap most founders fall into: You believe every decision is your decision.

I get it. You're driven. You're confident. You built this thing from nothing. Nobody cares about the business like you do, right?

That mindset will kill you.

If you want transformational growth, you'll eventually hit the wall of your own capacity. You can't be in every meeting. Can't approve every decision. Can't be the bottleneck for everything that matters.

Delegation isn't about offloading tasks you don't have time for. That's just dumping.

True delegation—delegate to elevate—means transferring authority to elevate performance. It's trusting someone to achieve an important goal. Nothing builds oxytocin more than being trusted with something that matters.

And here's the deeper reason: You need to transfer the trust that clients have in you to your team. Someday you won't be around. Your business flourishes only if your clients trust your team as much as they trust you.

That's the foundation of a multigenerational business.

## THE DECISION TREE

Most delegation models mirror org charts—top-down. The Decision Tree flips that.

Imagine a tree. At the roots, the trunk, the branches, and the leaves—four levels of decisions.

- **Root decisions:** These stay with me. I'm not willing to delegate them. At ICG, one root decision is who becomes an equity partner. Even then, other equity partners participate—it's never mine alone.
- **Trunk decisions:** I delegate these, but check with me before you act.
- **Branch decisions:** I delegate these. Act on your decision, then report back later.
- **Leaf decisions:** Make the decision. Act. No need to report.

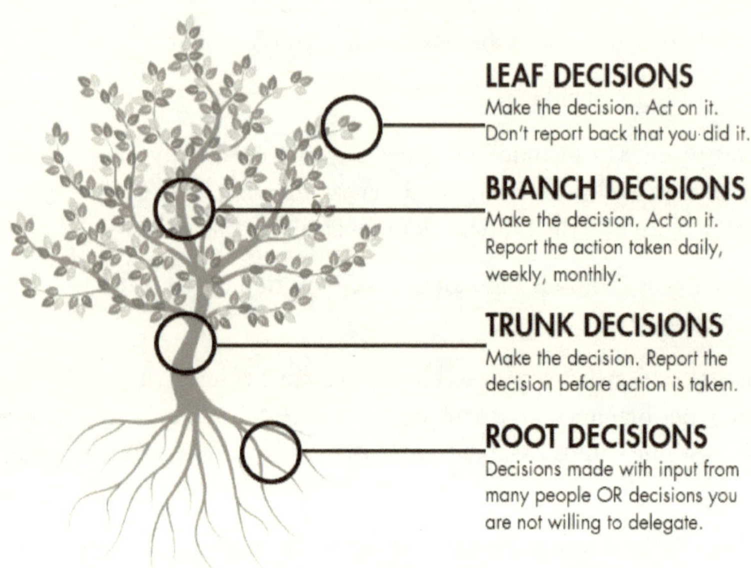


For a long time, I treated every decision like a root decision. Everything ran through me. Every call, every approval, every detail—I was the bottleneck, and I told myself it was leadership. It wasn't. It was *control* wearing *leadership's* clothes.

Building trust meant learning to label authority differently. I started deliberately moving decisions up the tree—from roots to trunk, trunk to branches, branches to leaves. Not all at once. Gradually. Intentionally. Because rockstars and leaders don't just want a paycheck and a job description. They want autonomy. They want to express themselves, own something, and leave their fingerprint on the work. The Decision Tree is how you give that trust to them structurally—not as a favor, but as a design.

When people are empowered to make decisions at the right level, something shifts. They stop waiting to be told. They start trusting their own judgment. They take action, learn from mistakes, and start teaching each other. Confidence builds. Ownership deepens. The tree grows because the whole team is tending it—not just you.

I know it's working when someone solves a problem I never heard about. That's the goal. To build something that doesn't need me for everything.

Mismatched delegation kills trust. Alignment builds it.

> **Shoulder Tap:** Delegate authority to elevate performance. Delegation isn't dumping. It's transferring trust.

## FEEDBACK IS A GIFT

In our culture, failure is not an option.

It is a requirement.

We empower people to take action. When they fail, we facilitate learning. When someone makes a mistake, the instinct is to tell them what they did wrong. Don't. Instead, ask, "What did you learn?" And then, "What would you do differently next time?"

Telling them what went wrong and showing the right answer can feel like helping. It isn't. It takes the lesson away from them.

Our team members are missionaries. They have a strong commitment to our purpose. They take failure hard. That initial sting usually transforms into something powerful—a deeper thirst to learn. The questions create space for that transformation. Telling them what they did wrong just creates shame.

Feedback is a gift. But only if it's wrapped in trust.

> **Shoulder Tap:** Don't tell people what they did wrong. Ask what they learned. Create space for growth, not shame.

## EVERYTHING MOVES AT THE SPEED OF TRUST

General Jim Mattis led Marines into Afghanistan in the weeks after 9/11. In his memoir *Call Sign Chaos*, he describes how they planned, organized, and put boots on the ground in twenty-eight days. From concept to execution—less than a month.

How? Multiple branches of the military operating with such deep trust that they could move without the usual friction of bureaucracy and turf protection.

Stephen M.R. Covey calls it "the speed of trust." When teams trust each other, things accelerate. Decisions happen faster. Execution sharpens. Clients feel the difference.

Without trust, every interaction generates heat. Every handoff requires double-checking. Every decision gets relitigated. You're driving with the parking brake on.

With it, operations flow. People cover for each other without being asked. Problems get solved before they escalate to your desk.

Your whole future as a small business depends on trust. The memorable client experience that differentiates you? Only a trusting team can deliver it.

Trust is the currency of leadership. Spend it wisely. Invest it often. And never forget, someone has to go first.

## BEFORE YOU MOVE ON → SHOULDER TAPS FROM THIS CHAPTER

- Trust is the currency of leadership. Without it, you're bankrupt before you start.
- The trust problem you can't name is usually the one sitting next to you.
- Trust is given first. Someone has to go first. That's the leader's job.

- The conversation is the relationship. Schedule the coffee time. Protect it.
- Delegate authority to elevate performance. Delegation isn't dumping. It's transferring trust.
- Don't tell people what they did wrong. Ask what they learned. Create space for growth, not shame.

Trust is earned through regular practice. When you've built it, people tell you the truth, even when it's hard to hear.

Perhaps the biggest test of trust comes when swim buddies—or the whole team—see things differently. What happens when you disagree? Is it safe to be honest? Will you be heard? Or dismissed?

These questions keep teams ordinary.

Trust gets you honest. Honesty gets uncomfortable. That's where we're going next.

NINE

# Embrace Conflict

## THE TOUGH LOVE THAT CHANGED EVERYTHING

Back in 2014, we had what Ray Kelly would call a control-based culture. That was the year my business partner sat in my living room four days after my hip surgery and read me the feedback that changed everything.

*"You change things constantly. The team is frustrated. Demoralized. You're impossible to work for. It's falling apart. And it's your fault."*

What does that mean, control-based? Everything went from the top down. Conflict was initiated by me—some people embraced it, most people avoided it. Every decision needed to be run by me. I felt stuck. My team felt worse. They were exhausted from the constant changes, demoralized by having their ideas picked apart, and frustrated that nothing they did seemed to matter.

As you read about in Chapter 7, one of my most talented team members resigned.

She was a rockstar. She was a leader. I thought she had a great future with us.

During her exit interview, she said something that landed like a punch to the gut: "All this talk about how we're all leaders is nice. But at the end of the day, it's always going to be 'Do what Saša says.'"

I felt the blood drain from my face.

She was right.

In a control-based culture like ours at the time, I wanted people to be empowered, but I also wanted to be in control of every single move. Team members felt that every initiative they brought in, I would pick apart. They stopped bringing their ideas because they felt it didn't matter.

I paid a lot of dumb tax because of this. Every time someone left, I had to rebuild. Every time I changed direction, the team had to scramble. Every time I overrode a decision, I taught my people that their judgment didn't count. The cost wasn't just turnover—it was the slow death of initiative across the entire company.

The control culture helped us grow very fast to a million-dollar business. But it created a bottleneck that slowed our growth and drove a lot of people out.

**Shoulder Tap:** If everyone agrees with you all the time, you're not leading. You're controlling.

## THE OPPOSITE EXTREME

The feedback was clear: it was my fault. So I overcorrected. Hard. We went from one extreme straight into the other: appeasement culture.

I asked Maureen and other leaders on the team to lead through solving issues while I sat back.

The team was conditioned to my control. They were used to me making the final call on everything. Now, suddenly, someone else was leading, but did I still have the final say? I thought stepping back meant staying quiet, but silence from the founder isn't empowerment. It's confusion.

People, myself included, didn't know who had authority. They didn't know if decisions would stick. They started second-guessing everything because they'd been burned when I changed things on them. The difference between control-culture change and appeasement-culture change was that in control culture, I changed things because I wanted to; in appeasement culture, direction changed because nobody knew who was actually in charge.

Eventually, it eroded the trust between all of us. People stopped believing that any decision was final and stopped investing in outcomes because they'd learned that outcomes could shift at any moment.

> **Shoulder Tap:** You don't have the full picture. Neither does anyone else. That's the point.

## THINKING TIME LEADS TO SOLUTION

When I'm trying to figure something out, my most effective thinking happens on long walks. Long bike rides. In the pool, swimming laps. That's where my brain does its best work—away from the noise, away from the urgency, away from the inbox.

That's what I did after the appeasement culture failed. I walked. I biked. I swam. I read everything I could get my hands on. I went back to my experiences on previous elite teams. I sought coaching.

What kept coming back to me was every elite team I'd ever been part of. The military. Rugby. None of them were conflict-free. They were conflict-proficient. The difference wasn't that people got along. It was that they knew how to fight for the right things, together.

After the 2018 breakup, I didn't want to rebuild this ever again. This was going to be the last rebuild, and we were going to make it right.

So we established our credo and guiding principles as our North Star. Every single decision we make as a team needs to align with our promise to our clients and team members.

*Inspire Confidence, Simplify Life, Reduce Stress.*

On a high level, it's a very simple thing. On a deeper level, I learned that it's my responsibility to create an environment where people are empowered, encouraged, and celebrated when they challenge the status quo, especially when they challenge me.

Empowerment without structure is just chaos with better intentions. People needed a way to disagree that didn't feel like insubordination. A framework everyone understood and trusted. Not rubber-stamping. Not anarchy. A way to fight for the right answer together.

**Shoulder Tap:** In elite teams, conflict isn't avoided. It's required.

## THE EMBRACING CONFLICT MODEL

The model we use at ICG comes from Susan Scott's book, *Fierce Conversations.* It starts with a beachball.

Picture a beachball. The kind with colored stripes—red, green, yellow, blue, orange, white. Now imagine everyone on your team is standing on a different stripe.

They experience reality from that position. If you're on the blue stripe, your whole world looks blue. You're not wrong. You're just seeing what the blue stripe shows you. Your teammate on the red stripe sees something different—not because they're less smart or because they don't care, but because they live somewhere else on the same ball.

My view of reality is just one version. Everyone else has a different angle. When challenges hit, one person sees it from their white stripe, another from their red stripe, yet no one's stripe is better or more valid.

Five steps. Simple to understand. Hard to execute.

**Step 1: View Reality Like a Beach Ball.** Let go of the need to be right. Accept that everyone has a piece of the truth.

**Step 2: Be Radically Open-Minded.**
This is about interrogating reality—not just challenging others, but challenging yourself. Stay quiet. Listen. Sit with what you hear before responding.

Being radically open-minded only happens during a conversation. How we talk to each other defines our relationship. When we really listen to someone's perspective, we strengthen our connection. We show we are willing to understand them. That builds trust.

**Step 3: Be Radically Assertive.**
Tackle tough issues to solve differences and get in sync. Listen aggressively—with your eyes, ears, and all your senses, like you're walking alone in the woods at night.

Here's where it gets hard. You have to be open to others' ideas and take ownership of working through problems together. Ray Dalio calls this "thoughtful disagreement"—the skill of being assertive and open-minded at the same time.

**Step 4. Build Rituals that Embrace Conflict to Enhance Relationships.**
As we solve issues, I like to create shortcuts to remind us of the conflict that we just went through. That way, next time we don't litigate the same issue. I call those shortcuts "rituals." Rituals create safety and rhythm for conflict to be productive.

**Step 5. Repeat.**
This is not a one-time exercise. It's a discipline. The cycle never stops. Every new issue, every new decision—back to Step 1. Time is the most powerful force in leadership.

Most of the time we need to **take** the **time,** and occasionally we have to **seize** the **time**.

Most of us struggle with this balance. We push our view because it's easier than understanding someone else's. Or we give in too quickly to avoid discomfort. Elite teams do both. Take in information. Engage with each other. Challenge assumptions. Form a collective opinion. Then decide. And remember, the people who change their minds are the winners. They learned something. The ones who stubbornly refuse to see stay stuck.

If you hit a stalemate, go back to your credo. Your guiding principles. Your business *why*. That's your tiebreaker. Not ego. Not tenure. The mission. That's productive conflict. It generates fresh ideas, builds trust, and delivers better results.

**Shoulder Tap:** Thoughtful disagreement means holding your view loosely while holding your values tightly.

## THOUGHTFUL DISAGREEMENT IN ACTION

Our Investment Committee is built on the premise of the embracing-conflict model. It's where we put thoughtful disagreement into practice every week.

We have six voting members and one support advisor—I'm the oldest; Maria, as my business partner, is second; and then we have four advisors in their twenties and thirties who are passionate about investments and money management and doing great work for our clients.

When you look at our TUG Cards™, something I'll cover in the next section, we cover the gamut of talents, unique geniuses, and different perspectives. Every one of us has our own side of the beach ball. That's step one of the model in action—we start by recognizing that each person sees reality from their own stripe. They were selected because of their passion and because of their conviction in their opinions and ideas.

I'm in my late fifties. I've been an advisor for thirty years. I've been through the tech bubble bursting in 2000. September 11th. The 2008 financial crisis. Multiple elections that shook the markets. COVID-19. The Fed raising rates to levels not seen in decades.

The youngest member of the committee is twenty-five years old. Her experience is different. She came into this profession during COVID-19 and navigated the Fed's rate hikes in real time. She brings a perspective shaped by those events, combined with fresh research and direct insight from her clients.

Everyone in between has their own angle too. We recognize that our points of view might be different, but we have the same mission.

To interrogate reality—step two of the model in action—we start with data. Helios, our research partner, sends us a weekly report—forty-nine pages of information relevant to understanding where things are. Not opinions or algorithms or if-this-then-that analysis. And each of us is expected to do our own research on top of that. We never take any recommendation blindly.

Every Tuesday, we have Investment Committee meetings where we argue points of view to get a better understanding of how different people look at things differently. We have youth, and we have experience. All of it is part of the decision-making.

Twice a month, Helios makes recommendations on whether we should move our portfolios in any direction. Eighty-two percent of the time, we follow their direction because it makes sense.

The other eighteen percent? That's step three in action. That's when opinions, arguments, and embracing conflict come in. That's when we all come together on the same side of the table against the problem. How do we guard our clients' assets through tough markets, tough political situations, pandemics, and anything else that might come?

We created a thoughtful disagreement principle. Regardless of tenure, knowledge, or percentage ownership of the company, each member has one vote.

We intentionally have an even number of members so that one vote will be a tiebreaker. At this point, I have the tiebreaker vote because I have the highest percentage ownership and the most skin in the game.

When we know a decision isn't going to be straightforward, there's additional preparation. All of us elevate our game. And we've had plenty of decisions that are four-to-two in either direction.

Sometimes I'm part of the four. Sometimes I'm part of the two.

And that's okay.

We've had situations where my vote was part of the four, and that investment committee decision turned out to be a good one. And in 2024, I was one of the two who were overruled on de-risking our portfolios coming into the election. That was a good move for our clients.

The art of thoughtful disagreement is this: we make decisions based on the merits of the ideas and the situation. At the end of the day, it comes down to the vote. And if I feel very strongly that my opinion should guide us in a certain direction, I have a responsibility to whip the votes.

But if I don't have them, I don't have them.

Every member has a fiduciary responsibility toward clients. We're all selected because we're leaders with the highest integrity, and we work with clients every day.

We walk out of that meeting and straight into client conversations. The portfolios we just argued about belong to real people. That's not abstract. That keeps us honest.

We take that very seriously.

**Shoulder Tap:** The best decisions come when everyone has a voice—and everyone has skin in the game.

## KNOW THEIR TUG LANGUAGE BEFORE YOU TACKLE THE PROBLEM

You are not in conflict with the person. You are in conflict with the problem.

This is where TUG Cards™ come in.

TUG stands for Talent and Unique Genius. It's our way of combining the Working Genius assessment, Kolbe, and PrinciplesYou into something practical, a tool that helps us see each person's natural wiring.

I use TUG Cards™ to suspend judgment and focus my mental energy on the person I'm working with so we can embrace conflict with the problem together. I focus on their talents, unique genius, and their Triple E's: environment, education, and experience.

Derek is our defensive coordinator. He's the CFO of our business. He grew up in a family where frugality and responsible stewardship of resources were the key to his upbringing. That's how he's wired. I, on the other hand, prefer offense. I'm the "let's go for the hill, and we'll deal with the consequences later" kind of leader.

Derek and I could not be more different.

Derek was one of the people who said in 2018, "I'm there with you." I trust him, not to be a yes-man or rubber-stamp every decision, but because he *is* my opposite. And together, with that level of trust and shared values, we make decisions that are better for the business.

Over the years, our conflicts in the partners' meetings and leadership meetings became legendary. And not always in a good way.

I'm very passionate. I want what I want. I don't necessarily like it when people say no to me. But through the power of his example—standing up and saying no to me on things that mattered, like "This is not in the budget," "We need to be financially responsible," and "Our business won't survive if we're not paying attention to profitability"—I learned something important.

If there's no defense, offense can't win championships.

That conflict, Derek holding the line while I pushed for the hill, is what resulted in the development of TUG Cards™.

Everyone on the team has their own stripe. Laura. Maria. Derek. Every one of them sees something I can't see from where I'm standing.

It's critical to have everybody's TUG card in front of you during conflict to understand why they make decisions the way they do and why they hold the positions they hold.

The TUG card helps me suspend my own judgment. It tricks my brain out of blaming somebody for not being like me and into understanding their talent and unique genius so we can find a solution that becomes our solution. One where one plus one equals three.

We developed a TUG card app with all kinds of capabilities for individual people and for teams involved in decision-making.

TUG Cards™ taught me that I don't like too many details. I think too many details are confusing. But eighty-eight percent of my partners need as much specificity as possible, and I've learned to adjust my ways to help people understand what we're trying to do.

Kayla—one of the OGs I mentioned earlier—her natural genius is wonder and discernment. She constantly asks, "I wonder about this…" and, before TUG Cards™, I thought that was extremely annoying. Laura's genius is galvanizing and tenacious. In the book *Who Moved My Cheese?*, she's Scurry—ready to go, even when we don't know where we're going.

Everybody has their own point of view, and TUG Cards™ help us see that as a strength, not a problem.

When you understand someone's genius, you stop taking their resistance personally. You stop hearing their caution as obstruction. You start hearing it as information. That's when conflict stops being combative and starts being useful.

**Shoulder Tap:** Know their TUG Language before you challenge their thinking.

## BEST INTEREST OF THE BUSINESS

Because of who Derek is and how we leaned into his genius, we made him the CFO of the company.

In 2022, we went through a very tough time as a business—markets were going down, most companies' revenue was down, and coming out of that, we entered into the biggest acquisition in the history of our company.

Derek's conflict proficiency and our ability to know each other well through TUG Cards™ resulted in a decision we made as partners—unanimously: We would not take any profit distributions until we built financial emergency funds to a certain level, which in 2024, meant a lot of us paid taxes on profits we didn't receive.

That's what it looks like to put the best interest of the business first. When we're on opposite ends—offense versus defense, growth versus protection—we ask what the business needs in that moment.

Not what I want, not what feels comfortable, but what's best for the business.

And here we are at the end of 2025, two years later, experiencing the highest profit we've ever had as a company, not just distributed to the owners but shared with the team. Everyone who stayed through the hard years got to see what the hard years built.

**Shoulder Tap:** The hardest conversations today create the best outcomes tomorrow.

## WHOLE MESSAGE: TOUGH LOVE RITUAL

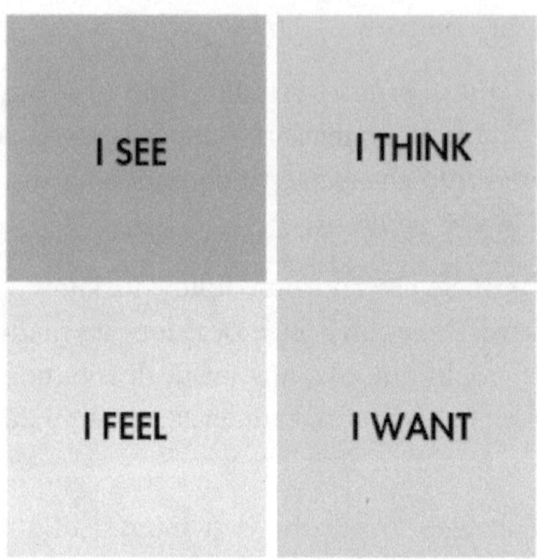


**THE WHOLE MESSAGE = CONTENT + EMOTIONS**

- **I SEE** - List 2-3 undeniable facts that illustrate the issue.
- **I THINK** - "You may not be aware of the impact of your actions..."
- **I FEEL** - Frustrated, Disappointed - **name the real feeling.**
- **I WANT** - To work together to resolve issues and get in sync.

Susan Scott says it best: "The conversation is the relationship. One conversation at a time, you are building, destroying, or flatlining your relationships."

The hardest part of embracing conflict is starting.

That's why we use the Whole Message Model. It's a ritual for delivering tough love—content plus emotions, delivered face-to-face.

Here's how it works:

**I See:** List two or three undeniable facts that illustrate the issue. Not opinions. Facts.

**I Think:** You may not be aware of the impact of your actions.

**I Feel:** Name the real feeling. *Frustrated. Disappointed. Concerned.* Don't hide behind corporate language.

**I Want:** Start with what you want the outcome to be and work backwards. If you don't know what you want, don't start the conversation.

The opening should take no more than two minutes. Write it out. Read it aloud if you need to. The discipline of writing forces clarity.

When people stop giving you feedback, they've already left. Not physically—emotionally. They've decided you're not worth the discomfort of honesty. Silence isn't peace. It's abandonment.

Willingness to embrace conflict is a sign that people care about your mutual success.

People ask us constantly, "How do you live and work together?"

The answer might surprise you.

We love each other enough to risk pissing each other off.

Every tough conversation Laura and I have—every "you were being an asshole" moment—deepens our relationship. Because tough love is proof of care. It's saying, *I love you too much to let you stay stuck here.*

Here's my tough love formula: Tell it to me straight.

No sugar. No yelling. Just truth.

That's what works for me. I need a little pain to separate tough love from casual conversation. Without that sting, I can't tell when someone's coaching me versus just chatting.

But not everyone is built like me.

Some people need gentleness first, warmth before the hard words land. Others need data and logic before emotion. Others need time to process alone before discussing anything face-to-face.

Tough love isn't one-size-fits-all.

What works for you may destroy someone else.

That's why understanding TUG profiles matters. It's not about softening the truth—it's about delivering truth in a way the other person can actually receive it.

I made almost every mistake you can make here. As a business owner. As a husband. As a father. I avoided the hard conversations. I let things fester. I told myself silence was kindness.

It wasn't kindness. It was cowardice dressed up as patience.

The people who changed me were the ones willing to be uncomfortable for my sake. That's not a small thing. That's love with some spine in it.

**Shoulder Tap:** If you love someone, tell them the truth. If you can't do that, you don't love them as much as you think.

## THE BOOSTER IN MARIO KART

Derek and I don't come out of conflict as different people. We come out as better versions of the same ones. Still standing on our own stripes. But we've picked up a few speckles of each other's colors along the way.

Derek says working with me has made him more proactive about seeking growth opportunities. Thanks to him, I've become more disciplined about the financial implications of my wild ideas.

That's the booster. Not the peace after the conflict. The conflict itself. Handled right, it doesn't cost you momentum; it creates it. Like hitting the speed strip in Mario Kart. You go in at one speed. You come out faster.

**Shoulder Tap:** Trust turns conflict into a multiplier.

## BEFORE YOU MOVE ON → SHOULDER TAPS FROM THIS CHAPTER

- If everyone agrees with you all the time, you're not leading. You're controlling.
- In elite teams, conflict isn't avoided. It's required.
- You don't have the full picture. Neither does anyone else. That's the point.
- Thoughtful disagreement means holding your view loosely while holding your values tightly.
- The best decisions come when everyone has a voice—and everyone has skin in the game.
- Know their TUG Language before you challenge their thinking.
- If you love someone, tell them the truth. If you can't do that, you don't love them as much as you think.
- The hardest conversations today create the best outcomes tomorrow.
- Trust turns conflict into a multiplier.

Conflict handled right doesn't just solve problems.

It builds something. A way of working together. A shorthand. A shared language for hard conversations that didn't exist before.

That's not an accident. That's culture. And culture doesn't maintain itself—it's built, on purpose, through the rituals your team practices every single day.

TEN

# Ritualize to Actualize

## RITUALS ARE SYSTEMS WITH HEART

I paid a lot of dumb tax because I relied on blue-brain systems too much.

In *The E-Myth*, Michael Gerber defines a system as eliminating discretion at the operating level. A system takes the thinking out of the work. You build a process. People follow it. One step leads to the next. Nobody has to decide anything.

I defaulted to that for everything. I even heard myself say, "Thinking weakens the team."

I knew better. I'd learned better—the hard way, years before I ever ran a business.

I learned this in the military. On elite teams I was part of, rituals brought harmony. So much so that sometimes we ignored the systems. Those rituals got me through the toughest moments of my life.

But somewhere along the way, I forgot. I built a business on blue-brain systems and wondered why the culture felt flat.

The systems I built were good at getting things done. But those things might not have been the things that needed to be done—or the best things to be done. And when you build systems that ignore how people feel about them, or why they're doing them, something dies. We began to operate on autopilot because I didn't understand the difference between a system and a ritual.

A system is mechanical. Step one leads to step two, which leads to step three. It reduces the need for thinking, and that's the point. Systems create consistency. They create efficiency. They create outputs.

But do you know what systems don't create? Teams.

A ritual creates emotional connection. A ritual creates a team. And in times of crisis, transition, and huge change, when pressure is at its peak, that emotional connection is what helps teams weather the storm, move through adversity, and ultimately win.

Pressure is essential—a team needs constant pressure to be elite and perform at the highest level—and rituals are what hold people together when the pressure comes.

**Shoulder Tap:** Systems create outputs. Rituals create a team. You need both—but don't mistake one for the other.

## START THE DAY AS A TEAM

Every elite team I've been part of (and that I've studied) has a ritual that brings the team together before the work begins.

The Ritz-Carlton has its daily lineup before they greet a single guest. Restaurants have pre-meal before the doors open. The All Blacks perform the *haka* before the first whistle. Will Guidara, in *Unreasonable Hospitality*, calls that thirty-minute pre-meal meeting the moment "when a group of people becomes a team."

That's the point. You don't become a team halfway through the shift or in the second quarter. You become a team at the beginning. The ritual is what makes that transformation happen.

ICG has always had some kind of ritual—from the stand-ups of the early days to the weekly team meetings and Level 10s. During COVID-19, we added daily check-ins to bring everyone on the same page, create belonging, share information, and support each other. Those rhythms kept us connected. No one was on an island. We exceeded expectations and accomplished things I didn't think were possible.

But rituals aren't static. They have to adapt. They have to scale. What works for one level of complexity doesn't automatically work for the next.

**Shoulder Tap:** You become a team at the beginning, not halfway through. The ritual that starts the day—or the game, or the shift—is what makes the transformation happen.

## BIRTH OF A SHARECON

One afternoon in October 2022, I received a text message from Andrea.

*"Mike is ready to go."*

That freaked me out.

Let me back up. I met Andrea when I started my career in Towson, Maryland. She had just graduated from college and had started a few months before me. I often say she coached me on how to create my first financial plan, and I have always looked up to her as an advisor. I admired her grace and resilience, and she was never afraid to put her grit to work and get out of her comfort zone.

When I became a district manager, one of the coolest things that happened was that Andrea became a member of my team. As her leader, I watched this young woman do things that required tremendous courage. As Bono said about the citizens of Sarajevo, "courage is grace under pressure," and Andrea exemplified that in some of the best ways.

We kept in touch over the years as I moved to New York and went on to start my own business. We talked about collaborating through our coaching business, Inspire Network. Then, during COVID-19, she and her business partner decided to part ways, and she needed support to rebuild.

We happened to have a check-in call around that time. During that call, I said, "Our team can provide support. We have the capacity. Let's see where this takes us."

She found space with Mike Shuck—another advisor from the Towson days who knew us both well—and ICG became her extended virtual team. At the end of 2021, Andrea became a coaching client of Inspire Network. In early 2022, ICG was providing full support as she transitioned to her next chapter. Over the course of the year, our team got to know her and appreciate her as a leader and advisor. Trust grew. Her business became integrated with ours. We all seemed to know that infusing her business with ICG was imminent. We just didn't know when or how it would play out.

Then she informed me that Mike Shuck kept coming to her office asking, "When are you guys going to buy me out?"

Andrea had her own ideas about how to handle it. As Mike was looking to retire, he was looking for successors. He saw Andrea daily and respected her immensely. Through Andrea's leadership in their conversations during 2022, Mike decided he wanted her and me to take over his business—with ICG as the team—as he transitioned into retirement.

So when Andrea texted me that October afternoon, *"Mike is ready to go,"* I knew what it meant.

This wasn't just an acquisition. This was a transformation. We wouldn't be doubling our team, but we'd be doubling the clients we served. Doubling the assets we steward. Doubling the complexity of everything. And Mike's way of doing business was different from ours. We'd need to transition his clients to our approach while helping a fairly young team mature in the process.

I knew our systems were good. But I also knew they weren't good enough for where we were going. So I did what I always do when I hit the ceiling of complexity—I hired a coach.

Coach General Stanley McChrystal cost me $29.95, and he didn't know he was my coach. I bought his book, *Team of Teams*, and went on long bike rides to digest it and think through how we could implement his ideas into our system.

McChrystal commanded special operations forces in Iraq, where traditional military hierarchy couldn't keep up with a fast-moving enemy. His solution was daily "operations and intelligence forums," a three-hour meeting where over seven thousand people from around the world came together to share information and stay focused on the mission.

Seven thousand people. Three hours. Every single day.

If General McChrystal could bring seven thousand people together for three hours, I figured we could bring thirty-five people together for thirty minutes.

It was the Wednesday before Thanksgiving when Kayla and I spent two days in Maryland with Mike and Andrea. The drive from Maryland to Albany takes about five hours. Kayla and I had a lot of "windshield time" on that drive, a long stretch where the road becomes a thinking space and the car becomes a conference room. Some of our best ideas have come from staring at white lines while the miles blur together.

That evening, we weren't celebrating. We were planning.

Our systems were good. But our rituals—the daily check-ins, the Level 10s—weren't built for this level of complexity. We weren't just onboarding new clients to our processes. We were bringing in new team members who lived five hours away. Team members we needed to get to know. Team members who needed to learn how we do things. And we needed to do all of that while serving twice as many clients.

Systems can move information. They can track tasks and flag problems. But systems don't create alignment. They don't help thirty people in five locations feel like one, unified team. They don't build the trust you need when everything doubles overnight.

What we needed wasn't better technology. We needed something that would hold us together when the pressure came. Something that would remind us, every single day, why we're here and who we're here with.

We needed a new ritual.

Shared consciousness. That's what McChrystal calls it, or the collective intelligence that emerges when everyone has the same information and can make good decisions without waiting for orders from above.

ShareCon.

## HOW SHARECON CODES OUR CULTURE

We launched ShareCon on January 3, 2023, the first workday of the new year.

The design was intentional. We combined what was working (the daily check-ins, the Level 10 meeting structure) with what we needed (McChrystal's shared consciousness principles). The result was something new. Something that belonged to us.

ShareCon does three things that code our culture:

**First, it builds a sense of belonging.** Every day, we check in. Not just with our tasks, but with our energy, our capacity, and our readiness to receive feedback. The ritual of showing up together, seeing each other's faces in those little squares on the screen, reminds us that we're not alone. We're part of something.

**Second, it creates shared vulnerability.** Anyone on the team can raise an issue. We identify problems together. We help each other solve them. This isn't about the boss handing down solutions but about rockstars with the same information making good decisions together. That's the heart of "delegate to elevate."

**Third, it creates a story of success.** We celebrate wins. We give kudos. We recognize the people who went above and beyond. Over time, those small moments of recognition accumulate into a narrative: we are a team that wins together.

> **Shoulder Tap:** Great rituals do three things: build belonging, create shared vulnerability, and create a story of success. If yours doesn't do all three, it's incomplete.

## THE SHARECON RHYTHM

We meet together as a team Monday through Thursday for thirty minutes. On Mondays, we go longer because we add leadership development and a culture component to the regular rhythm. On Fridays, all teams meet in small groups for deep work collaboration—no ShareCon, but everybody works together getting ready for the next week.

Every ShareCon starts with a video-on check-in. Our team members enter into the Teams meeting chat their energy levels, where they're working from, their workload, and whether or not their landing dock is open.

You might be asking yourself: *What's a landing dock?* In our culture, words are rituals. A landing dock is a shortcut for letting people on the team know whether or not you're open to feedback and tasks. Just like when a pilot wants to land a plane on the deck of an aircraft carrier, she calls the control tower and asks if the landing dock is open.

Because of this check-in, people see that chat throughout the day. If somebody has low energy or needs help, other team members jump in and cover and move. This simple ritual keeps our team connected.

Every day, we give people an opportunity to give kudos to team members for work well done. Creating an environment where people can share gratitude and recognition builds oxytocin flow and deepens trust. It also creates a culture in which people are seen, they see other people, and build strong emotional connections.

We don't have expectations or requirements. Anybody can give kudos in person or in chat. As a "gardener" of my team, I see kudos as an opportunity to pour in some water, add some sun, and provide good nutrients for hardworking people who are taking care of our clients, working through complexities, and performing under pressure.

As a leader of any team, I recommend coming to every ShareCon prepared to give kudos to someone. Not because it's required. Because when I started looking for wins and things people do really well, I helped them reframe their negative biases. There's a lot of neuroscience and psychological research confirming that focusing on small wins helps reprogram the generally negative biases most of us carry.

After kudos, we go to wins. The structure changes by day.

**On Mondays,** we share personal wins or business wins. We celebrate passing exams, licenses, and milestones. This year, some of our wins were announcements that people are getting married and announcements that they're expecting babies. It's also an opportunity for people to get to know each other and understand that there is a life beyond just work. This is how we live our credo—*Inspire Confidence. Simplify Life. Reduce Stress*—balancing life and work in a way that makes everyone's life better.

**On Tuesdays,** our wins are focused on team wins. Each team reports the wins it had to the greater team.

**On Wednesdays,** we have a question of the week. Most of our team is in their twenties and thirties, and we try very hard to take ourselves less seriously. The question of the week is to learn more about each other and break the seriousness of the situation. One Wednesday, the question of the week was, "If I won the lottery and didn't have to work, I would..." Another one was, "The last time I got really nervous at work was..." If you're reading this book, I strongly recommend getting the *Where Should We Begin?* cards by Esther Perel and the Culture Amp.

**On Thursdays,** we share client wins. This is the day we bring the five-star client reviews, or unsolicited reviews from clients, to celebrate them and recognize the teams that contributed to that five-star rating.

It's become incredibly powerful to see pride grow and the desire to do better work.

The check-in, kudos, and wins usually take about fifteen to twenty minutes. The last ten minutes focus on traction. Each day, we review a different scoreboard—looking back at what happened and how we performed—and we go over the full list of client visits scheduled for that day. We make sure every client is welcomed with hospitality and that our service is as excellent as it can be.

## ELITE LEADERSHIP CULTURE MONDAYS

Becoming an elite team doesn't happen by accident. It's built—Monday by Monday, conversation by conversation.

We took our cue from Netflix. Their culture deck laid out exactly what they valued and how they expected people to show up. We built our own version. The ICG Culture Deck. Not a poster. Not a PDF living in a folder nobody opens. A living document we actually use.

When someone new joins the team, they sit down with a senior leader and walk through it together. Usually, that's me. There's something that happens in that room—when you look someone in the eye and say *this is who we are*—that no onboarding checklist can replicate.

We've been doing focused leadership development since 2011. That's when Ray Kelly first sat with us. Ever since, there's always been a dedicated space for the whole team to grow together. The format has evolved as the team grew and the complexity rose. Today, it lives inside ShareCon—Monday mornings, the extra time we carve out specifically for this.

That's when we learn. We discuss. We argue a little. We grow.

We read together, too. *21 Irrefutable Laws of Leadership. Developing the Leader Within You. The Psychology of Money.* Not because someone assigned it. Because we're serious about the craft.

Every ShareCon is recorded. No secrets. No filtered version of reality. What you see is what we are.

## LANGUAGE AS RITUAL

I said at the beginning of this chapter that rituals are systems with heart. But nothing defines culture better than the words and language being used.

When teams ritualize language, they create shortcuts that everyone understands. We streamline communication, create trust, and reinforce what matters.

## THE S-WORD

One of the first things I discovered on my journey to become a more effective leader is that people often call non-advisor team members "staff."

I struggled with it before I even knew why. People were showing up, doing their jobs, collecting paychecks—and somehow the mission never fully landed. There was always a distance I couldn't close. And English not being my first language, I kept turning the word over in my head, trying to figure out what I was missing.

There was always a disconnect. Always an us and a them.

So I went to the Merriam-Webster Dictionary to find the definition. And what I found blew my mind.

“Staff” has two applicable definitions. One, a group of people who work together. And two, a group of military officers that support the commanding officer but do not take part in active fighting.

Let that second one land for a second.

We're a small business. We can't afford to have people who don't take part in active fighting. For me, the mission is the fight. It's making the promise of inspiring confidence, simplifying life, and reducing stress come through. And it takes every single one of us—all of our talents and geniuses and energy.

“Staff” is kryptonite. Superman doesn't struggle because someone punched him. He struggles because the wrong element got too close.

The word "staff" does the same thing to teamwork and trust—it poisons the environment before anyone even realizes what happened. You are sabotaging yourself without knowing it.

Self-leading teams are made of people who all take action in the fight. Not just the commanding officer. Everyone.

And—I always save this one for the room—the other definition of "staff"? A long stick you carry when you walk.

Every time I say that, the laughter erupts. And every time, the idea sticks.

So I ask you: Do you have a team or a staff?

Now, we call it the "S-Word." And once you hear it that way, you can't unhear it.

## TUG LANGUAGE

A great example of ritualized language is what we've created around TUG Cards™. We would say, "Oh, you say this because you're a high Fact Finder," or "I now know I need to provide more information because you're a 7 Fact Finder on Kolbe."

The Working Genius language has proliferated in every conversation and team discussion we have. People will say—I will say—"To complete this project, I need some Enablement and Tenacity," and people know exactly what I'm talking about.

When we use language as a ritual, we accelerate execution, build trust, and start finishing each other's sentences.

## ADVANCES, NOT RETREATS

Another example of language as ritual is the name we have for our off-site meeting, where we all get together once a year.

When we started our business—up until 2021, when Brent and his team joined us—we used to call it a retreat because that's what everyone calls them.

Then a friend asked a simple question: "Do you want to retreat or advance?"

The light bulb went on.

We renamed them "**advances**," and the word changed how we thought about them. We weren't getting away from work—we were moving toward something. Advancing our purpose. Building trust. Celebrating wins. Aligning on what's next.

Every elite team I've been part of and studied has its own unique language. What's yours?

> **Shoulder Tap:** Language codes culture. The words you ritualize become shortcuts for trust. TUG language. "Staff" versus "team." "Retreat" versus "advance." What's your team's unique language?

## PERSONAL ENERGY RITUALS BUILD CAPACITY FOR ELITE PERFORMANCE

My daily energy level reported in ShareCon is usually 9 or 10. It is that high because I built personal energy rituals that bring a full tank of energy to the day, but it wasn't always that way.

When I started my career, I was taught certain ways of doing things. And I was pretty successful by every measure.

Then in 2000, I got promoted to district manager, and in addition to being an advisor, my world included fifteen to twenty other people I needed to train and support. In order to make the money my wife and I needed to make, I had to keep my personal production going.

But I was faced with a conundrum. I couldn't do it. I didn't have the capacity.

Somebody told me to hire a coach who could help me organize. So I did. We went through my business model, my personal rituals, and how I worked as an advisor.

One of the things he told me was, "In order to make this kind of money, you need to have seven client visits a week."

I said, "It's impossible for me to have seven clients a week."

He asked, "Why not?"

"I don't have the time."

"It's pretty simple. You're going to do three on this day, two on this day, and two on this day."

"But my visits are two hours long."

He looked at me. And with a very cool Baltimore accent, he said, "Hon, nobody wants to talk to you for two hours."

From that point on, every time I hit the ceiling of complexity, I looked inward and asked, *What do I need to change?*

We're going to talk more about the process of change and creating capacity in the next chapter, but here I'll tell you: I treat my life as a personal laboratory. I do regular experiments on what rituals I can adopt to increase my capacity and energy. A good friend of mine, Marcus Ranger, calls this "extreme productivity."

I have the same twenty-four hours as anyone else. And I've been told I accomplish more in a day than some people do in a week or a month. Part of that is understanding that in order to perform at a high level, I have to bring my energy to the performance.

So how do I keep my energy at 9 or 10?

I get up at 4:30 a.m. The very first thing I do is transcendental meditation for twenty minutes. This is how I start my day.

After my meditation, I journal while drinking coffee. Ideas that popped up during meditation get captured. When I'm done journaling, I check my sleep number, Lumen, and other metrics to get my bearings before the day.

Most days, I attend the 6:30 a.m. CrossFit class. During nice weather, I go for a bike ride. By 7:30 or 8 a.m., I've been up for hours and filled my energy tank with good sleep, meditation, hydration, and exercise.

From 8 a.m. until 1 p.m., I work on deep thinking—long-term projects, activities, initiatives, and leadership development.

From then until about 5:30 or 6 p.m., my calendar is open for appointments. Most people have a link to my calendar and schedule time to work on anything they want to.

At 3 p.m., I have the most important appointment in my calendar: my afternoon meditation, where I shut down my lights, close my eyes, and meditate for twenty minutes. This time gives me six hours of energy to push through and give my best self, not only to the end of the day, but most importantly, to the most important people in my life: my wife and my kids.

Because I've been up since 4:30 a.m., around 8 p.m., I start to shut down. I'm in bed usually by 9 p.m. and try to hit a high sleep score, which usually requires between six and a half and seven and a half hours of sleep.

My plan is not to be an elite athlete today. My body is not built for that. I often joke that in the world of CrossFit, I'm going to age myself into elite status. My plan is to be the oldest athlete in a CrossFit Open so that when I'm ninety, I'm in the top decile of all members.

> **Shoulder Tap:** Personal energy rituals build capacity for elite performance. The energy you bring has to come from somewhere. Treat your life as a laboratory and experiment.

## BEFORE YOU MOVE ON → SHOULDER TAPS FROM THIS CHAPTER

- Systems create outputs. Rituals create a team. You need both —but don't mistake one for the other.
- You become a team at the beginning, not halfway through. The ritual that starts the day—or the game, or the shift—is what makes the transformation happen.
- Great rituals do three things: build belonging, create shared

vulnerability, and create a story of success. If yours doesn't do all three, it's incomplete.
- Language codes culture. The words you ritualize become shortcuts for trust. TUG language. "Staff" versus "team." "Retreat" versus "advance." What's your team's unique language?
- Personal energy rituals build capacity for elite performance. The energy you bring has to come from somewhere. Treat your life as a laboratory and experiment.

Rituals bring harmony to life.

I learned this early. My family had rituals. My teams had rituals. I brought rituals with me everywhere I went. We all have rituals. Your church has rituals. Your synagogue has rituals. Every organization worth anything has rituals.

Some are language. Some are actions. Some are songs.

Systems become rituals when we infuse emotional connection—the red brain—and make them purple.

This is how elite teams win most of the time.

But rituals have to evolve. What worked last year might not work next year. The world changes. Markets shift. People leave. The rituals that made you elite can become anchors if you refuse to adapt.

Brent, Jo, and Andrea were about to teach me what adaptation really looks like. And it started with an appendectomy.

## ELEVEN

# Adapt to Win

## KILL THE LEADER

Atlanta. April 14, 2023. A mild Friday at the end of a productive week.

I was sitting in the airport lounge, waiting for my flight home to Albany, when I logged onto a video call with two colleagues. They took one look at me and said I looked green. They weren't exaggerating. I felt like death—which, as it turns out, I nearly was.

*Must be food poisoning,* I thought. *Bad shrimp or something.* My colleagues begged me not to board the plane. But I was determined to get home no matter what.

Saturday felt better. Sunday morning, I woke up with pain so intense I knew something was seriously wrong. In the emergency room, the diagnosis came fast: a burst appendix and a life-threatening infection spreading through my abdomen.

Here's the thing about timing. My appendix didn't pick a random week to explode. It picked the most critical week in the most significant organizational transformation in ICG's history.

We'd just absorbed our largest-ever infusion—the Maryland firm that inspired ShareCon. Five hundred new clients. Three extra team members to handle them. A level of complexity that had thrown us into chaos for months.

And we were about to implement a complete restructuring of our business—something called "Diamond Teams"—at a quarterly business review scheduled for the day after my surgery.

Before they wheeled me into the operating room, Maria called. "Some of the leadership team is wondering if we should postpone the QBR," she said. "I think we should go forward. What do you think?"

I didn't hesitate. "Absolutely. Go."

This was the first quarterly review I'd ever missed. It also happened to be the most important one we'd ever held.

I woke up from surgery, still groggy. I spent four days in the hospital receiving round after round of antibiotics to clear the infection. My energy was down to a two out of ten.

After the first day of the QBR, the leadership team came to visit. When they walked into my hospital room, I could see it in their faces before anyone said a word. Things went well.

We went through the usual check-in. "How are you feeling? What's the prognosis?"

"I think I'm going to live," I said.

"Good." They smiled.

"How's the QBR going?"

"It's going great."

And then they started talking. The energy in that room shifted. I listened to the chatter, the updates, the problem-solving they'd done without me. It was something to witness from a hospital bed.

Our team had come a long way since that hip surgery in 2014. Back then, coaching clients sent flowers while my own team stayed silent. Now, my team was running the most important QBR in our history without me. They didn't just survive. They thrived.

We concluded this QBR was the best one we'd ever had—because I was not in the room.

Everyone had stepped into the void and filled it with their character, their talent, their unique genius. It was working. We were becoming a self-leading team.

Best news I could have received on what felt like my deathbed.

> **Shoulder Tap:** Kill the leader to create space. Remove yourself from the day-to-day to see how the team operates. The vacuum you create is where rockstars emerge.

## TRAINING FOR CHAOS

That result wasn't luck. And it wasn't my first kill-the-leader experience.

Coach K calls it "motion offense." No rigid play. No single path to the basket. You read what's in front of you, make the adjustment, find the gap, and move. The plan matters—but the read matters more. I've been playing that way my whole life.

Poor execution? Adapt. Opportunity in the field? Exploit it. Winning, to me, has always meant moving to the next stage of the game. We only have wins or lessons.

Since my days in theater, I've been conditioned to be prepared to step in if the lead actor isn't available. Every understudy knows the show must go on. On the rugby team, we always practiced eventualities—key players getting injured, positions shifting mid-match. Our coaches trained us for chaos long before we faced it in competition.

During the war in Sarajevo, I learned this lesson the hard way. When my mother died, I couldn't go to her funeral. My team was too dependent on me. I was stuck. That moment burned into my memory. I applied the kill-the-leader principle and started imagining the world without me. In every situation since, I've asked myself: *What will happen if I'm not here?*

During our first client advisory board in 2011, my dear friend Susan, one of our earliest clients, looked at me and said, "Saša, this is all going great while you're here. What happens if you're not around?"

Since then, I've instructed my team to prioritize training for chaos without me.

The elite teams I've studied all practice this. Navy SEAL teams train extensively before deployment. One of their mandatory drills removes the team leader early in a simulated mission. The drill ensures the team can adapt, complete the mission, and survive losing their point person.

The New Zealand All Blacks do something similar on the rugby field. They practice under conditions more challenging than actual matches —waterlogged fields, slippery balls, missing key players for extended periods. When chaos hits in competition, they've already felt it. They've already adapted.

Billie Jean King said it best: "Pressure is a privilege." It means you have something worth fighting for. Elite teams don't run from pressure. They train into it.

My appendix gave our team an unplanned kill-the-leader drill, and years of building an adaptive culture had prepared them.

> **Shoulder Tap:** Pressure is a privilege. It means you have something worth fighting for. Elite teams don't run from pressure. They train into it.

## TURNING STRESS INTO PRESSURE

Our most successful infusions shared something in common: a dedicated team that met weekly, solved issues together, and kept things moving forward.

I was on a call with Kayla, Phil, and Maria during the first meeting of our Maryland infusion team. Kayla would lead the operational component. Phil would lead the advisory component. Maria and I would step back to give them the opportunity to grow their wings and lead.

In the first few minutes of the conversation, Phil and Kayla were talking about the amount of stress the team would be under. All the different things that would cause that stress. The weight of it.

I asked for an opportunity to speak.

"What I'd like you to do," I said, "is change the word in your mind. Every time you feel you're under stress, change it. Say instead, I am under pressure."

I learned this trick in the military and applied it during my experiences in Bosnia and later in Sierra Leone. When I tell myself I'm under stress, I feel negative. Defeated. I resist things. But when I change the label—when I shift from "I am under stress" to "I am under pressure"—something happens in my head. I immediately shift into action mode. Problem-solving mode.

It's the same neurological chemical reaction in your body. Stress and pressure trigger identical responses. But the framing changes everything. Elite performers know this. Elite athletes know this. I learned it in rugby, in the military, in theater. Every time you're under stress, you find a way to turn it into, *I'm under pressure. I need to perform. What do I need to do?*

They both said, "That's brilliant."

Since that conversation, both Kayla and Phil have remarked that shifting the mindset from being under stress to being under pressure and coaching others to do the same has been one of the most important leadership tools in helping us adapt and transform.

**Shoulder Tap:** Change the word. When you're under stress, shift to "I'm under pressure." Same chemical reaction, completely different mindset. Action instead of resistance.

## WHAT GOT US HERE WON'T GET US THERE

Within weeks of the Maryland infusion starting, it became clear we needed to transition our organization into a new structure. ShareCon was working well. People were empowered to bring issues forward and talk about things that weren't working. The pressure was real.

As a visionary, I'd seen this coming months before. I'd been trying to influence Maria and Phil to think about adapting the Diamond Teams concept, a structure I'd learned from Bob Bonfiglio during an Elite Growth Forum the year before.

Although resistant at first, the pressure of the new situation pushed Maria and Phil to move. They went to work, taking the original Diamond Teams framework and making it our own. It was elite teamwork at its best, taking care of clients while introducing Mike to our ways of doing business and recognizing that things needed to adjust. We brought in some of the original concepts, a lot of what we already did, and practices that Mike, his team, and Andrea contributed.

Over two months, we worked on what the structure should look like. In early April, we gathered to align everyone. Our original plan called for four diamonds, with Maria and me each leading one. As we walked through how it would work, Mike looked at me and asked, "Saša, why would you be a diamond leader? You should let your partners lead the diamonds. You should be a floater, like I am."

Maria and I looked at each other. We both knew that was exactly the right thing to do. Neither one of us had the guts to say it out loud. When Mike said it, we both nodded. Done.

Since April 2023, we've changed the diamond structure several times. Today, we operate under what we call "Diamonds 3.0"—three diamonds made up of advisors and coordinators, plus one diamond called "Financial Wellness" that provides a completely different client experience. What we learned in this process confirmed that what got us here will not get us where we're going. Adaptation of systems is how you work through change and make your business fit the needs of the future.

**Shoulder Tap:** What got you here won't get you there. Successful teams hold their methods loosely. The systems that drove past success may be limiting your future.

## BUILDING THE ADAPTATION MUSCLE

Building an adaptive culture starts with understanding how change actually works.

There are four levels of change. And there are dynamics of change. The levels are the architecture—the stages you move through. The dynamics are how people react as they go through those stages. As a leader building self-leading teams, the dynamics of change are your roadmap. They prepare you for your team's reactions as you lead them through different levels.

I think of it as four levels.

**Level One: Knowledge.** We recognized that change needed to happen. At the beginning of the Maryland infusion, we saw that we had to change the way we worked in order to accomplish the mission—*Inspire Confidence, Simplify Life, Reduce Stress*—for twice as many clients and a book of business twice the size.

**Level Two: Attitude.** We adopted a positive stance toward the change that was needed. We created a shortcut: stress and pressure are the same stimulus, but the way we interpret pressure determines whether we perform at a higher level. When viewed correctly, being under pressure becomes a positive force. It also requires us to stay flexible so we can meet the challenges that come our way.

**Level Three: Behavior.** We actually changed what we did. We reorganized our teams, realigned people, and created new processes and ways to communicate. One of the most important additions was a weekly coffee between Mike and me, in addition to our weekly infusion team meetings. When Mike and I met, we worked through obstacles and maintained alignment across the organization. It wasn't my idea—it grew out of necessity. What didn't change was our commitment to the client experience and our overall mission: bringing Mike's and Andrea's clients into our way of doing things.

**Level Four: Culture.** Culture is what you repeatedly do and celebrate. When behavior changes—and results follow from that behavior—a new culture is formed. Today, we are infinitely stronger as a team at adapting to the world around us to accomplish our mission than we were at the beginning of the Maryland infusion.

> **Shoulder Tap:** Build the adaptation muscle. Levels of change are the architecture. Dynamics of change are the roadmap for how your people will react. Know both.

## WE GOT LUCKY

I paid a lot of dumb tax. Made a lot of mistakes. Over time, I trained my leadership brain to look for signs. Or as I like to say, sometimes when you work hard on your transformation to be an elite leader, you get lucky.

We got lucky in January 2020.

It just happened that Ray Kelly had done a leadership session with our team where he introduced us to the Seven Dynamics of Change. The model is simple but powerful: People feel awkward and self-conscious when change hits. They worry about what they're giving up. They feel alone, even when everyone else is going through the same transition. They can only handle so much at once. They feel vulnerable. They're concerned about resources. And when the pressure is off, they often revert to their old state.

That last one—dynamic number seven—is my frequent default. I have to remind myself constantly that progress isn't permanent. When things calm down, people drift back to what's comfortable.

The recognition that different people react to change in different ways is critical for leaders. How you lead through those dynamics is what builds trust. Less than three weeks after Ray's session, we tested those dynamics against a global event like no other.

## THE PANDEMIC STRESS TEST

On Monday, March 16, 2020, our leadership team made a decision that would reshape everything. We moved all operations online to keep everyone safe.

At 12:30 p.m., while the whole team was still in our Albany office, we ran a test to work out the kinks of virtual meetings. We told everyone we'd do a virtual check-in at 9:15 a.m. the following morning.

Then we sent everyone home.

At the time, we thought we were just making the right call for our team's well-being. We didn't realize that shift would become critical to handling future business infusions and driving a three-hundred percent jump in organic growth over the previous year.

Because we'd already internalized the Seven Dynamics of Change, we anticipated how our team would react. We knew people would feel awkward and self-conscious about video calls. We knew they'd worry about what they were losing—the casual hallway conversations, the in-person collaboration, the sense of being together.

So we started daily check-ins the very next day—9:15 a.m. and 3 p.m. These weren't status updates. They were about supporting each other. Mental well-being. Open discussions of thoughts, feelings, and needs. A space where leaders could step up and take action.

When team members felt resource-strapped—and many did—we delivered food and supplies to their homes. We acknowledged the limitations everyone faced and worked to support work-life balance in real, practical ways.

By June, optimism had returned. We felt a positive shift in energy. And we decided not to get comfortable. We applied FranklinCovey's 4 Disciplines of Execution model to client referrals, creating weekly accountability for referral conversations.

By the end of 2020, we'd seen a three-hundred percent increase in new clients.

## THE MISSION GUIDES ADAPTATION

Self-leading teams have a mission. It's clearly defined. And it's the mission that guides what needs to change in order to accomplish it.

Our credo card—*Inspire Confidence, Simplify Life, Reduce Stress*—is that mission, in which we put clients first, create family-focused experiences with integrity always, and pursue excellence through leadership and teamwork while seeking life balance.

Without that mission, adaptation becomes chaos. You're just reacting. With the mission, adaptation becomes purposeful. You're making reads, like running a motion offense in basketball. You see the play, but you also see the gap. You take advantage of the opportunity for your team to win.

Distraction and opportunity are two sides of the same coin. When something comes at you, is it pulling you away from the mission, or is it a gap you need to exploit? Knowing what you're trying to accomplish as a team, through building your adaptation muscle, is how you answer that question in real time.

## PRIORITIZE AND EXECUTE

We all have a mission. We all have a plan. And you go into that plan, into that mission, into that day, thinking, *This is what's going to happen.*

I have many days where my must-dos are appointments on the calendar, my should-dos are written on the right side, and I'm looking at my day review thinking, *This is going to be a busy day.* And as soon as I'm done with that review—sometimes while I'm still in it—an email arrives that blows the whole thing up.

A client issue. A team emergency. A curveball from nowhere.

"Prioritize and execute" is using your blue brain to counteract your red brain's emotional reaction. It's how you stay in purple when everything around you is trying to knock you off balance.

"Prioritize and execute" means asking, *What do I need to do now? Is the thing coming at me a distraction or enemy fire?*

If it's enemy fire, you drop the mission and survive. If it's not, you continue on your mission and put a pin in what needs to be addressed later. More often than not, it's not me who needs to react. It's delegating to elevate, letting others handle what they're capable of handling.

You can't go into the day winging it. You need a plan. And you need to be prepared that the plan is going to blow up at any point. You still need to deliver.

When you do that over time—when your whole team does that over time—you become resilient. That's the adaptation muscle working. That's how you build a team that leads itself.

## PLANNING IS ESSENTIAL. PLANS ARE WORTHLESS.

Not every day is a win. Some days are devastating. You lose important clients. You miss out on opportunities. Your best people move on.

When that happens, leaders have to be brutally honest about the setbacks while giving the team real reasons for hope. When things don't go as planned, your job is to find another way. To get creative. To come up with an even better Plan B. To help your team shake off discouragement and get ready for the next challenge.

Nothing is permanent. The good things and the bad things will change. The second hand on my watch, back in the military, was a reminder that time is passing—and the worst of things will pass. And if the bad things pass, so will the good.

The world we live in is not linear. It's more like a jungle gym. You're not climbing a corporate ladder. You're climbing El Capitan. Sometimes you have a rope. Sometimes you don't.

Adaptation isn't about surviving one crisis. It's about building a team that thrives on pressure and that sees every disruption as an opportunity to get stronger. "Killing the leader" creates a vacuum. People step into it. They grow. You create new challenges, new pressure. They become dependent on you again. So you kill the leader again. And again.

This is how you build rockstars. This is how you build a team that leads itself.

## BEFORE YOU MOVE ON → SHOULDER TAPS FROM THIS CHAPTER

- Kill the leader to create space. Remove yourself from the day-to-day to see how the team operates. The vacuum you create is where rockstars emerge.
- Pressure is a privilege. It means you have something worth fighting for. Elite teams don't run from pressure. They train into it.
- Change the word. When you're under stress, shift to "I'm under pressure." Same chemical reaction, completely different mindset. Action instead of resistance.
- What got you here won't get you there. Successful teams hold their methods loosely. The systems that drove past success may be limiting your future.
- Build the adaptation muscle. Levels of change are the architecture. Dynamics of change are the roadmap for how your people will react. Know both.

The adaptation muscle only matters if it produces something real.

Purpose. People. Trust. Conflict. Rituals. Adaptation. Six elements. Years of work. A hospital bed in Albany proving it held together when everything went wrong.

But proof isn't a feeling. Proof is a number. A client who stayed. A leader who stepped up. A business that grew while its founder was flat on his back.

TWELVE

# Inspiring Results

## RESULTS ARE PROOF OF A COMMITMENT

Every gardener knows the secret. You don't get tomatoes by accident. You don't wake up one morning to find roses climbing your fence because the universe decided to be generous. You plant what you want to harvest. Then you wait. You tend. You trust.

Leadership works the same way.

Some of the most expensive dumb tax I ever paid came from not tending the garden.

What do I mean by that? Not paying attention to what seeds I was planting and not pulling the weeds that needed to be pulled.

For as long as I can remember, I was mission-driven. Purpose-driven. A guy who wanted things to matter. But the seeds I kept planting were bringing me a harvest I didn't want.

Results are proof of our efforts. I had to learn the hard way that profit is not a purpose. It's a result. An important one, yes. But not the whole thing.

I was always competitive. Driven to do more, to be the best. My mother's voice still in my head. *You missed a spot.* That drive never left me.

But I was never willing to do whatever it takes to achieve the results that most people recognize as success—profit margins, sales numbers, the stuff that fits on a spreadsheet. For me, since Sarajevo, since my work with Catholic Relief Services, making a positive impact has always been the most important part of results. The thing is, in order to keep doing good over the long haul, you absolutely have to achieve the sales metrics and profit, too. The duality matters. Winning by doing good.

That pairing came from the war. In Sierra Leone, working with CRS, I kept saying it to myself: *I want to do good for people, but I also want to do good for myself and my family. I want to help people who want to be helped.*

And the driving force behind all of it was defining what result would be inspiring and worthy of my best efforts.

Scarcity is the default setting. It's what naturally comes to us. The hoarding. The protecting. The fear that if someone else wins, I lose.

In order to accomplish inspiring results, I learned that I have to reject scarcity. Actively reject it. Embrace abundance.

It's like going to the gym—I don't want to do it. But when I start doing it, it feels so good that there's no other way I'd have it. And if I don't practice abundance, the weeds of scarcity grow so fast I have to pull them all the time.

**Shoulder Tap:** Profit is not a purpose. It's a result. Get clear on what seeds you're actually planting—because you will harvest exactly what you tend.

## THE RESULTS TRIFECTA

In my second year as an advisor and my first year as a district manager, I had lunch with Scott DiGimarino, a leader of our market group. The big boss. Over plates of cheddar biscuits at Red Lobster in Owings Mills, Maryland, he got us all fired up about results.

I will never forget what he said that day.

"You measure success as a financial advisor in three ways. People have to love you. Peers have to respect you. And you make a boatload of money."

That lunch in 2000 became my enlightenment. Simple. Clear. And it covered the duality of how I think about results—the doing well and the doing good, all in one frame.

Over time, I refined it. I've never met a good idea I didn't want to tinker with until it felt like mine.

In 2005, I almost got fired for poor results on a scorecard. The results were black and white. On seven different metrics, I fell below the Mendoza line. I had to turn things around—meet the numbers in recruiting, production, and results. It put a lot of stress on me, but worse, it created this sense that I was doing it not for any greater purpose, but just to keep my job. I felt trapped. I proved to myself I could do it, but I knew it had to be something more than that.

And then there was 2008. Two years into our new business, I burned through all of our savings to keep the team together. I didn't realize it at the time, but I was putting the livelihood of my family at risk.

I remember an exchange with Laura sometime in the fall of that year. She told me I'd been snapping at the kids. Snapping at her. Short. Under stress. And I remember responding, "But this is our livelihood."

She looked at me and said, "But this is your family."

That hit me. Hard. I needed to find the balance. Balancing doing good with doing well—that's what the trifecta of results is all about.

I define inspiring results as a trifecta. People love you—your team, your clients, your community. Peers respect you—not your competitors, but your rivals, the ones who make each other better. And the business outlasts the founders. It plays the long game.

**Shoulder Tap:** Measure results three ways: people love you, peers respect you, business outlasts its founders. Hit one without the others, and you're running on fumes.

## PEOPLE LOVE YOU

Will Guidara, in his book *Unreasonable Hospitality*, talks about how service is black and white, but hospitality is in color. Service is how we deliver on the promise—inspiring confidence, simplifying life, reducing stress. The mechanics. Our service, I'd like to think, is excellent. But the way we make people feel? That's hospitality.

A client whose husband was dying of cancer told us, tears in her eyes, how much she appreciated the Spoonful of Comfort box we sent. Her husband didn't want to eat anything else. So we sent more.

A client who got laid off, in a moment of despair, called Brent. By the time he got home, there was a note in his mailbox. Brent had beaten him there. The note said they were going to be okay, that they'd planned for this, and that Brent would be there every step of the way.

Ten years ago, a couple walked through our door carrying the kind of fear that doesn't announce itself loudly—it just sits quietly in your chest. Their advisor was a friend. When he retired and joined ICG, they followed him—cautiously, skeptically—the way you follow anyone into unfamiliar territory when you're not sure the ground will hold. It held. And over the next decade, the trust that had started with their friend slowly expanded. First to me. Then to our team. That's what succession is supposed to look like. Not a handoff. A transition.

Last year, our conversations shifted from "having enough" to "dying with zero regrets." We started nudging them toward gifting now, while they could still see what it did to their kids. While they could feel it themselves. The gratitude that comes back from those conversations doesn't show up on any results report. There are tears. Long pauses. And more than once, they've walked out the door saying "I love you" to each other, as though the weight of decades of frugality had finally lifted and they remembered what the money was actually for. That's the result I'm most proud of. Not the number. The moment.

We give love. We get it back.

The same is true for our team. We have people who met at work and are getting married later this year. During an advance, on the bus ride back from karaoke night, a spontaneous chant broke out: "ICG! ICG!" Like we were their favorite soccer club.

One of our rituals at the advance is called "opening presents." It has nothing to do with wrapping paper.

We sit together—the whole team—and we acknowledge what we've been given. Not bonuses. Not promotions. The other stuff. The stuff that doesn't fit on a performance review. Gratitude for the people sitting in the room. For families back home holding it down. For the moments when someone showed up for us, and we didn't have to ask.

Every member of the team has the opportunity to share. Some write it down and read from the page, voices cracking halfway through. Some stand up in front of everyone, no notes, just the weight of what they need to say. This ritual can stretch past an hour. There are almost always tears.

People get vulnerable. Really vulnerable. They talk about what scared them. Where they felt weak. The moment they thought they might not make it, and the person who helped them through. It's not performance. Nobody's required to speak. It's people choosing to be seen because they trust they're safe enough to do it.

We've had guests in the room for Opening Presents. They walk in expecting a team meeting and leave wiping their eyes, saying they've never felt anything like it. The camaraderie. The realness. The way people hold space for each other without flinching.

That feeling, the one guests can't quite name when they leave the room—that's what it means to be loved by your team.

We give our community our time, treasure, and talents. Our team members volunteer with organizations focused on education, entrepreneurship, financial literacy, and food security—Junior Achievement,

Regional Food Bank, Boys and Girls Club, and others. Community service and making a positive impact are part of our credo.

**Shoulder Tap:** Your clients don't remember your portfolio returns on a Tuesday. They remember that you showed up when their world was falling apart. Love is a result you earn with presence, not performance.

## PEERS RESPECT YOU

There's a difference between being liked and being respected. As humans, we all want to be liked. But elite teams earn respect.

The respect that matters to me—the respect I value—is given when my team and I accomplish hard things. Things most people wouldn't attempt. When we create new solutions, open new pathways, and innovate in ways that make life easier for the people around us.

It doesn't matter if I'm at the top of the scoreboard or somewhere in the middle. What matters is whether I'm the kind of person who creates new pathways. Who makes life easier for my colleagues. Who does the hard things the right way.

But accomplishing hard things and innovating don't really matter if I don't have the abundance mindset to share what I've learned. Not because I get paid to. Because it's the right thing to do. Because a rising tide lifts all ships.

Before the war in Sarajevo, I had an idea of becoming a relevant thinker on subjects of marketing and business. But I didn't like the politics of academia. When I came to the United States, some important people told me I didn't have to get a Ph.D. I could do it by being an entrepreneur—learning things, developing, innovating, and then sharing with others. If I did a good enough job, I could actually make a living.

So from the very beginning of ICG, I considered it to be a training hospital. The lab. The crucible where I imagine things, test them, break them, fix them, and figure out how they actually work. Part of my mission of making a positive impact has always been testing, learning, and sharing—influencing others. This became a very natural thing.

When we arrived at "Inspire Confidence, Simplify Life, Reduce Stress" as our purpose, it resonated. I was invited to speak at conferences, showcasing our work, our results, our culture. After presentations, people would come up to me and say, "I love that. Can I use it?"

Absolutely, I'd tell them. ICG is trademarked—you can't use that. But the purpose statement? Take it. Make it yours.

Laura used to give me grief about it. Compliance would call, asking if we knew people were using our *why*. And Laura would ask, "Why are we giving that away?"

I told her the biggest compliment you can get is when people want to use your stuff. It's not about the words. It's about what actions people take with those words. Teams have copied our credo card and made it their own. Many of them are tremendously successful, some at the very top of our organization.

Being respected by your peers is a sign you're doing something worth emulating. The accolades we've received—Best in State, Chairman's Advisory Council, Experience Award, and one of the Best Places to work—result in that respect. And that recognition gives us the opportunity to share what we're doing.

**Shoulder Tap:** If the people doing the work beside you don't respect how you got here, it doesn't matter what title's on your door. Respect is built in the trenches—not in the corner office.

## PROJECT 9ZERO

It was 2011. I read an article by Dan Sullivan about breaking the ceiling of complexity. The success we accomplish over time creates a ceiling. The complexity of all the different things that got us there becomes a limiting factor. We get stuck. Sullivan's solution? Put an outrageously crazy goal way out of any realm of possibility. Reframe the thinking. Get out of the rut.

I felt we were in a rut. And as I was thinking about what could be an outrageously crazy goal, something popped into my head.

Reaching a billion dollars under management.

At the time, we were less than $100 million. It was ten times more than we managed at the time. That was the goal.

I was sitting with my coach, Ray Kelly, wrestling with a question I couldn't shake. We had incredible talent on the team. But we weren't growing like we should have been. Something was missing.

Ray reminded me of John Maxwell's Law of Explosive Growth, which says to achieve explosive growth, your team should be adding leaders, not just followers.

That landed. Hard.

I went home that night and did the math. Not the safe math. The real math. Where could this team actually go if we stopped hiring help and started developing leaders?

I sat with one billion for a while. It felt ridiculous. It also felt right.

But I needed to make it sticky. Memorable. Something the team would carry in their heads when the days got long and the work got hard.

"How many zeros are in a billion?" I asked my partners at our next meeting.

They looked at me. "Nine."

"That's the project. Project 9Zero."

They looked at me like I'd lost my mind.

Good. That meant it was big enough to matter.

Here's what I didn't do then that I know now: I kept it to myself. The initial reactions I got were skeptical, and I was afraid that would create confusion. So I didn't bring the team along. I didn't inspire the performance or unify us around the common goal.

That was a mistake.

Seven years later, in 2018, as Maria and I were envisioning the future of ICG, we brought Project 9Zero back. This time we did it right. We put it in our Vision/Traction Organizer as a big, hairy, audacious goal and started working backwards on what was required to accomplish it.

Project 9Zero wasn't just about hitting a number. It became tied to how well we delivered on our promise. I connected every outcome to the credo, to the commitments we made to our clients and team members.

Our people were aligned. We were building trust through challenges. Along the way, we built a team with more than sixty percent of its members in their twenties and thirties. Sixty percent female. Fifty-nine professional designations.

We embraced conflict and stood together against the problem. We recognized that what got us here wouldn't get us where we needed to go. So we changed. We built rituals like ShareCon to keep the team connected. We kept getting more and more into the flow.

In 2022, we hit $415 million. The ten-year mark. Halfway there.

And then came the Maryland infusion. It took us from $450 million to $1 billion in less than three years.

We accomplished Project 9Zero.

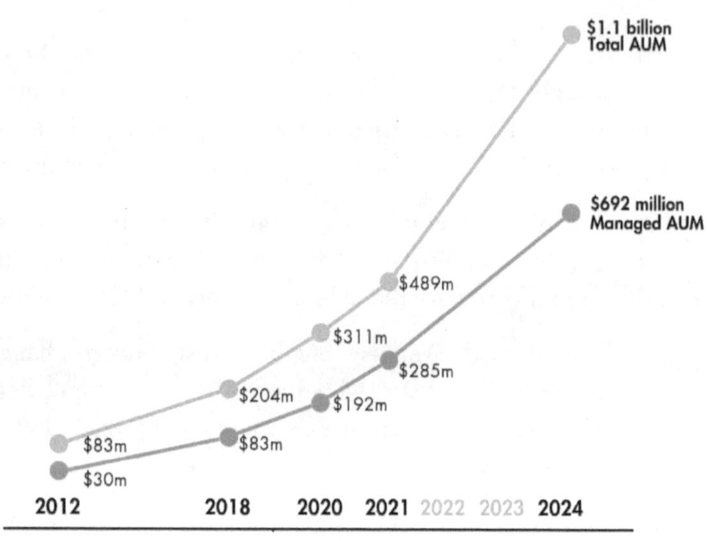


**PROJECT 9ZERO**

By hitting it, we hit just about every other target our peers would recognize. Chairman's Advisory Council. Best in State. I was inducted into the Ameriprise Hall of Fame and received the Outstanding Leader Award.

The lesson? Growth is not linear. It takes time. The effort you put into accomplishing extraordinary results often won't be visible. But you have to keep going. And sometimes, like in our case, you complete the 10X leap by doubling in two years.

Because of our results—and the innovation we either initiated or helped facilitate—we've been asked, again and again, to share how we do what we do. Coaching other teams became the ultimate measure of that respect.

We built a leadership development and business coaching company called Inspire Network. Today, we support twenty-eight different teams across various industries, helping them transform into self-leading teams and build multi-generational ownership structures. (Take a closer look at Inspire Network by scanning the QR code at the beginning and end of this book.)

> **Shoulder Tap:** Set goals big enough that the people around you think you've lost your mind. If it doesn't scare you a little, it's not a vision—it's a to-do list.

## BUSINESS OUTLASTS THE FOUNDERS

The ultimate measure of success for a leader of self-leading teams is this: the business survives the founders and lasts for generations.

There is no success without succession. For years, I owned one hundred percent of a business that owned one hundred percent of me. I was the bottleneck, the single point of failure, the guy who couldn't take a vacation without his phone buzzing every hour. That's not a business. That's a job with overhead.

The shift happened when I stopped thinking about what I could control and started thinking about what I could cultivate. When I stopped asking, "How do I grow this?" and started asking, "How do I grow the people who will grow this long after I'm gone?"

When I think about building a business that outlives its founders, I have a visual in my mind.

> **Shoulder Tap:** You don't build a self-leading business by holding tighter. You build it by giving it away. I went from owning one hundred percent of a business I couldn't escape to thirty-eight percent of a business that runs without me—and my personal stake tripled. Do the real math.

## THE AIRPLANE

Think of your business as an airplane.

If you're like most founders, your business is a single-engine plane. You are that engine. The whole thing flies because you're generating thrust. Your relationships. Your expertise. Your hustle. Your name.

If something happens to you—if you get sick, burn out, or just want to take a damn vacation—that airplane loses altitude. Eventually, it crashes.

I didn't want a single-engine plane anymore.

In 2018, I realized that, more than ever, I wanted to build a plane that would fly long after I was gone. So I started building.

Maria became a partner in 2020. She grew into the second engine on the plane. Shortly after we signed the paperwork making her a twenty percent owner, I asked her, "So, do we build a tax business, or do we bring Brent in?"

The first decision we made as partners was to bring Brent in. We needed another engine.

Brent and his team joined us in 2021, adding a third engine to the plane. The very first decision the three of us made as business partners was that our plane needed a better structure and a better crew to fly it.

We brought in Derek as a fourth partner at the end of 2021. He's our uncompromising navigator. He doesn't let us stray from financial responsibility. All three of us—Maria, Brent, and I—are driven by accomplishing things, taking the hill. Derek makes sure we always have the support to keep the hill.

But engines and navigation aren't enough. You also need a crew—a team that knows how to fly the plane even when you're not in the cockpit. That means building leadership capabilities across the organization, not just at the top.

Coach K (Mike Krzyzewski, the Hall of Fame basketball coach) says it. A lot of great leaders say it. Leadership is the most underleveraged capability in business. Most of us, as practitioners and business owners, suck at leadership. The good news? You can actually get better.

Then there's the body of the plane. The systems, the technology, and the infrastructure that keep everything connected and functional. You can't fly from New York to New Zealand without a solid fuselage. That structure is the responsibility of two of our business partners—Kayla and Jo.

And finally, there's energy. Sustainable energy that keeps the plane flying indefinitely. Your credo card, your narrative, your culture, the right clients, financial strength—these are the components that keep the engines running without burning you out.

It's through this work that we attracted Mike and Andrea to join our team in 2023, who have only added more energy to our plane.

Today, we have a plane with multiple engines. Three diamonds led by partners—Brent, Andrea, and Maria—each with two lead advisors growing into their own engines, supported by relationship advisors, support advisors, and diamond coordinators. Laura and our marketing team and Kayla and the operations team keep things together.

As we closed out the Project 9Zero journey, I learned that if I go to the directional point, things present themselves that I could not have imagined. And as you close in on a big milestone, new milestones start popping up. If you're brave enough to go for them, new relationships start popping up, too.

A relationship I'd been cultivating as a friendship for fourteen years became a partnership. Mark joined our team as the second part of the visionary-integrator duo. In the book *Rocket Fuel* by Gino Wickman and Mark C. Winters, they talk about the power of the visionary and integrator working together. Mark and I started fortifying systems, making sure the plane runs correctly, and navigating our next 10X journey.

Our conversations, especially at the beginning of working together, often started with, "So, how do we minimize the impact of Saša on day-to-day operations?"

This piece—and having constant kill-the-leader conversations in the cockpit—is a critical component of what we're going to talk about in the next chapter.

The one hundred to thirty-eight percent story isn't a story about giving something away. It's a story about watching something multiply. When you build a team of owners—not employees, but people who think and act like the business is theirs—the math changes. You stop playing for quarters and start playing for decades.

In the chapters that follow, I will outline all the important things we did—and are still doing—to transform our team. From a control-based operation driven by one person to a self-leading business. A business that grows itself. A business that leads itself.

## BEFORE YOU MOVE ON → SHOULDER TAPS FROM THIS CHAPTER

- Harvest What You Plant: Profit is not a purpose. It's a result. Get clear on what seeds you're actually planting—because you will harvest exactly what you tend.
- The Results Trifecta: Measure results three ways: people love you, peers respect you, business outlasts its founders. Hit one without the others, and you're running on fumes.
- People Love You: Your clients don't remember your portfolio returns on a Tuesday. They remember that you showed up when their world was falling apart. Love is a result you earn with presence, not performance.
- Respected by Peers: If the people doing the work beside you don't respect how you got here, it doesn't matter what title's on your door. Respect is built in the trenches—not in the corner office.
- Project 9Zero: Set goals big enough that the people around you think you've lost your mind. If it doesn't scare you a little, it's not a vision—it's a to-do list.
- Business Outlasts Its Founders: You don't build a self-leading business by holding tighter. You build it by giving it away. I went from owning one hundred percent of a business I couldn't escape to thirty-eight percent of a business that runs without me, and my personal stake tripled. Do the real math.

That's the harvest. Twelve chapters of planting, tending, pulling weeds, trusting the process. Purpose. People. Trust. Conflict. Rituals. Adaptation. All of it working together like a flywheel—each piece reinforcing the next until the whole thing builds a momentum you can feel in your chest.

But here's the thing about gardens. You can stand in mine all day. You can admire the tomatoes. You can take pictures of the roses. And none of that helps you grow a single thing in your own yard.

I didn't write this book so you could tour my garden.

I wrote it so you could build yours.

Everything in Act Two—every framework, every principle, every story about the people who made this real—that's *what* elite leadership looks like. The next five chapters are about *how*. The tools. The rhythms. The uncomfortable conversations. The systems that make the right behavior the easy behavior and the wrong behavior impossible to hide from.

I paid a lot of dumb tax getting here. Decades of it. The kind that costs you sleep and marriages and partnerships and years you don't get back.

You don't have to pay all of it.

That's the deal I'm offering. Not theory—testimony. Not a textbook—a recipe from someone who burned the first twelve batches and finally figured out the temperature.

Results aren't the point. They're the proof. The proof that your purpose was real, your people were right, and the garden you planted was worth tending.

Walk with me.

# ACT III
# The Business

## INTRODUCTION

You're still here. That means something.

The work is in front of you.

Act Two gave you the framework. Purpose. People. Trust. Conflict. Rituals. Adaptation. Results. Seven elements. The beach ball that holds it all together. The shift from chess master to gardener. The proof that elite leadership isn't about control—it's about cultivation.

Now comes the part that most leadership books skip. Not the "what." The "how."

Act Three is the story of developing leaders. Not just on my team, but on other teams. Other organizations. Other founders who are standing where I stood, wondering how the hell they're supposed to build something that doesn't collapse the moment they take a breath.

Everything that follows came from fifteen years of building teams that lead themselves—first at ICG, then through the coaching business we built to help other founders do the same. Not a textbook. A workshop. Not someone else's case study. Ours.

The work is organized around four things that create real, lasting value in a business. Not just revenue. Not just profit margins. The stuff that makes a company worth something to the next generation—whether that generation comes from inside the firm or outside it.

Social capital. Human capital. Client capital. Structural capital.

Think of them as the four systems that keep the plane in the air. Each one connected to the others. Each one, essential. Ignore one and you feel it everywhere.

Chapter 13 is where we introduce the specific frameworks we use to build all four. But I want to give you a sense now of what you're walking into.

There's a framework from the Heath brothers—*Switch*—that shapes how we think about getting things done when change is hard. They break it into three moves: direct the rider, motivate the elephant, shape the path. The rational brain needs a destination. The emotional brain needs to feel something. The environment needs to make the right behavior the easy behavior.

That's the lens for everything in Act Three. More on it in Chapter 13.

Now—who is this for?

If you're a founder who's stuck where I was stuck: you've hit real milestones, but you're realizing the habits that built this business are the chains keeping you from the next level. There's a path through. I walked it. These pages will show you how.

If you're a next-gen leader—someone stepping into ownership or preparing to take over—your job isn't to become a copy of the founder. Your job is to help your founder cross the chasm. Your words and actions should be building trust and deepening it so the founder can hand over control, knowing the mission is safe.

And if you're neither—if you're just someone who wants to lead better, wherever you are—the principles still apply. The framework scales down as easily as it scales up.

What follows is the work. Not theory—practice. Not motivation—traction.

I paid a lot of dumb tax getting here. Decades of it. The kind that costs you sleep and partnerships and years you don't get back.

This book exists so you don't have to pay all of it.

Let me show you how it works.

# THIRTEEN

# Leadership Lab

In 2010, when Ray Kelly and I started talking seriously about transforming my leadership and transforming our team, he put two things in my head that I've never been able to shake.

The first: to get the most out of your people, you have to give them a purpose worthy of their best efforts. Give them the *why*.

The second: exponential growth—results that actually inspire others—happens when you build teams full of leaders. Not teams with one leader and a bunch of followers. Teams where leadership lives at every level.

Ray introduced me to what I now call Leadership in Action. The five levels. And at the top, Level 5 leadership, he defined it simply: the ability to tie everything to the *why* and the ability to develop other Level Four-plus leaders.

That became my "North Star."

And the story of how that North Star became a business started, like most good things, with someone who wouldn't take no for an answer.

**Shoulder Tap:** Level 5 leadership isn't about being the best performer on the team. It's about developing other leaders who can develop leaders. That's how one person becomes a movement.

In 2011, I was asked to deliver a workshop as the keynote speaker and facilitator for Ameriprise as part of their senior partnering program. King of Prussia, Pennsylvania. The usual drill—drive down, set up, deliver the content, drive home.

Shortly after the first break, a guy named Brent approaches me. Big energy. Direct eye contact.

"This is awesome," he says. "Are you coaching other people?"

I said no. I hadn't figured that out yet. I was still building my own business, still learning the ropes. I didn't think anyone should listen to what I had to say at that point.

"Okay," he said. "Would you let me know if you change your mind?"

Sure. Fine. Whatever.

About ninety minutes later, the second part of the session finished. Brent comes over again.

"So," he says. "Have you thought more about coaching?"

I looked at him. "We just talked two hours ago."

"I know. Maybe you changed your mind."

By the time the day ended, Brent had approached me four times. Same question. Same answer. No.

Part of that program involved me coming back to King of Prussia about a month later. The very first person I saw when I walked in to set up? Brent.

"Hey. Did you decide about coaching?"

No.

We had four breaks that day. Every break, same conversation. Man, this guy is relentless.

The event ended. I drove back to Albany. About a week later, I got an email from Brent.

*"Hey, have you thought about coaching again?"*

*"No,"* I typed back.

*"Okay. Are you licensed in the state of Pennsylvania?"*

*"Yeah."*

*"I need a financial advisor."*

I paused. *"Do you want to hire me as your financial advisor so that I can coach you?"*

*"Whatever it takes, man."*

> **Shoulder Tap:** Pay attention to the people who won't leave you alone. Persistence is a signal. The ones who chase you down aren't desperate—they're ready. Your next leader might be the person you keep saying no to.

In that conversation, I learned what was driving Brent's persistence.

He had inherited his financial advising practice from his father. His dad had been a pillar of the community—the kind of advisor people trusted with their life savings, their retirement dreams, their family's future. And he had just died from leukemia.

Brent was trying to keep the business afloat. Everything he knew about being an advisor, he'd learned from watching his dad. He didn't have any formal sales training. No business education. His younger sister worked for him, but there was no mentor, no support system, no one to show him how any of this actually worked.

He told me he'd been looking at Monster.com for jobs before we met that first time in King of Prussia.

He wasn't asking me to coach him because he thought I had all the answers. He was asking because he was drowning, and I seemed like someone who might know how to swim.

When I hear stories like that, it's impossible for me to say no.

So Brent and I started working together. I helped him first as his financial advisor. Then, over time, as something more.

He became my first coaching client. And eventually, he became a partner at ICG.

That's Level 5 leadership in reverse. Brent didn't need a boss. He needed someone who could develop him into the leader his father's legacy deserved. And helping him showed me something I hadn't fully understood until then—that the work of developing leaders might be the most important work I'd ever do.

---

I HAD a partner (Derek) at the Ameriprise Home Office to help with those events, like the one in King of Prussia, and he helped coach the advisors across the Northeast region. We were collaborating on different components of the senior partnering program, and it became clear to me pretty quickly that I wanted him on my team.

I asked him. "What would it take for you to move to New York?"

Derek was living in Minnesota at the time. He gave me one of those long "Minnesota nice" answers that basically translates to "not happening."

"I have deep roots in Minnesota," he said. "I love my family. I'm tied to the land as much as to the people."

I think I actually blinked a few times. *Tied to the land?* Okay then.

I said, "Well, if you change your mind, let me know."

Two years later, I got a call. "So what would it take for us to work together?"

I asked if he was moving to New York. He said no. I said, "Then we need to be creative."

Six months after that, I went through the hard work of telling Derek's leaders at our home office that he would be leaving their team in corporate to join mine out in the field, and we created Inspire Network together, the leadership development and coaching business that would help facilitate change for other founders, other teams.

It takes two to tango. And it took two years for the music to start.

**Shoulder Tap:** The best partnerships don't happen on your timeline. Plant the seed. Be patient. Be creative. Sometimes it takes two years for the music to start.

## WE FACILITATE CHANGE

By this time, I already knew the lesson Ray had drilled into me—that I needed a purpose worthy of my best effort. Not just any purpose. One that would inspire others to bring their best effort too. One that could answer a simple but ruthless question: *Why do you get up in the morning, and why should anyone care?*

In 2016, Ray took a leadership position with Ameriprise Financial. And I had the privilege of having Doug Lennick—the founder of Think2Perform—become my coach. Working with Doug, I crystallized my own purpose and credo in a way I hadn't been able to before.

Facilitating change. That's what I believe God put me on this earth to do. Developing leaders. Building self-leading teams. Helping people become who they were always capable of becoming.

As I looked around the coaching and consulting landscape, I saw a gap. Most leadership coaching is about telling people what to do. Handing over a playbook. Charging a fee. Moving on. Very few coaches actually walk the walk with their clients. Very few have skin in the game. I didn't want Inspire Network to be like every other coaching company. I wanted us to be the ones who actually lived it.

Inspire Network was built to fill that gap. It became a testing lab for the ideas we were developing at ICG—but it became something more than that, too. It became a platform for our own leaders to grow in their leadership capacity. A place where they could stretch toward Level 5. You don't develop Level 5 leaders by lecturing them. You develop them by putting them in the arena.

How? By leading from the front and by example.

Here's what I noticed over the years: most people already know what to do. They don't need more information. They need someone to walk alongside them—to nudge, to encourage, to hold the mirror up when they're avoiding it. When you do that, something shifts. The journey becomes transformational. The relationship becomes deeper. Personal. Just like Ray became my friend through this work, many of the teams and leaders Inspire Network coaches have become more than clients. The relationship is deeper because the transformation is real.

In the context of Simon Sinek's Golden Circle, Inspire Network's *why* is to facilitate change. That's the core. Everything radiates from there.

The *how* is a framework I learned from the Heath brothers…

**Shoulder Tap:** Most people already know what to do. They don't need another playbook. They need someone willing to walk alongside them and hold the mirror up when they're avoiding it. That's the difference between coaching and consulting.

There's a framework I learned from the Heath brothers that shaped how we built Inspire Network—and how I think about everything in Act Three.

They wrote a book called *Switch* about how to change things when change is hard. They break it into three moves.

**Direct the rider.** That's your rational brain. It needs a clear destination. Without one, it just spins in circles, analyzing options forever, never actually moving.

**Motivate the elephant.** That's your emotional brain. The big, stubborn part that actually controls whether you move or stay stuck. You can't reason with the elephant. You have to make it *feel* something.

**Shape the path.** That's the environment. You make the right behavior the easy behavior. You remove friction from the thing you want to happen.

I'm going to use this framework throughout Act Three because it's the most useful lens I've found for actually getting things done. Envisioning is how you direct the rider. Narrative is how you motivate the elephant. Traction is how you shape the path.

And the *what*—everything we do to build the four capitals—is where the rest of Act Three lives.

But there's something underneath all three. Something that makes the whole system work.

And it took us ten years to figure it out.

> **Shoulder Tap:** Logic alone won't move people. Emotion alone won't sustain them. You need both—a clear destination for the rational brain, something that makes the emotional brain *feel* it, and an environment that makes the right behavior the easy behavior. Direct the rider. Motivate the elephant. Shape the path.

The first ten years of Inspire Network were trial and error.

We built systems. We created models. We developed frameworks and assessments and all the fancy stuff you'd expect from a coaching business.

But we discovered that people weren't drawn to us because of the fancy systems. They were drawn to us because of the power of our example. Because we walked in their shoes. We lived their lives. We'd made the same mistakes they were making. We'd paid the dumb tax already—and they believed we might be able to help them avoid writing that same check.

Since Inspire Network was created in 2013, we've developed dozens of leaders. We've helped dozens of teams. We've facilitated the entire journey—from triggering event to value acceleration to exit—for founders who were ready to build something that could outlast them.

Here's something important to understand about how this works.

Inspire Network lived a parallel life to ICG.

We learn ideas and test them in ICG. We coach Inspire Network clients using what we've learned. Most of the time, the direction flows from ICG to INET—we figure something out in our own business, then we teach it to others.

But not always.

At the times of biggest struggle as an advisor—when our own team wasn't ready to implement something new—I was testing ideas in Inspire Network. Working with other business owners. Learning from what they were doing. Taking their insights and bringing them back to our team.

It's a feedback loop. We coach, we learn, we apply, we refine. Then we coach again with better tools.

Today, Inspire Network and ICG are both part of Inspire Holdings Company. And last year, we added Inspire Tax. It's a completely unique offering that we created for our clients—because most of the problems our target clients face—founders trying to build value, prepare for transition, create legacy—involve complexity. Financial complexity. Tax complexity. Succession complexity. Human complexity.

ICG handles financial planning and wealth management. Inspire Network handles business coaching and value acceleration. Inspire Tax handles smart tax decisions and builds financially resilient teams.

Three businesses. One integrated solution. All built on the same foundation of elite leadership and self-leading teams.

> **Shoulder Tap:** Don't coach what you haven't lived. Test ideas in your own business first. Then teach from experience, not theory. The feedback loop—coach, learn, apply, refine—is what separates credibility from commentary.

The biggest obstacle to personal agency—to actually doing things differently—isn't lack of motivation. It's confusion.

People are confused. They're confused because they don't know where they're going. Or they don't know how to get there. Or they don't know how to bring everyone along for the journey.

The Exit Planning Institute—the folks who train advisors to help business owners prepare for transition—talks about four intangible capitals. These are the things that create real value in a business. Not just revenue. Not just profit margins. The stuff that makes a company worth something to the next generation of owners, whether they come from inside the firm or outside.

The four capitals are Social, Human, Client, and Structural. We've built five chapters around the work we do every day inside these four areas—practical, tested, no-theory-without-application.

Structural Capital gets two chapters. The volume alone earns it. And honestly? Financial resiliency and entity structures get overlooked by almost every founder we've ever worked with. Not anymore. The next five chapters are where we stop talking about the framework and start doing the work.

- **Social Capital.** The health of your culture. The heartbeat of the organization. How people work together. How the brand is experienced inside and outside the firm. Social capital is the integrating force. It's what connects the other three. When your culture is strong, human capital develops faster. Customer relationships deepen. Systems actually get followed instead of ignored.
    - **Chapter 14: Practice Envisioning.** Making the dual focus a reality. In my opinion, this is the most important of

the four capitals—the thing that ties everything else together. It's about connecting the ten-year vision with what happens today.

- **Human Capital.** The knowledge, skills, and capabilities of your people. Can they perform under pressure? Do they develop themselves? Are they the kind of people others want to follow?
    - **Chapter 15: Leadership is a Force Multiplier.** Building Elite Leadership Culture. This is where the abundance mindset lives. Developing leaders at every level. The multiplication effect that happens when you stop being the bottleneck.
- **Client Capital.** The strength of your client relationships. Are they transferable? Would your customers stick around if you disappeared tomorrow?
    - **Chapter 16: Growth is a Team Sport.** Winning Hearts by Doing Good. Your narrative. Your jug lines. The relationships that make your business worth something beyond the spreadsheet.
- **Structural Capital.** Your systems, processes, and infrastructure. The playbooks. The technology. The documentation that lets someone new come in and understand how things work without having to live inside your head.
    - **Chapter 17: Technology, Traction, and Scaling with Compassion.** Empowered Execution. Traction. Rituals and rhythms. The systems that turn good intentions into consistent behavior. Financial Resiliency and Governance. The path to ownership. Building a resilient legacy through financial discipline and governance structures that let you play for decades, not quarters.
    - **Chapter: 18: Play for Decades, Not Quarters. Financial Resiliency and Governance**. The path to ownership. Building a resilient legacy through financial discipline and governance structures that let you play for decades, not quarters.

> **Shoulder Tap:** Revenue and profit margins are lagging indicators. The real value in your business lives in four capitals—human, customer, structural, and social. Social capital is the integrating force. When culture is strong, everything else accelerates. When it's weak, nothing else matters.

The framework ends here. The work begins.

This is not what I think. It is what I've done. What I've coached others to do. What I've watched succeed and fail and evolve over fifteen years of building teams that lead themselves.

We've tested everything in our leadership labs and training hospitals. We've implemented every single thing I'm going to talk about. We're not fancy consultants who got an MBA and read about this stuff in a case study. We live it. Every day. In the same trenches you're standing in.

Here's what I want you to walk away with.

If you're a founder, you're probably standing at a crossroads right now. You've built something. Maybe it's successful by most measures. But you're tired. Or stuck. Or starting to wonder what happens next—when you want to step back, or bring in partners, or hand the keys to someone else.

## BEFORE YOU MOVE ON → SHOULDER TAPS FROM THIS CHAPTER

- Level 5 leadership isn't about being the best performer. It's about developing leaders who develop leaders.
- Pay attention to the people who won't leave you alone. Persistence is a signal—your next leader might be the person you keep saying no to.
- The best partnerships don't happen on your timeline. Plant the seed. Be patient. Be creative.
- Most people know what to do. They need someone to walk

alongside them and hold the mirror up when they're avoiding it.

- Logic won't move people. Emotion won't sustain them. You need both—direct the rider, motivate the elephant, shape the path.
- Don't coach what you haven't lived. The feedback loop of coach, learn, apply, refine separates credibility from commentary.
- The real value in your business lives in four capitals. Social capital is the integrating force—when culture is strong, everything else accelerates.

The chapters that follow will show you how to build the four capitals. How to envision a future that's worth pursuing. How to find and develop the people who can execute that vision. How to create the rhythms and systems that keep everything moving even when you're not pushing.

If you're a next-generation leader—someone who's stepping into ownership or preparing to take over—these chapters will show you what to look for. What questions to ask. How to partner with the founder in a way that honors what they built while creating space for what you'll build next.

And if you're neither—if you're just someone who wants to lead better, wherever you are—the principles still apply. The framework scales down as easily as it scales up.

I paid dumb tax so you don't have to.

Now let me show you how it works.

FOURTEEN

# Practice Envisioning

## SOCIAL CAPITAL: MAKING THE DUAL FOCUS A REALITY

### Dual Focus

There are four intangible capitals that create real, transferable value in a business. Human capital gives you the crew. Client capital fuels the engines. Structural capital holds the fuselage together. But social capital—the shared vision, the alignment, the navigation system—is the one that connects the other three. Without it, you have talented people pulling in different directions. Great client relationships attached to a business that doesn't know what it's becoming. Systems executing on last year's priorities. Social capital is where envisioning lives. It's the first thing we address because everything else builds on it.

There's a quote from Simon Sinek that makes vision sound like a mystical gift. Some people have it; most don't. You either see the future, or you stumble through the dark.

That's not how this works.

Envisioning isn't a lightning bolt from the heavens. It's not reserved for the chosen few who wear turtlenecks and stare dramatically out of floor-to-ceiling windows.

Envisioning is a discipline. A practice. A ritual you commit to the same way you commit to brushing your teeth.

Here's what I mean.

To be an effective CEO—to actually lead a business instead of just running one—there are two timeframes that matter. Everything else is a blur.

The first is the ten-year timeframe. Where do you want to be a decade from now? What does success look like? What are you building toward?

The second is today. What happens in the next eight hours? What's the one thing you need to move forward right now?

Envisioning is about connecting those two. As frequently as possible. You look out—ten years, maybe twenty. You ask yourself what you actually want. Not what's realistic. Not what's safe. What you want.

Then you come back to today. You look at where you are right now—the revenue, the team, the chaos, the wins, the stuff that keeps you up at night. You see the gap between here and there.

And then you do the hard part. You keep going back and forth. Future. Present. Future. Present. Making adjustments. Turning the idea of what you want into something real.

That's dual-focus thinking. It's not a one-time exercise you knock out at an offsite and never look at again. It's a continuous practice of oscillating between where you're going and where you are until the distance between them starts to shrink.

**Shoulder Tap:** Envisioning isn't magic. It's maintenance. The businesses that fly the farthest are the ones that build multiple engines, train their crew, strengthen their fuselage, and bring the whole operation into the hangar every quarter for inspection. You don't need to be a visionary. You need to be disciplined about the practice of envisioning. Look up. Look down. Adjust. Repeat.

## FINDING YOUR VISIONARY-INTEGRATOR DUO

In 2018 or 2019—the timeline blurs a bit—I hired a coach named J.T. Wiederholdt to help me build the structure of our firm. One of the first things he told me to do was read *Rocket Fuel.*

*Rocket Fuel* describes the visionary-integrator duo. The two essential roles that make a business actually function. Part of the book is an assessment that tells you which role you're better suited for.

My result explained why I had led through organized chaos for so long.

I'm eighty-five percent visionary and seventy-five percent integrator.

I'm one of those people who can perform both roles pretty effectively. But I definitely lean toward visionary. I see possibilities. I start things. I get bored with maintenance.

Maria naturally became the integrator of our business. She and I led the firm from complete rebirth—after the 2018 partnership split-up—up through Project 9Zero. We built something real together.

But both of us were playing two full-time roles.

I was a full-time advisor and a full-time visionary. She was a full-time advisor and a full-time integrator. And that can only go so far.

Eventually, we both hit a ceiling of complexity. We knew something had to change.

Here's the thing most people miss about the visionary-integrator duo: it's not a permanent pairing that never changes. Businesses evolve. Relationships evolve. A partnership that works brilliantly for three or four years might naturally shift as the business grows and people's callings change. We've been through multiple iterations at Inspire Holdings—and each time, it was the right move for that stage of growth. The key is naming the roles clearly, understanding the natural fit, and being willing to reconfigure when the business outgrows the current structure.

**Shoulder Tap:** The visionary-integrator duo isn't a marriage. It's a season. The partnership that builds your business from zero to five million probably isn't the same one that takes you from five to fifty. Name the roles. Understand the fit. And be willing to reconfigure when the business outgrows the current structure.

## THE MARK DECISION

In August of 2023, Maria texted me from Minneapolis.

"I think Mark Keeling is ready to join the firm."

My response was skeptical.

I'd been talking to Mark for fourteen years. Trying to recruit him. Pulling out all the stops. At one point, I even got his wife on board to help convince him. Nothing worked.

So when Maria said he was ready, my first thought was, *What the hell changed?*

But before I could get excited about Mark, I needed to answer a different question. What role does Maria want to play?

I asked Maria to complete her calling cards. This is an exercise I learned from Doug Lennick years ago. It helps you understand your calling—what you're actually built for.

My calling cards are: facilitating change, performing in events, solving problems, starting things, and seeing the big picture.

The simple idea is that if I spend most of my time doing those five things, I'll be fulfilled. If I can make enough money doing them, that's the ultimate freedom scenario. Freedom of time, money, relationships, and purpose.

Maria's number one calling card? Building relationships. Bringing joy. Being present with people.

So I asked her directly: "Being the integrator of a business that's ten times bigger than we are now—is that your calling?"

Her answer: "Hell no."

Now I was excited about Mark.

When I looked at Mark's TUG card compared to mine, it became clear that we could be an amazing visionary-integrator duo. His Values, Working Genius, his Kolbe, his PrinciplesYou archetypes—everything lined up.

It took about four months to finish everything. Convince my other partners. Figure out the structure. We didn't have the money, and we also didn't want him to go anywhere else.

TUG Cards™ became the critical component in explaining how we'd all fit together. When you can show people—visually, on paper—how their genius complements someone else's, the conversation shifts from politics to possibility.

## THE ACCOUNTABILITY CHART

The next piece of building a plane that flies without you is establishing who sits in what seat and who plays what role.

We practice a combination of the Entrepreneurial Operating System (EOS), CEPA methodology from the Exit Planning Institute, and our own Elite Leadership Framework.

Elite teams have captains. These are the people who carry out the mission and lead by example so others can follow.

In EOS terminology, this is the accountability chart. Not an organizational chart—those are full of titles and egos and communication breakdowns. An accountability chart answers a simpler question: Who is accountable for what?

The first two roles are visionary and integrator. They have to work together. After that, most businesses break into three core functions: sales and marketing, operations, and finance.

But I don't know any business with an accountability chart that simple. Ours certainly isn't.

Here's how our structure looks:

**Laura** leads marketing and tells the story of our firm.

**Kayla** leads technology and people capital—systems, integration, talent development.

**Jo** leads Inspire Network, our coaching and value acceleration business.

**Chris** leads Inspire Tax.

**Maria, Andrea, and Brent** each lead one of our three diamonds at ICG.

**Derek** is the CFO for the entire business.

And when we were going through chaos and it could have broken us, we added G3 leaders. Next-generation leaders. We included them in decision-making and gave them accountability before they technically "earned" it by traditional standards.

I call this "Saša Math." It's counterintuitive. Traditional leadership development says people earn responsibility over time—you prove yourself, then you get the title, then you get the seat. Saša Math flips the sequence. You give people accountability first, and they rise into it. Not everyone will. But the ones who do become the leaders who build your next level of the game.

**Phil** leads our advice quality lane. Not direct client relationships, but ensuring we give world-class advice.

**Will** leads our investment committee.

**George** leads our tax and Platinum One integration.

**Ryan** leads advice production integration.

None of them has a one-to-one direct relationship in those roles. But they have leadership, management, and accountability for their functions. They're developing as leaders by actually leading—not by waiting for permission.

Each of these leaders operates at a different level. Some are at Level Two—solving problems and making decisions within their lane. Others have grown to Level Four—galvanizing people and driving results across teams. The goal is to develop every captain toward Level Five, where they're not just leading but developing other leaders. That's when the multiplication effect kicks in. That's when a team starts to lead itself.

This team is the team that leads our business. Mark, as integrator, has functional accountability for the ICG component until someone emerges who can oversee the whole enterprise.

We have the vision. We have the people. And we have a team that continuously works on making sure the plane is healthy, flying in the right direction, and has enough energy to get there.

Every one of those leaders has their own TUG card. Their own calling. Their own genius. Building a business that leads itself is about synchronizing all of these things together under the same flag, for the same vision.

> **Shoulder Tap:** Saša Math works. Give people accountability before they've technically earned it. Not everyone will rise to it. But the ones who do become the leaders who build your next chapter. Stop waiting for permission to develop your next generation.

## THE TRIGGERING EVENT

The Heath brothers wrote a book called *Switch* about how to change things when change is hard. They talk about three moves: direct the rider, motivate the elephant, and shape the path.

The rider is your rational brain. It needs a clear destination, or it just spins in circles, analyzing options forever.

The elephant is your emotional brain. The big, stubborn part that actually controls whether you move or stay stuck. You can't reason with the elephant. You have to make it feel something.

And the path? That's the environment. You make the right behavior the easy behavior.

I'm going to use this framework throughout Act Three. But for now, let's start with the triggering event.

The triggering event is the moment you decide that, in order to grow, you have to do things differently.

Not just in a leadership context. In a practical, structural, money-on-the-table context.

For me, that moment came in August of 2020. I made a decision. I would no longer commingle business assets and revenue with my personal finances.

Up until then, I considered business revenue my revenue. I owned one hundred percent of the company. All the assets, all the income—it was all commingled with my personal finances. I used business revenue to pay the bills, hire people, and fund my life.

That's how most founders operate. The business is you. You are the business. The line between personal and professional doesn't exist because you drew it with disappearing ink.

But you cannot build a business that leads itself if you are the business.

The business would have its own money. Its own identity. Its own future that didn't depend entirely on me showing up every single day.

But just saying that wasn't enough. I'm human. Humans don't change because they intellectually understand they should change. They change when something shifts inside them.

I had to motivate the elephant. And that started with getting the right people in the right seats.

## REGULAR MAINTENANCE AND UPGRADES

Even the best airplane in the world needs maintenance.

I've established that I'm not the smartest guy in the room. But I'm smart enough to be dumb enough to do what smarter companies did.

When I discovered how Toyota and Lexus handle service, it became a no-brainer.

Every five thousand miles, you bring the car in. Whether you think you need it or not. They do their thing—maybe it's a 164-point inspection, maybe it's 730 points. I don't know what they check, and I don't care. What I care about is that my car gets me from where I am to where I need to go without breaking down.

Same with our business.

Once a quarter, we do what we call a quarterly business review (QBR). We conduct a 194-point inspection of the entire operation. Check the brakes. Rotate the tires. Tighten whatever's loose. Then we get back on the road.

Part of the CEO's job—maybe the biggest part—is recognizing that you're flying a plane. There are engines, body, crew, technology, and energy. All of these components need attention. You can't just push the throttle and hope for the best.

There's an ideal sequence for all of this work—the envisioning, the workshops, the disciplines. We've designed it in the lab. TUG Cards™ first, then credo card, then the V/TO (Vision/Traction Organizer), then talent density, then the cultural work. But I've never seen it executed in that exact order. Not once. Every business has its own complexities, its own dynamics, its own fires that need putting out before you can build the system. The sequence is the blueprint. Making reads and adapting to what your business actually needs right now—that's the coaching. What doesn't change is the commitment to addressing all of it over time.

## THE DUAL-FOCUS CHECK-IN

As part of our envisioning practice, I meet monthly with the leaders of the company for what I call a dual-focus check-in.

**Focus One:** How are the engines and the plane? What's working? What needs adjustment? Are we on track toward the vision or drifting off course?

**Focus Two:** What's occupying their mind? Concerns, issues, problems, fears—the stuff that's keeping them from performing at their highest level.

You can't separate performance from well-being. A leader carrying invisible weight will eventually drop something important. The dual-focus check-in gives us space to address both.

We do the same with the integrators of the business. And we back it up with rituals and rhythm—the regular cadence of meetings and touchpoints that keep everyone aligned.

**Shoulder Tap:** You can't separate performance from well-being. A leader carrying invisible weight will eventually drop something important. Build the check-in. Ask the second question. The one about what's occupying their mind—not just what's on their scorecard.

## WDYWFY: WHAT DO YOU WANT FOR YOURSELF?

On a personal level, there's a ritual we call WDYWFY—pronounced "woody-woofy."

Personal readiness, known as "Lifestyle Plan" in CEPA methodology, is one of the main obstacles to value acceleration. Seventy-six percent of business owners decide not to go down the path of value acceleration because they have not figured out their personal goals, objectives, and reasons to work on the exit. The WDYWFY ritual is our way of facilitating change and moving the ball down the field.

This isn't a business exercise. It's a human exercise. And if you don't know what you want for your own life, you'll build a business that serves everyone except you.

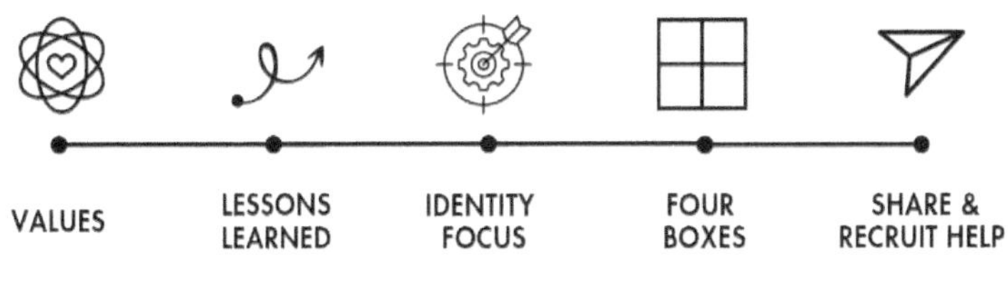


WDYWFY RITUAL

The WDYWFY ritual has two parts.

The first is about values and reflection. You write down your top five values, in order. Then you rate yourself on a scale of 1–10 for how well you're actually living each one. Not how well you want to live them. How well you are living them right now.

Then you ask: *What were the biggest lessons I learned this year? And what's my identity focus for next year?*

The second part is about the four quadrants of life: Family & Friends, Meaningful Work, Health & Fitness, and Mind/Spirit/Personal Development. You take stock of each area. Then you set quarterly goals—not annual goals that you'll forget by February, but ninety-day targets you can actually track.

We do this every year, usually between Thanksgiving and the first week of January. It's a reset. A recalibration. A way to make sure your business ambitions aren't slowly crushing the parts of your life that actually matter.

**Shoulder Tap:** If you don't know what you want for yourself, you'll build a business that serves everyone except you. Do the WDYWFY. Rate yourself honestly. Set the ninety-day targets. The business doesn't exist in a vacuum. You do.

## CALLING CARDS

As a founder, if you're reading this, it's going to be important for you to know your calling. So you can build your life in the next stage of your career around what actually fulfills you.

Every time I have a coaching client or a leader on our team going through a transition, I recommend the calling card exercise. It helps inform what their natural drive is—what they're called to do, not just what they're capable of doing.

TUG Cards™ tell you how to apply your talent and unique genius eighty percent of the time. Calling cards tell you why it matters to you.

Not everyone needs both. TUG Cards™ are the baseline for every member of the team. When people go through transitions—career changes, leadership shifts, life inflection points—that's when calling cards come in. They provide additional data points so people can make decisions in alignment with what they actually want for themselves.

This is how, at age fifty-nine, I feel like I can live for another eighty years. I know what I'm built for. I spend most of my time doing it. And I've surrounded myself with people who are doing the same.

## THE CREDO CARD AND V/TO

On an enterprise level, one of the first things we do with leadership teams is the credo card development exercise.

We don't send a deck and ask people to fill it out remotely. We bring the leadership team to our office. It's not a presentation. It's not a sales pitch. It's a working workshop.

We recommend the entire leadership team—all the key players—spend a full day with us. Part of that day is finalizing the credo card. The other part is creating the ritual and cadence around the Vision/Traction Organizer, putting regular plane maintenance on the schedule.

The V/TO comes from EOS. It's built around eight questions:

1. What are your core values?

2. What is your core focus?
3. What is your ten-year target?
4. What is your marketing strategy?
5. What is your three-year picture?
6. What is your one-year plan?
7. What are your quarterly rocks?
8. What are your issues?

Most businesses have a strategy. Most businesses have some version of a vision. But not everyone knows what it is. Not everyone agrees on it. The V/TO gets everyone in sync, so you're all flying the same plane in the same direction.

## What This Looks Like

At ICG, our V/TO includes:

*Core Values:* Clients Come First. Family-Focused. Integrity Always. Excellence Through Leadership & Teamwork. Pursue Life Balance.

*Purpose: Inspire Confidence, Simplify Life, Reduce Stress.*

*Niche:* We are a multi-generational elite team. Our culture empowers the selection, development, and growth of future-minded advisors while meeting the needs of retiring advisors through leadership development and teamwork.

*Ten-Year Target (2031):* eighteen million dollars in GDC, 1.8 billion dollars in client AUM, fifteen percent organic growth, ten percent net flows, and thirty-four client-facing advisors.

These aren't abstract wishes. They're specific, measurable, and they create energy for everyone on the team. The target should make you a little uncomfortable. Remember, growing 10X is easier than 2X. When you aim for 10X, you have to reimagine everything. When you aim for 2X, you just try to work harder at what you're already doing.

Be bold. Go for the 10X future.

**Shoulder Tap:** The biggest obstacle to personal agency is confusion. Envisioning cuts through it. You know where you're going. You know who's getting you there. You know the rhythms that will keep you on course. That's how you direct the rider.

## TIPS FOR THE V/TO PROCESS

Get your team involved. The V/TO should not be a form that you fill in alone and hand down from the mountaintop. It's an envisioning exercise that connects the future with today and builds buy-in.

Caution: You may lose some team members—even partners—who don't buy into the vision. That's a good thing. Celebrate the past and embrace the future.

Your future is at stake. G1 leaders should be radically open-minded. G2 leaders should be radically assertive. If both sides show up that way, this becomes a transformational experience.

If only one side shows up? You'll get a document that nobody believes in.

## BEFORE YOU MOVE ON → SHOULDER TAPS FROM THIS CHAPTER

- Envisioning isn't magic. It's maintenance. The businesses that fly the farthest are the ones that build multiple engines, train their crew, strengthen their fuselage, and bring the whole operation into the hangar every quarter for inspection. You don't need to be a visionary. You need to be disciplined about the practice of envisioning. Look up. Look down. Adjust. Repeat.
- The visionary-integrator duo isn't a marriage. It's a season. The partnership that builds your business from zero to five million probably isn't the same one that takes you from five to fifty. Name the roles. Understand the fit. And be willing to reconfigure when the business outgrows the current structure.

- Saša Math works. Give people accountability before they've technically earned it. Not everyone will rise into it. But the ones who do become the leaders who build your next chapter. Stop waiting for permission to develop your next generation.
- You can't separate performance from well-being. A leader carrying invisible weight will eventually drop something important. Build the check-in. Ask the second question. The one about what's occupying their mind—not just what's on their scorecard.
- If you don't know what you want for yourself, you'll build a business that serves everyone except you. Do the WDYWFY. Rate yourself honestly. Set the ninety-day targets. The business doesn't exist in a vacuum. You do.
- The biggest obstacle to personal agency is confusion. Envisioning cuts through it. You know where you're going. You know who's getting you there. You know the rhythms that will keep you on course. That's how you direct the rider.

*Now let's talk about what happens when you build leaders at every level—not just the top. That's where human capital comes in.*

FIFTEEN

# Leadership Is the Force Multiplier

## HUMAN CAPITAL: THE SECRET SAUCE THAT MAKES EVERYTHING WORK

### The Abundance Shift

The biggest shift I had to make on my journey was to reject scarcity, control, and micromanagement and replace them with abundance.

Shifting from a scarcity mindset to an abundance mindset is shifting from one leadership identity to another. From chess master to gardener.

The chess master controls every piece on the board. He knows where everything should go. He makes all the moves. And he burns out trying to play against opponents who have figured out that life isn't chess—it's a garden.

The gardener creates conditions for growth. She tends. She trusts the process. She knows that a tomato plant doesn't need someone screaming at it to produce tomatoes. It needs good soil, water, sunlight, and time.

Here's what that shift looks like inside the airplane metaphor we've been using. Most founders are in the cockpit alone. Everyone else is buckled into their seat, waiting for you to decide the altitude, the heading, and the speed. They can't adjust course. They can't read the instruments. They don't touch the throttle. Not because they're incapable—because nobody empowered them to fly.

Your team isn't dead weight. They're untapped thrust. They want ownership, not just assignments. But wanting it isn't enough—they need a leader willing to move them from crew to engine.

Crew gives you an addition—more hands on the same work. Engines multiply your thrust.

Leadership culture is a force multiplier. That's not a metaphor. Every capable Level 4 and Level 5 leader on your team is another engine on what used to be a single-engine Cessna.

Everything I'm going to talk about in this chapter is about making that shift—and how to facilitate that shift within your leadership team first and then throughout your whole culture.

## WHY MOST LEADERSHIP DEVELOPMENT FAILS

Let me tell you why most leadership training doesn't work.

Teams invest in workshops. They read books. They bring in speakers. Everyone leaves feeling inspired, maybe even transformed. Two weeks later, nothing has changed.

It's not because the content was bad. It's not because people don't care. It's because most leadership development focuses entirely on the blue brain—the mechanics, the frameworks, the engineering of how things should work.

I learned a long time ago that there are three levels of learning and change. Leadership training is no different.

The first level is **recognition**. Most of the things I'm going to talk about here won't be radically different—with the exception of maybe TUG Cards™.

The second level is **understanding**. Understanding is when you grasp the concepts well enough to explain them to others.

But the third level—the most important one—is **integration**. Integration is when learning becomes part of your day-to-day activity. It's burned into how you actually operate.

Everything I'm going to describe next is about that third level. Recognition is easy. Understanding takes effort. Integration takes rituals, repetition, and relentless practice.

I know this because my mother drilled it into me before I had the language for it.

In high school, I wanted to study philosophy. Acting. Theater. Anything but electrical engineering—which is what I went to school for. I put minimum effort into my classes and somehow pulled a B average. But the stuff that lit me up? Books. Ideas. Theater. I'd come home buzzing and start talking my mom's ear off.

She'd look at me with this face. Part love. Part disgust.

"Yes, but how are you going to make that practical?"

Every. Single. Time.

Didn't matter what it was. A philosophy I'd read. A technique from a play. A big idea about the world. Her response never changed.

"Yes, but how are you going to make that practical?"

Things that weren't practical didn't compute for her. I thought my ideas were brilliant. She thought they were useless until they touched real life.

Turns out, she was right. But you have to hear it from someone other than your mother before you believe it.

## THE ACT FRAMEWORK: HOW LEARNING BECOMES PERMANENT

Enter Ray Kelly.

In 2011, Ray started facilitating monthly leadership sessions for our team. He shared an idea that transformed how I think about learning—the three levels I just described. Recognition. Understanding. Integration. Most of us stop at recognition. We hear something smart and nod. But ideas are only worth the investment you put into them through practical application.

My mother's voice echoed in the back of my head. Make it practical.

Some lessons need a different messenger. The principle stays the same.

Here's the problem with most training: People recognize good ideas but never integrate them.

The gap between recognition and integration is action.

That's why we use the ACT framework:

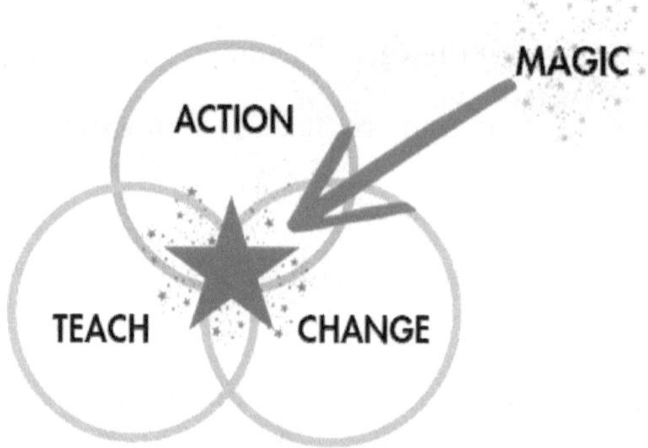


A—Action within twenty-four hours. Don't wait until next week. Don't wait until the timing is perfect. Within twenty-four hours of learning something, do something with it. Apply it. Test it. Make it real.

C—Change something. Based on what you learned, change one thing about how you operate. It doesn't have to be big. Small changes compound over time.

T—Teach someone else. This is the secret weapon. When you teach something, you have to understand it well enough to explain it. Teaching forces integration.

ACT is my answer to the question my mother asked a thousand times. How are you going to make that practical? You act on it within twenty-four hours. You change something because of it. And you teach it to someone else—because teaching is where recognition finally becomes who you are.

When Ray Kelly started working with us on leadership development, we met monthly for masterminds. We established a basic understanding, built a new language, and constantly referred back to the framework.

But the key was ACT. After every session, people had to act within twenty-four hours, change something based on what they learned, and teach it to someone else.

Over time, we evolved. Now, leadership development is weekly, built into ShareCon. We review things we know. We bring in new ideas. But the nudge is always the same: ACT.

This is how learning becomes permanent. This is how transformation happens.

## DIRECT THE RIDER, MOTIVATE THE ELEPHANT, SHAPE THE PATH

The Heath brothers nailed it: You have to direct the rider (give the rational brain a clear destination), motivate the elephant (make the emotional brain feel something), and shape the path (make the right behavior the easy behavior).

Most teams only do the first one. They explain what great leadership looks like. They draw org charts and accountability matrices. They define roles and expectations.

Then they wonder why nothing sticks.

What I'm going to describe in this chapter is the infrastructure we've built to actually move people—from Level 1 to Level 5 leadership. Not through lectures and laminated posters, but through rituals, rhythm, and relentless practice.

This is the stuff that transforms teams from "above average" to elite.

## THE ARCHITECTURE OF ELITE LEADERSHIP CULTURE

Building elite leadership culture has an architecture. It's built on leadership in action.

It's about recognizing where people are on that journey and helping them move through each level to reach the fifth.

Levels 1 to 4 + Ability to **Tie Everything to the Team's Why. Develop Level 4+ Leaders!**

Levels 1 to 3 + Ability to **Galvanize People & Drive Results**

Levels 1,2 + Ability to **Solve Problems**.

Level 1 + Ability to **Identify Problems**.

Perform tasks with competency when given direction - **Be Coachable.**

## FIVE LEVELS OF LEADERSHIP IN ACTION

The Five Levels of Leadership in Action is inspired by Ray Kelly's version that he taught our team starting back in 2011. It is different from John Maxwell or Jim Collins. We use it as a progression track in developing Level 4 and Level 5 leaders. Its emphasis is on practical application of concepts and taking action to elevate our leadership capacity. That's why we call it "The Five Levels of Leadership *in Action.*" Where most leadership models describe what great leaders look like, this one is built around what great leaders do. Core competencies. Daily behaviors. A progression you can see, measure, and develop.

The goal is an organization full of Level 4 and Level 5 leaders.

Level 1: Be coachable. Perform tasks with competency when given direction.

Level 2: Level 1 plus the ability to identify problems. See what's not working and raise it.

Level 3: Levels 1 and 2 plus the ability to solve problems. Don't just flag the issue—bring a solution.

Level 4: Levels 1 through 3 plus the ability to galvanize people and drive results. Lead others toward outcomes.

Level 5: Levels 1 through 4 plus the ability to tie everything to the team's *why*. Develop Level 4-plus leaders.

Each level builds on the ones before it. A Level 5 leader doesn't skip problem-solving to go straight to purpose—they embody every competency underneath and add the ability to develop other leaders who can do the same.

Most teams have a Level 4 to 5 founder surrounded by Level 1 and 2 team members. That's the real reason the founder can't leave the cockpit. The crew hasn't been developed to fly the plane.

Level 4 and Level 5 leaders are the people who become additional engines on the plane. They don't just keep it flying—they give it more thrust. They share the load so the founder isn't white-knuckling every decision alone. And they diversify the risk. When your business depends on one engine—you—a single failure grounds the whole operation. When you have four engines, five engines, eight engines, one can go down for maintenance and the plane keeps flying. That's the force multiplier. That's when the plane flies without you.

Everyone starts somewhere. The trick is creating an environment where movement happens naturally—not through force, but through cultivation.

The foundation is TUG Cards™.

## THE FOUNDATION: TUG CARDS™

Before we talk about culture, standards, rituals, or leadership development, we have to revisit TUG Cards™.

Here's why.

Elite teams are built on two things: character and natural ability. Not credentials. Not experience. Not who you know or what school you went to. Character and natural ability.

The ultimate trick is recognizing that business is simple. People are complicated.

You can optimize your systems all day long. You can buy the best software, implement the tightest processes, create the most elegant org charts. And all of it will break down if you don't understand the humans operating inside those systems.

TUG Cards™ are the user manual for your team.

Think about it. You can get an instruction manual for every piece of equipment you'll ever buy. Your coffee machine has one. Your car has one. Your printer—the one that jams constantly—came with a two-hundred-page manual nobody read.

But the people on your team? The humans who actually determine whether your business succeeds or fails? No manual. You're supposed to figure them out through trial and error. Through years of awkward interactions and misread signals and round pegs jammed into square holes.

That's insane.

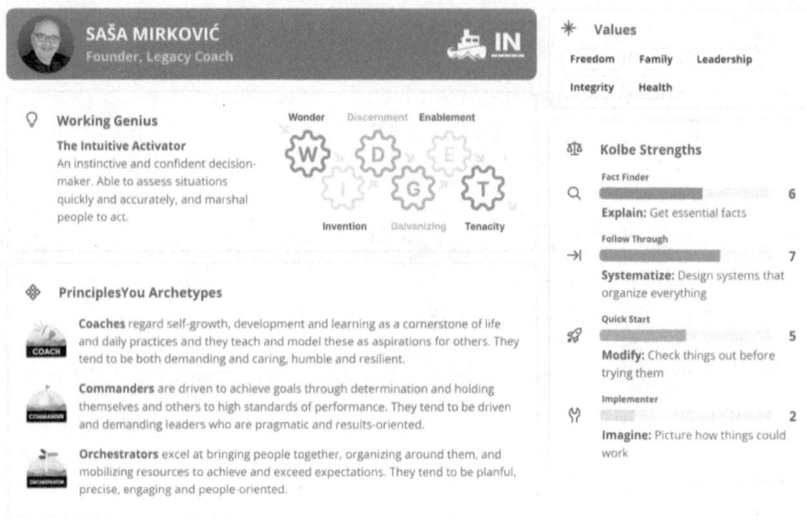


TUG stands for Talent and Unique Genius. The TUG card is a digital profile that combines four assessments into something profoundly simple—a single view of how a person is wired.

**The first dimension is *Values*.** This gives us a picture of alignment—what someone believes, what guides their choices, what matters to them when nobody's watching. Values come first because they're the foundation everything else sits on. You can have all the talent in the world, but if someone's values aren't aligned with the team's purpose, nothing else on the card matters. When alignment is there, talent and unique genius get pointed in the same direction as the mission—and people don't just perform, they multiply everything around them. When there's a misalignment, no amount of genius saves you.

**The second dimension is *Working Genius***, from Patrick Lencioni. This gives us a picture of someone's energy—which types of tasks fuel them and which types drain them. There are six types of genius: Wonder, Invention, Discernment, Galvanizing, Enablement, and Tenacity. Everyone has two that give them energy, two that are neutral, and two that deplete them. It's about eighty percent productivity assessment and twenty percent personality.

**The third dimension is *Kolbe*.** This gives us a picture of someone's drive—their instinctive way of taking action. How they gather information, how they organize, how they deal with risk and uncertainty, and how they handle tangible problems. It's not about what you can do—it's about what you will do when you're free to be yourself.

**The fourth dimension is *PrinciplesYou***, Ray Dalio's assessment. This gives us a picture of someone's attitude—how they think about themselves, how they make decisions, and how they show up in a team. Are you a shaper? A planner? Do you lead with your head or your heart?

Put all four together on one card and you have the clearest picture you'll ever get of how someone operates. Alignment, energy, drive, and attitude—all in one place. Their strengths. Their blind spots. Where they'll thrive. Where they'll struggle.

We built the TUG card app so that every person on our team can access this data instantly. Not once a year during a review. Not when HR pulls a file. Daily. When we're solving problems in a meeting, someone can pull up a TUG card and say, "Wait—who on this team has the right genius for this project?" When we're navigating a conflict, we can look at the card and understand why two people are seeing the same situation completely differently. The app makes TUG Cards™ a working tool, not a document that sits in a drawer.

When leaders are empowered to perform in their talent and unique genius, they become rock stars. Not overnight—over time. When people spend eighty percent of their time in their genius zone, there's no limit to the exponential growth a company can achieve.

## TUG LANGUAGE: TRICKING YOUR BRAIN OUT OF JUDGMENT

Here's what most people don't realize about TUG language. It's not just shorthand. It's not just a more efficient way to talk about people.

TUG language is a way to trick your brain out of judgment and guilt—and into focusing on talent and unique genius.

Think about what happens in most teams when someone struggles with a task. The judgment kicks in immediately. They're lazy. They don't care. They're not detail-oriented. They're too scattered. The labels come fast, and they stick.

Now think about what happens when you have TUG language. Instead of "Brent can't focus," you say, "Brent's a 7 on Quick Start—he moves fast from one thing to the next. That's not a flaw. That's his wiring." Instead of "She's too slow making decisions," you say, "She's a high Fact Finder. She needs more information before she commits. Give her the data and watch what happens."

The guilt works the same way. People carry shame about the things that drain them. They think they should be good at everything. TUG language gives them permission to stop pretending. You don't have to be great at Tenacity if your genius is Wonder. You just need to be on a team where someone else carries that load—and you carry theirs.

What we've done is build this language into our daily conversations. Going back to it becomes the act of creating an identity. A leadership culture where everyone is empowered to be in their talent and unique genius most of the time.

## What This Looks Like

We talk about, "Oh, you say this because you're a high Fact Finder," or "I now know that I need to provide more information because you're a 7 Fact Finder on Kolbe."

On the other side, we all know that Brent flies from one item to another, partially because he's a 7 on Quick Start. It's not bad. It's just who he is.

TUG language has proliferated in daily conversations as we embrace conflict with a problem and build teams to solve them. People say things like, "To get this done well, we need a high Fact Finder to do the research and some Tenacity to get it done in time," and everyone knows exactly what they're talking about.

When we use the language as a ritual, we accelerate execution, deepen trust, and start finishing each other's sentences.

As I mentioned in the beginning, if you don't use it, you lose it. And if you lose it, you can go back to the app, pull up the cards, and use them again. That's why we built it. Not as a one-time exercise. As a daily practice.

## CULTURE IS A SIMPLE FORMULA

Culture is a simple formula. It's a set of values and behaviors that people in the team embody.

But culture doesn't happen by announcement. It happens through a progression.

The first level is knowledge. Recognizing that change needs to happen. This is where most teams start—and where most teams stall. Knowing isn't doing.

The second level is attitude. Adopting a positive stance toward the change. Shifting from "we have to" to "we get to." This is the mindset shift.

The third level is behavior. Actually changing what you do. New processes. New rhythms. New ways of communicating and making decisions. This is where leadership development gets real.

The fourth level is culture. Culture is what you repeatedly do and celebrate. When behavior changes produce results, and those results get recognized and reinforced, a new culture is created.

Most leadership programs target that first level—knowledge—and hope culture magically follows. It doesn't. You have to build through all four levels, deliberately, with the right tools and the right rhythm.

Values without behaviors are just posters on walls. Behaviors without values are just motions without meaning. Elite culture happens when your values translate into visible, daily behaviors that everyone can see and hold each other accountable to.

## LEADERSHIP DEVELOPMENT RITUALS

So how do we develop leaders? What are the rituals that make leadership development and moving through the five levels of leadership part of our regular rhythm? Below is a roundup of a few we've discussed.

- **ShareCon Leadership Development**

  During ShareCon on Mondays, we have a leadership development component every week. We teach the Elite Leadership Framework in different ways to keep it fresh.

  Sometimes I use YouTube videos that talk about culture and have a discussion about it. Sometimes we use training materials we've developed for our leaders and the teams we coach. And sometimes we just have an open mic conversation on a very particular subject.

  The content is secondary. The discussion—and the impact that discussion has on people—is primary.

  I've learned that you cannot develop leadership culture by giving people a book. Modeling that behavior and giving an opportunity for the leaders on your team to model that behavior in front of others is the key component of rituals for leadership development.

- **Masterminds**

  We have several masterminds going on across our teams.

  The very first mastermind we started in 2011 was a monthly session with the entire team where we talked about leadership, learned the principles, and moved that learning into action.

  Currently, we facilitate several monthly masterminds for our coaching clients. We found that the most impactful mastermind is when everybody on the team is involved, but often it starts with a leadership team—people on your accountability chart—and getting them on the same page.

- **Roundups**

We have other masterminds that we build and facilitate called "roundups." Roundups are twice-monthly sessions facilitated by leaders, including myself, that create an opportunity for people to master their leadership capability and move towards the next level of leadership.

One mastermind is focused on developing advisors of the future. We call it **Second Chair Academy**, where Maria and Olivia facilitate one-to-many coaching on implementing principles of advice and building the capabilities of future advisors.

The second is a **leadership mastermind for next-gen owners and leaders.** It's facilitated by coaches at Inspire Network with the intent of creating an opportunity for people who are further along in their journey to stay brilliant at the basics—and to learn and teach what they've integrated into their lives.

The most effective way of facilitating these starts with focus time—or spotlight time—where, in every session, a different leader is in the spotlight. We discuss things they're struggling with. They ask for help from fellow members of the mastermind, who give advice and facilitate learning.

- **The Nudge**

A lot of our teams and people who receive a nudge have given me feedback that sometimes that is the only type of leadership development that happens within their teams. And even if they don't do anything other than just a nudge and have the conversation, they feel like they're making progress.

It's leadership development at the atomic level, as James Clear would say. Atomic habits. The moves that you make become the votes toward the identity that you build.

- **Advance**

As you learned earlier, this is a two-and-a-half-day event where Inspire teams go off-site to advance. We build a sense of belonging, deepen trust, work on issues that need to be addressed, and advance our leadership through specific new leadership learning.

The entire event is the annual meeting of leaders to come together, work together, and build trust so that we can have better, more empowered execution.

- **Coffee Time**

Every system, every workshop, every mastermind—they create the container. But the human connection that makes people feel seen, heard, and invested in? That happens in the quiet conversations. The thirty minutes with a coffee where you ask someone what's actually going on.

I can't schedule trust. I can't put it in a framework. Trust gets built in the unstructured space—the hallway conversations, the check-ins that don't have an agenda, the moments when you stop being a CEO and start being a human who gives a damn about the person sitting across from you.

If you skip the relationship and go straight to the system, the system won't hold. Rituals without trust are just meetings.

## BUILD YOUR LEADERSHIP PIPELINE

Leadership development isn't just about the people you have. It's about the pipeline you're building.

Liverpool FC doesn't win championships by buying finished talent at market rate. They develop players through an academy system that identifies potential early, develops it systematically, and creates a culture where the next generation is always rising.

Your business needs the same thing.

Internship programs aren't a nice-to-have. They're where the future rockstars come from. When you build an academy—a deliberate pathway for emerging talent to learn your culture, your language, your standards—you stop being dependent on the job market to deliver fully formed leaders to your door.

This is where TUG Cards™ pay compounding dividends. When you understand someone's talent and unique genius early—during an internship, during their first year—you can position them for exponential growth instead of the slow, expensive process of trial and error that most organizations default to.

The companies that invest in developing leaders from the ground up are the ones that build multigenerational enterprises. The ones that don't are always one resignation away from crisis.

## BEFORE YOU MOVE ON → SHOULDER TAPS FROM THIS CHAPTER

- Leadership is a force multiplier. Passengers give you addition. Pilots give you multiplication. Every Level 4 and 5 leader on your team is another engine on the plane—sharing the load, diversifying the risk, giving you thrust you can't generate alone. The question isn't whether you have enough people—it's whether you've empowered them to fly.
- Make it practical. My mother knew that before I did. Ray Kelly gave it a name. ACT gives it a system. Recognition is easy. Integration takes rituals, repetition, and relentless practice. Within twenty-four hours, act on it. Change something because of it. Teach it to someone else. That's how learning becomes who you are.

- Know your people before you try to lead them. TUG Cards™ start with values—alignment—because without it, no amount of talent saves you. Then energy, drive, and attitude. Put all four on one card, and you have the user manual that most teams never bother to write. Pull it up daily. Use the language. Watch judgment turn into understanding.
- Culture isn't installed. It's cultivated. Knowledge, attitude, behavior, culture—in that order. Most teams stall at knowledge. The ones that break through build rituals that make the right behavior, the easy behavior, and they celebrate the results until the behavior becomes identity.
- Build the pipeline, not just the team. The companies that develop leaders from the ground up—through academies, internships, and deliberate pathways—are the ones that last for generations. The ones that don't are always one resignation away from crisis.
- Don't skip the coffee. The thirty minutes without an agenda might be the most important leadership development you do all week.
- Human capital is where the rubber meets the road. Social capital requires leaders who can envision. Client capital requires leaders who can serve. Structural capital requires leaders who can execute. None of that happens without capable, developed leaders at every level of your organization. When you build a leadership culture, everything else accelerates.

Culture and leadership mean nothing without execution. In the next chapter, we'll talk about how to create clear roles, radical accountability, and the systems that turn good intentions into actual results.

SIXTEEN

# Growth is a Team Sport

## CLIENT CAPITAL: FROM FOUNDER HUSTLE TO TEAM GRAVITY

### Your Vibe Attracts Your Tribe

Most businesses think about growth backwards.

They build the product or service. Then they hire a marketing team—or worse, hire an agency—to figure out how to convince people to buy it. Marketing becomes a separate function. A cost center. Something you do *to* people rather than *for* them.

Then they wonder why growth feels like pushing a boulder uphill.

Here's what I've learned: Your client experience is your marketing.

The actual experience of being your client—how it feels to work with you, how you make people's lives better, safer, easier, what they tell their friends at dinner parties—that's your marketing.

Everything else is just amplification.

## THE MUSCLE WE LET ATROPHY

Let me tell you how I learned this the hard way—again.

2023 and 2024 were years of explosive growth for ICG. We'd completed the Maryland infusion—bringing hundreds of new client families into our firm. And make no mistake, an infusion is not an acquisition. An acquisition is a transaction. An infusion is an integration. You're not just buying a book of business—you're welcoming real people into your ecosystem, earning their trust, proving that the experience you promised is the experience they'll receive. That takes everything you've got.

So we were laser-focused on two things: integrating those new clients into our experience and leveling up that experience at the same time.

We did both. And we did them well.

But while we were heads-down on integration, something else happened. Our organic growth muscle atrophied. Like a runner who stops training for a year because they're rehabbing an injury—the cardio is gone. The legs aren't there. You can remember what it felt like to run fast, but your body can't do it anymore.

Mark and I saw it. As we looked at the future of our business and at the importance of organic growth in the context of building something healthy and resilient (we'll talk about that in the next two chapters), we knew we had a gap. Not a crisis. A gap. And gaps, left unaddressed, become crises.

As a founder, I was always able to attract new clients. That is my gift. My personality, my relationships, my energy in the room—clients came because of me. But growing and marketing as a team? That's a completely different game.

This wasn't just Mark and me. This wasn't just Maria, Andrea, or Brent, the diamond leaders. This was an opportunity for everyone, on every team, to contribute in their own way, using their own TUG language. We didn't want a growth initiative. We wanted a growth culture.

This is the ultimate Level 4 and Level 5 leadership work. The hardest kind. Because it requires you to stop being the answer and start building the machine that creates its own answers.

To get it done, Mark and I had to apply everything we talked about in chapters 14 and 15. We needed to direct the rider—give the team a clear destination. Motivate the elephant—make them *feel* why this mattered. And shape the path—build the systems that made organic growth the natural behavior, not an extra effort.

And then we had to trust the team to execute.

Mark worked with Andrea, Maria, and Brent on how to solve the physics problem inside the diamond teams. How to tier the experience. How to build capacity for growth without diluting the hospitality that made us who we are.

Laura and her marketing team took the lead on the "bloom-where-you-are-planted" strategy, building the "surround sound" that would make our narrative visible in every corner of our natural markets.

Kayla and the operations team provided the empowered execution support—the systems, the tracking, the infrastructure that turned good intentions into disciplined activity.

And our G2 lead advisors—Phil, George, Will, Alex, and Ryan—did the hardest thing of all: they stepped into organic growth as *their* responsibility, not just the founder's.

What you see in the rest of this chapter is what we built together and what worked. The frameworks, the disciplines, the rituals that turned organic growth from a founder's instinct into a team capability. As a result, we achieved a twenty-plus percent average annual growth rate over the next two years.

But the most important outcome wasn't the numbers.

The most important outcome was watching our business partners and our G2 lead advisors go from skeptics to believers. Phil and George and Will and Alex and Ryan—people who thought organic growth was the founder's job, that it required some special charisma they didn't have—

discovered they could attract clients, build relationships, and grow the business on their own terms, in their own voice.

That's client capital. And client capital accelerates the value of your business when there's a high level of diversification and a low level of dependency on the founder. The magic isn't the person running the company. The magic is when the team becomes the attraction.

That's the flywheel. And here's how you build it.

## EXPERIENCE IS THE MARKETING

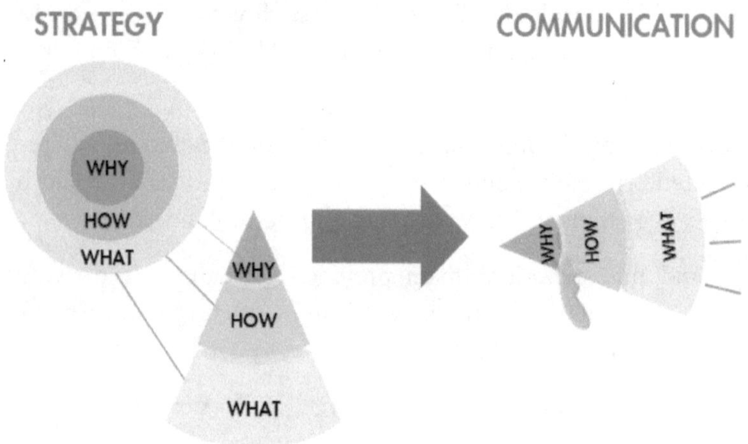


Early in my career, someone told me that marketing was about reaching as many people as possible. Cast a wide net. Get your name out there. The more people who know you exist, the more clients you'll get.

So I did that. Networking events. Cold calls. Advertising. Sponsorships. I was everywhere, talking to everyone, trying to be all things to all people.

You know what happened?

I attracted a lot of people I didn't want to work with. People who didn't share my values. People who were looking for the cheapest option.

People who drained my energy and my team's energy. Growth happened, but it was exhausting. And the clients who came through that wide net? They didn't stay. They didn't refer. They were always shopping for something better.

The turning point came when I stopped trying to reach everyone and started trying to attract *my* people.

Your vibe attracts your tribe. This isn't just a catchy phrase. It's a business strategy.

When you're clear about who you are—your values, your purpose, your way of doing things—you naturally repel the wrong people and attract the right ones. You stop wasting energy convincing skeptics and start building relationships with believers.

But your vibe has to be real. It has to show up in the actual experience of working with you.

You can't say clients come first and then make them wait three days for a callback. You can't claim to be family-focused and then burn out your team with seventy-hour weeks. You can't lead with integrity on a poster and cut corners when nobody's watching.

The experience is marketing because the experience is where your values become visible.

At ICG, we obsess over the client experience. Not in an abstract, strategic way. In a "What did it feel like to be in that meeting?" way. Did the client feel heard? Did they leave with clarity or confusion? Did we make their life simpler or more complicated? Would they tell their best friend about us?

Every touchpoint is an opportunity to demonstrate who we are. The way we answer the phone. The way we follow up after a meeting. The way we handle mistakes. The way we celebrate wins.

When the experience is consistently excellent, marketing becomes almost unnecessary. Clients become evangelists. They do your marketing for you—not because you asked them to, but because they genuinely want to share something good.

That's scalable growth. That's growth that compounds.

## THE PHYSICS PROBLEM

But here's the problem nobody talks about until it's too late.

One person can be in one place at one time. That's the physics problem.

Most founders built their businesses around one personality. Theirs. The clients came because of them. The trust was built by them. The relationships lived inside their head, their handshake, their presence in the room.

That works—until it doesn't.

Information overload. Commoditization of services. The increasing complexity of the problems your clients need solved. All of it means the same thing: what got you here is not going to get you where you're going. If the brand lives inside one person, growth has a ceiling. And that ceiling is the founder's calendar.

This is the tension at the heart of every growing business. You built something remarkable on the back of your personality, your relationships, your hustle. And now that very thing—*you*—is the bottleneck.

The shift is clear. Marketing built around the personality of one person has to transition to the personality and power of the team. Not someday. Now.

But that transition doesn't happen by telling your team to "take ownership of client relationships." You've been in those meetings. You've said those words. And nothing changed, because words without structure are just wishes.

It happens by solving the physics problem—deliberately, structurally, with the same rigor you'd bring to any operational challenge.

Here's what solving it unlocks. For the founder—freedom of time, money, and relationships. The space to lead instead of being consumed by every client interaction. For the next generation on your team—an opportunity to grow professionally, financially, and as leaders. Not just supporting the founder's book of business, but building their own. And for the client—the security of knowing they're being served by a team they trust, not a single point of failure.

This is exactly the work Mark brought to Andrea, Maria, and Brent. As our Diamond Leaders, they were responsible for the client experience inside their diamond teams. Solving the physics problem wasn't an abstraction for them. It was a daily reality—figuring out how to maintain platinum-level hospitality while building the capacity for new growth. They had to look at their teams, their client maps, and their own habits and ask: *Where is the bottleneck?* Where am I still the single point of failure? And what has to change?

## NOT EVERYONE FLIES FIRST CLASS

Solving the physics problem starts with defining what your clients actually experience.

Not all client relationships are the same. Pretending they are is one of the most expensive mistakes a growing firm makes.

Think of it like an airplane. Business class is a different experience than economy plus, which is different from basic economy. All three passengers get to the destination. But the service, the attention, the feel of the experience—those are intentionally different.

Your clients need the same clarity. Platinum. Gold. Silver. Each tier defined by the level of hospitality, the depth of relationship, the frequency of contact, and the complexity of the work.

Without tiering, your best advisors are spread thin across every client—delivering a diluted version of what should be a remarkable experience. Your platinum clients get the same attention as your silver clients. Which means your platinum clients aren't getting what they deserve, and your team is exhausted trying to deliver high-touch service at every level.

Here's the part leaders miss: when you grow as a team, you have to communicate by a factor of ten to keep alignment. If you don't keep repeating that you're flying Delta with different classes of service, your younger team members will assume you're flying a low-cost carrier—because that's what they'd book when they buy their own tickets. Most of them will go for the cheapest flight. You built a premium brand. You deliver a premium experience. As a leader, you have to continuously educate your team on what that means and keep it front of mind. Every day.

And your pricing has to match. Take-out prices should not be the same as a high-end dining experience. If you're delivering platinum-level hospitality—deep relationships, proactive planning, white-glove service—your pricing should reflect that. Mismatched pricing erodes trust in both directions. Clients paying premium fees for average service feel cheated. Teams delivering exceptional service at commodity prices burn out. Neither is sustainable.

The capacity math matters here, too. Research is specific: sixty to eighty platinum client relationships is the optimal load for a lead advisor. Beyond that, the quality of hospitality starts to degrade. The Dunbar number—150—is the maximum number of meaningful relationships one person can sustain if you want to deliver a hospitality experience, not just a service.

Know your numbers. Revenue per lead advisor. Revenue per all advisors. Revenue per all team members. These ratios tell you whether your capacity is built for growth or whether you're running hot with no room to scale.

## DIAMOND TEAMS

Once you've tiered the experience, you need clear ownership at every level.

This is not a top-down reorganization where the founder redesigns the client map and hands out new assignments. This is empowered execution. The Diamond Leader owns the platinum relationship. The associate advisor owns the gold experience. The service team—with Kayla and the operations team providing the infrastructure and accountability—owns the operational touchpoints that make every tier feel seamless. Everyone knows what "excellent" looks like at their level. Everyone is accountable for delivering it.

Without clear ownership, client tiering becomes a spreadsheet exercise. Platinum clients get neglected because nobody's sure whose job it is to follow up. Gold clients absorb resources meant for platinum. The physics problem comes back—except now it's everyone's problem and nobody's responsibility.

This takes all seven components of the Elite Leadership Framework executed with sustained pressure. Not a one-time restructuring. An ongoing discipline—with regular review of client tiers, capacity ratios, and experience quality. Monthly, not quarterly.

Remember the seventh dynamic of change: when the pressure is off, people revert to their preferred comfortable state. That's human nature. It's the leader's role to keep the pressure on and weed the garden—to make sure the right people are providing hospitality for the right clients at the right time.

## What This Looks Like

Create a financial wellness experience for your next-generation and lower-complexity gold clients. Transfer silver clients and a portion of gold to that team. Build diamond teams to support your platinum and higher-complexity gold clients with the depth of service those relationships require. Align compensation and incentives so the economics reward the new behavior. And provide weekly recognition for the job well done. Not quarterly. Not annually. Weekly. People repeat what gets noticed.

And sometimes—this is the hard part—consider transferring twenty percent of your client base to different businesses entirely. Not every client belongs with you. Letting go of the wrong fit creates capacity for the right one.

## YOUR CREDO IS YOUR FILTER

Your credo card isn't just an internal document. It's the heart of your narrative.

We talked about the credo in earlier chapters—how to develop it, why it matters, how it aligns your team. But the credo is also your story.

Think about the brands you love. The companies you're loyal to. The people you follow. They all have a clear story. You know what they stand for. You know what they're against. You know what it feels like to be part of their world.

That story isn't manufactured by a marketing agency. It emerges from the credo—from the authentic values, purpose, and standards that guide everything they do.

Your credo answers the question every potential client is asking: "Why should I trust you with something that matters to me?"

Not "why are you qualified?" Not "why are you better than competitors?" "Why should I *trust* you?"

Trust isn't built through credentials. It's built through alignment. When someone sees your credo and thinks, *Yes—that's what I believe, too,* that's when trust begins.

Our credo—Inspire Confidence, Simplify Life, Reduce Stress—isn't a tagline. It's a filter. Every piece of communication we put into the world gets run through that filter. Does this inspire confidence? Does this simplify or complicate? Does this reduce stress or create it?

When we talk about our services, we don't lead with features. We lead with the feeling: "Most people find money stressful and confusing. We make it simple. We take the weight off your shoulders so you can focus on what matters to you."

That's not marketing speak. That's our credo translated into a story that resonates with the people we're meant to serve.

## THE "YOU KNOW HOW" APPROACH

Here's where the narrative becomes portable.

We hired Derrik Kinney—author of *Good Money Revolution*—to help our team articulate the narrative of our experience in their own words. That's one of the best investments we made. Derrik has a framework for this. He calls it the "you know how" approach. Turns out the right words were there all along. We just needed someone to help us find them.

The "you know how" approach gives them that language. It's simple:

*You know how most people find money stressful and confusing? We make it simple. We take the weight off their shoulders so they can focus on what matters to them.*

That's not a tagline. That's your credo translated into a story that anyone can repeat—at a dinner party, on a golf course, in a conversation with a friend who just went through a divorce, lost a spouse, or got laid off.

But knowing the framework isn't enough. You have to practice it. We built it into our ShareCon meetings and our Level 10s until everyone on the team had their own version—not a script they memorized, but a story they owned. If only the founder can tell the story, the story stops when the founder leaves the room.

Every member of your team should have their own version of "you know how." Not a script. A narrative they believe, delivered in their own voice, grounded in the credo. When the whole team can tell the same story in different words—that's when the narrative tips.

Your clients and centers of influence need the "you know how" too. When you help your best clients tell your story in their own words, you're not asking for referrals. You're equipping advocates. The story spreads not because you pushed it but because it's true, and people want to share things that are true.

## KNOWN BEFORE NEEDED

Here's a principle that changed how I think about growth. And it didn't come from me.

Walter Thorne of the Albany Business Review said it first: *be known before you are needed.* Laura heard it and never let it go. It became the foundation of everything her marketing team built at ICG.

Most professionals wait until someone needs them to start building the relationship. A prospect has a problem, they search for a solution, you show up and compete with everyone else who showed up at the same time.

That's a losing game. You're a commodity. You're competing on price and promises. The prospect has no reason to trust you more than anyone else.

But what if they already knew you? What if, when the need arose, you were the first person they thought of—not because you happened to rank well on Google, but because you'd been building a relationship for years?

That's what it means to be known before you are needed.

It means showing up consistently, adding value, and staying visible long before someone is ready to buy. It means investing in relationships that may not pay off for months or years. It means playing the long game when everyone else is playing the short game.

Growth is not linear. It takes time. The effort you invest today in building visibility will feel disproportionate to the results—until it doesn't. There's a crossover point where your success curve overtakes the time invested. Most people give up before they reach it.

How to do this:

Tell your story. Not once. Continuously. Through whatever medium feels authentic to you—writing, speaking, video, podcasts, social media. Share your credo. Share your values. Share what you're learning and what you believe. Let people get to know you before they need you.

Be useful. Don't just promote. Add value. Teach something. Solve a small problem. Give people a reason to pay attention that has nothing to do with selling them something.

Stay consistent. Showing up once doesn't build trust. Showing up every week for five years builds trust. The compound interest of consistency is enormous. Most people give up too early.

Build your "surround sound." Your website, your email cadence, your social media, your events—these are your marketing air support. They work together to amplify the same narrative. Not four separate campaigns. One integrated message showing up everywhere your people already are.

This is why we publish The Nudge every week. It's not a sales pitch. It's a leadership principle, a story, a call to action. People in our ecosystem read it, share it, and think about it. When they're ready to work with us —or when someone asks them for a recommendation—we're already known.

And this isn't just the founder's job anymore. Laura and her marketing team built the surround sound at ICG—the digital presence, the content strategy, the visual identity that carries our narrative into every channel. But the whole team plays a role. Everyone lives the credo. No contribution is too small. When one team member does a keynote at your annual advance and galvanizes the whole team to find their own voice—that's the narrative coming alive. When every team member is posting, sharing, showing up authentically—that's surround sound working.

## SPREAD YOUR GLITTER

Laura doesn't explain things. She makes you feel them.

She introduced the concept at one of our advances. She stood up in front of the whole team and reframed something we'd been doing instinctively into something we could actually teach. And once she explained it, we couldn't unsee it.

Glitter isn't just a noun. For us, it's also an adjective.

Your team *is* the glitter. Think about what glitter actually does. It's the shiny part of the celebration. Glitter is the sparkle that makes the moment feel like something. It's the ray of hope in someone's lowest moment. It catches light when everything else feels dim.

And it sticks. Once glitter lands somewhere, it spreads to everything it touches. You find it in places you have never put it. And it sticks around forever.

That's your team. That's your expertise, your passion, your presence in someone's life at exactly the right moment. When your people show up authentically, not as polished professionals reciting credentials, but as real human beings who genuinely love what they do and why they do it. That's the gift. That's the shine. That's the glitter spreading.

How do you spread it deliberately and with intention?

Bio videos. Team videos. Personalized posts that let people see not just what you do, but who you are and why it lights you up. Every new follower is another piece of glitter landing somewhere it can sparkle. Create things worth sharing. Content, experiences, and ideas that people want to pass along, not because you asked them to, but because sharing them reflects well on them too. Make it easy to share. Celebrate your clients publicly. Let the world see what kind of people you work with.

The goal is a flywheel where your best clients attract your next best clients. Not through referral incentives or awkward "who do you know" conversations. Through genuine enthusiasm. Through glitter that spreads on its own.

## BLOOM WHERE YOU ARE PLANTED

We already talked about how words matter, and language is a ritual. Laura introduced "Bloom where you are planted" as a mantra for all of us.

It was built specifically for people on our team who don't naturally flex their marketing muscles. The ones who never thought of themselves as people who *could* market. Here's what most marketing strategies miss:

Not everyone's talent and unique genius shows up in a room full of strangers or behind a camera or on a social media post. But everyone has a natural market. Everyone already *belongs* somewhere. Her message to them was simple: You don't have to be everywhere. You have to be *undeniable* where you already are.

That's Level 4 leadership. She didn't just have a good idea. She made the idea teachable, handed it to people around her, and made herself unnecessary to it. The strategy now belongs to the whole team.

You don't need to be everywhere. You need to be unmistakably present where you already are.

Tap into your natural market. The boards you sit on. The golf leagues. The CrossFit gym. The community organizations you already support. These aren't networking opportunities you have to manufacture—they're relationships you're already in. The question is whether you're showing up intentionally.

This is the work Laura and her marketing team drive at ICG. Mapping out quarterly networking goals per advisor. Not corporate networking—real human connection in the places your team already lives and works. Convey your expertise and your compassion. Bio videos, team videos, personalized social content with a manageable cadence. Invite more followers. Let people in.

Your vibe attracts your tribe. Stop trying to reach everyone. Start trying to be unmistakably yourself in the places you're already planted.

## JUG LINES

Mark's grandfather used to fish with jug lines.

If you've never seen this, here's how it works: You take a bunch of plastic jugs, tie a line and a hook to each one, bait them, and float them across the water. Then you go do something else. Check back later. Some jugs will have fish. Most won't. But you've got lines in the water working for you while you're doing other things.

That's how I think about relationship marketing.

Think of your digital marketing—your surround sound—as the air force bombing the beach. Softening the targets. Creating visibility, building familiarity, making sure your narrative is in the water before anyone needs you.

Jug line management is the infantry and special forces going in to take the wins.

Digital marketing creates the space. It's how you attract people. But jug lines are how you actually turn people into clients. One without the other doesn't work. Air support without ground troops just makes noise. Ground troops without air support are fighting blind.

Jug lines are the relationships you're tending that may not produce anything today. The coffee meetings. The check-in calls. The LinkedIn comments. The conference conversations. You're not trying to close anyone. You're baiting hooks and setting them in the water.

Most of those jug lines won't produce anything. That's fine. You're playing a numbers game and a long game simultaneously.

But some of those jugs will bob. Someone you had coffee with two years ago will remember you when their friend needs help. A comment you left on someone's post will lead to a conversation that leads to a partnership. A conference contact will change companies and suddenly have a budget for exactly what you do.

## YOUR 3X'ERS

Not everyone in your network has the same reach.

There are three types of people who drive how ideas—and businesses—tip past the point of organic growth. Connectors have wide relationship webs and naturally bring people together. Mavens carry deep knowledge and help others make informed decisions. Salespeople have the charisma and persuasion to influence action.

Some people in your tribe are one of these—a 1X. Some are two—a 2X. The people who are all three? Those are your 3X'ers. They are the most important relationships in your jug line.

Identify your 3X'ers and work backwards. Build the jug line so you are constantly tending the relationships that have the most gravitational pull. Then layer in your 2X and 1X contacts.

The discipline comes down to a simple ritual: BCLs. Breakfast. Coffee. Lunch. A regular, non-salesy touchpoint with the key players in your network. For your 3X'ers, the best practice is once per quarter.

Here's what a BCL looks like:

The segue—wins since the last time you met. Progress updates. Headlines about things they should know.

The ask—one question: "What is the greatest service I can do for you?"

The follow-through—do that service. Actually deliver on whatever they asked for.

Be prepared that the greatest service won't always be an introduction. Sometimes it's connecting them to a resource. Sometimes it's solving a problem that has nothing to do with your business. That's the point. This is how you become genuinely useful—not transactionally useful. The introductions come because the relationship is real, not because you engineered a referral conversation.

Beyond BCLs, maintain your wider jug lines with regular, non-salesy touches. Birthday notes. Congratulations on a promotion. "Saw this article and thought of you." Stay present without being pushy.

Add new jug lines consistently. Your network should be growing, not static. Every month, new people, new conversations, new lines in the water.

Track it. Not in a creepy way. But know who's in your ecosystem. Know when you last connected. Have a system so people don't fall through the cracks.

This is slow work. It doesn't have the dopamine hit of a closed deal or a viral post. But over time, jug lines create a sustainable pipeline of opportunities that doesn't depend on advertising spend or algorithm changes.

## THE LEAD MEASURES THAT MAKE THE FLYWHEEL SPIN

Jug line management without a system is just good intentions. You need a scoreboard.

The wildly important goal is simple: new clients with a plan. That's the WIG. It moves the organization forward. It solves net flows. It moves you upmarket. Everything else is noise unless this number is growing.

The lead measures that drive the WIG are specific:

One prospect contacted per day. That's five per week, twenty per month. Consistent outreach, not bursts of activity followed by silence.

Two BCL meetings per week. Tending the jug lines with your connectors, mavens, and salespeople. Building the relationships that produce referrals.

Three engagement visits per month. Deepening existing relationships through face-to-face interaction. Bloom where you are planted.

Hit those three numbers consistently, and the math works. The target: one net new platinum client per month.

But the measures only matter if you track them. What's measured improves. Track referral asks, prospects received, engagement visits set and seen, intro calls, new clients, new clients with a plan, and net flows. Make the scoreboard visible. Make the team own it. The scoreboard creates accountability without requiring the leader to police every activity.

This is where Kayla and the operations team made it real at ICG. They built the tracking infrastructure, the reporting cadence, the systems that turned "we should be doing this" into "here are the numbers, and here's who owns them." Without that operational backbone, the lead measures are aspirational. With it, they're accountable.

Then lock in the cadence. Diamond team meetings—where Andrea, Maria, and Brent review the scoreboard with their teams. One-on-ones—individual coaching conversations on pipeline and activity with Phil,

George, Will, Alex, and Ryan. Quarterly business reviews—zoom out and assess whether the system is producing results. And ShareCon—sharing wins, celebrating progress, reinforcing the behaviors that drive the flywheel.

The cadence of accountability will surface gaps. Some team members will hit their lead measures. Some won't. The discipline is addressing that—not quarterly, not at annual review time, but in real time. The scoreboard makes it visible. The cadence makes it unavoidable. The culture of embracing conflict we built in Chapter 9 makes it productive instead of punitive.

## WINNING BY DOING GOOD

Let me tie all of this together with a principle that sounds naive until you see it work.

Teams that put serving clients first—teams that focus on making people feel good through hospitality—are the ones that win.

They win trust. They win hearts. They win minds. And yes, they win wallets.

This isn't a trick. You can't fake hospitality. You can't game your way to genuine care. Either you actually want to make people's lives better, or you don't.

But when you do—when serving clients well is genuinely your priority—growth takes care of itself.

Here's why.

Happy clients stay. Retention is the foundation of scalable growth. Every client you keep is one you don't have to replace. The longer they stay, the more profitable they become, and the less you spend on acquisition.

Happy clients refer. Not because you ask them to. Because they want their friends to have the same experience. Word of mouth is the most powerful marketing force on the planet, and you can't buy it. You can only earn it.

Happy clients forgive. You're going to make mistakes. Everyone does. When clients trust you—when they know you genuinely care—they give you grace. They tell you about problems instead of just leaving. They let you make it right.

Happy teams serve better. This is the flywheel. When your team believes in the mission, they serve clients better. When clients are happier, the work is more rewarding. When the work is rewarding, your best people stay. When your best people stay, clients get even better service.

Winning by doing good isn't charity. It's strategy. The most sustainable competitive advantage you can build is a reputation for actually giving a damn.

## THE FLYWHEEL

Here's the formula in plain language.

Build an experience worth talking about. Make working with you so good that clients become advocates without being asked.

Solve the physics problem. Tier the experience, build diamond teams, and get clear on who owns what. Stop being the bottleneck.

Clarify your credo and let it become your narrative. Know what you stand for and communicate it consistently. Give your team and your clients the "you know how" language to carry the story forward.

Be known before you're needed. Show up, add value, and stay visible—long before anyone is ready to buy.

Spread your glitter. Create things worth sharing and let your best clients attract your next best clients. Bloom where you're already planted.

Maintain your jug lines. Identify your 3X'ers. Run your BCLs. Hit your lead measures. Keep the scoreboard honest.

Win by doing good. Put serving clients first and trust that the growth will follow.

This isn't a funnel. It's a flywheel. Each element reinforces the others. The better your experience, the more your clients share it. The more visible you are, the more jug lines you set. The more you win by doing good, the better your experience becomes.

Once the flywheel is spinning, growth becomes sustainable. You're not burning yourself out chasing leads. You're attracting the right people through the gravity of who you actually are.

## BEFORE YOU MOVE ON → SHOULDER TAPS FROM THIS CHAPTER

- Your experience is your marketing. Not your brochures, your website, or your ad spend. The actual experience of being your client—how it feels to work with you, what they tell their friends at dinner—that's your marketing. Everything else is amplification. If the experience isn't worth talking about, no amount of marketing will fix it.
- Solve the physics problem before it solves you. One person can be in one place at one time. If the brand lives in you, growth has a ceiling—and that ceiling is your calendar. Tier the experience. Build diamond teams. Get clear on who owns what at every level. The transition from founder-driven to team-driven isn't optional. It's the difference between a business and a job.
- Make the narrative portable. Your credo isn't a poster on the wall. It's the script your whole team carries. Give everyone the "you know how"—the plain-language version of why you exist that anyone can repeat at a dinner party. When the whole team can tell the same story in different words, the narrative tips.
- Your vibe attracts your tribe—but vibes don't scale without systems. One prospect contacted per day. Two BCLs per week. Three engagement visits per month. Identify your 3X'ers. Keep the scoreboard honest. Lock in the cadence. The flywheel doesn't spin on inspiration alone. It spins on discipline.

- Tend your jug lines. Not every relationship has the same gravitational pull. Find the connectors, mavens, and salespeople in your network—especially the rare ones who are all three. Run your BCLs. Ask the only question that matters: "What is the greatest service I can do for you?" Then actually do it. The referrals come because the relationship is real, not because you engineered a conversation.
- The magic is the team, not the founder. Client capital accelerates the value of your business when there's high diversification and low dependency on any one person. When Mark and Andrea and Maria and Brent and Phil and George and Will and Alex and Ryan and Kayla and Laura and the entire team built organic growth together—when skeptics became believers—that was the chapter's lesson lived out in real time. Your team doesn't need your charisma. They need the mindset, the intentionality, and the systems to grow in their own voice. When the team becomes the attraction, the flywheel spins on its own.

You've got vision, culture, execution, narrative, and growth. But none of it lasts without resilience—the financial strength and governance structures that let you play for decades, not quarters. That's where we're headed next.

SEVENTEEN

# Technology, Traction, and Scaling with Compassion

## STRUCTURAL CAPITAL, PART ONE: THE EXECUTION ENGINE

### Where Vision Meets Reality

All the envisioning in the world means nothing if you don't do things.

I've watched teams spend months crafting the perfect vision. Beautiful V/TOs. Inspiring credo cards. Values that would make a philosopher weep. And then… nothing changes. The document goes into a shared drive. People go back to doing what they were doing before. The vision becomes a relic, something you dust off once a year to remind yourself what you were supposed to be building.

Execution is where most teams die.

Not because they don't know what to do. Because they haven't built the infrastructure to actually do it.

Think about the airplane metaphor we've been building throughout this book. If your vision is the destination and your people are the crew, then execution is the fuselage—the body that holds everything together when turbulence hits. Your engines can be powerful. Your crew can be world-class. Your fuel can be abundant. But without the fuselage, everything falls apart mid-flight.

That fuselage is what I call structural capital. It has two sides, and they're important enough that I'm giving each its own chapter.

This chapter—technology and traction—is about the systems, roles, rhythms, and accountability structures that turn vision into daily execution. It's the operational side of the fuselage. How the work actually gets done.

The next chapter—financial and entity resilience—is about the money, the governance, and the structures that keep the plane in the air for decades. It's the durability side of the fuselage. How the business endures.

You need both. Traction without financial resilience means you're executing beautifully on a business that's one bad quarter from collapse. Financial resilience without traction means you've got a healthy balance sheet and a team that can't get anything done.

Both sides. That's the fuselage. Let's start with traction.

## TECHNOLOGY

Before we talk about people, roles, and accountability, let me address the accelerator underneath all of it: technology.

I'll be honest with you—I'm not going to write a technology manual. Whatever specific tools I name today will be outdated before this book hits its second printing. That's the nature of technology. But the principles underneath the tools? Those don't change.

The keyword is integrated. Not more tools. Not better point solutions. Integrated systems where data flows smoothly, where people aren't re-entering information in three different places, where the technology serves the work instead of creating more work.

Here's our standard, and I'll fight anyone who tries to change it: If it's not in the CRM, it didn't happen.

In integrated teams where multiple people are involved in producing a client experience, communication on client-related items is essential. Everything needs to live in one place—the place where it can be easily accessible and turned into action. That's the foundation of strong client capital. When three different people touch a client relationship, you can't have critical information living in someone's head or buried in an email thread. It has to be in the system.

AI accelerates all of this. AI summarization and AI-enabled client intelligence keep the team informed without requiring anyone to dig through notes. Business intelligence through dashboards creates the bedrock of empowered execution—when you can see you're steering off course, the whole team can course-correct instantaneously.

And one more rule that I will die on this hill for: Keep the cameras on. Text messages and emails don't activate the oxytocin that fuels high-performing teams. Use the highest-bandwidth communication platform available. If you can be face-to-face, be face-to-face. If you can't, be on video. The screen is the last resort, not the default.

## What This Looks Like

Your accountability chart should be reflected in your technology. If someone owns a function, the systems should give them visibility into that function without hunting through five different dashboards.

Your scorecards should update automatically wherever possible. If people have to manually compile their numbers every week, they won't do it consistently. Reduce the friction.

Your meeting rhythms should be supported by tools that make preparation easy. Level 10s work best when the issues list, scorecard, and rocks are all in one place, visible to everyone, updated in real time.

Technology isn't the strategy. Technology enables the strategy. When it's integrated well, it disappears into the background. When it's fragmented, it becomes another source of friction and confusion.

Simple is scalable. That applies to technology, too.

## WHO, NOT HOW

To transform a team or a business into a self-leading one, founders need to embrace *who*, not *how*.

I didn't know it at the time, but this is exactly what I did when I started the business. I needed to deliver client experiences that were remarkable—so remarkable that clients would remark about them, and we could grow. That advice needed to be at the highest possible level. The service needed to land exactly when it was needed, to whom it was needed, and at the moment it was needed.

That included production of client visits. Creating recommendations. Having meetings. Delivering those recommendations. Executing everything we talked about. Making sure it was compliant.

When Laura and I decided to build the business together in 2006, she was clear about what she needed. She wanted work that let her be fully present as a mom to Oscar, Stella, and Kosta—and she wasn't willing to sacrifice the professional gifts she'd spent years developing. She didn't want to choose. She wanted to design.

So we designed.

I said to her, "There's one thing I know I cannot afford to drop: marketing. And you're the best person I know to own it. You will be my *who* to get this going."

She looked at me like I had five heads on my shoulders.

"You are an execution master," I told her. "You don't drop any balls. You do communications and marketing better than anybody I know. You won a national award from the Direct Marketing Association. I'm counting on you to be my marketing *who*."

She became a leader at Ameriprise in executing marketing strategies, building something remarkable while living the life she'd been intentional about creating.

A similar thing happened as we grew. In 2008, I called Christin, my collaborator on this book, and said the business was growing and that I needed someone I could delegate the authority of building systems and making the vision come through. She was an advisor. She understood the concept. There was a high level of trust between us. And off we went.

As we were writing this book, she shared with me a document titled "19 Things I Keep." Meeting prep. Client follow-up. Transactions. Planning communication. Case management. Payroll. Leadership. Nineteen different functions she was responsible for.

That's a great example of how stupid I was. No one leader should have nineteen things on their plate. But I was able to delegate that authority to the very first integrator of any of my businesses. We didn't call it that at the time. But she was my *who*.

In 2015, months after the conversation I described at the beginning of this book, I was able to delegate the authority of making things work to Maureen. She became my *who*.

In 2019, as we learned about Traction and V/TO, Maria and I decided she would be the Integrator, and I would be the Visionary. She became the *who* of getting things done, making sure we stayed compliant, making sure we didn't end up in jail.

As we grew further, we delegated responsibility for financial management to Derek. He became our CFO, our *who* when it comes to resilient business and responsible stewardship of resources. Maria and I knew, and Brent knew, that where we're going would be way bigger than any of us had the interest or capacity to handle alone.

The latest iteration started in January 2024, when Mark became the *who* of seamlessly integrating all the businesses we work with. And when I wanted to build our coaching business to the next level, I brought in Jo and delegated the authority of an integrator for the next phase of growth.

All of these were 10X moves. I delegated authority for things I'm not good at, or not interested in, to a *who*, and worked with them to figure it out.

Here's what I've learned: When people are ready to move to the next level of development, founders lack *whos* to delegate authority to. They lack the infrastructure for transformation.

Empowered execution is about defining clear roles and ownership. Then, radical accountability to get things done.

And every bit of it runs on trust. Finding your *whos* is an act of trust. You're not transferring tasks—you're transferring authority to another human being. Nothing builds oxytocin more than being trusted with something that matters. Delegation isn't dumping. It's transferring trust to elevate performance.

## FRACTIONAL *WHOS* HELP MOVE THINGS

Several years ago, our coaching clients started saying something that stopped me cold.

"I really enjoy talking once a month. But I never get anything done. I don't have time. I don't have people on the team that you have."

Jo and I looked at each other. We could offer a fractional integrator experience for clients. Today, Jo is leading eight different businesses, each having achieved a transformation that would not have been possible without her as a fractional integrator.

Just this week, I met with a client named Michael. Before we even started the conversation, he said, "I have to tell you, your team—Jo, Laura, Jenna, and all the other coaches—has my team flying in formation. They are telling me what I need to do. They're telling me to get out of the way and stay in my lane. I freaking love it."

The best part? Michael is a founder who brought in his daughter Jill and his son John to build a multi-generational legacy business, and our coaches and leaders are helping his kids become effective leaders. Getting things moving.

This is what empowered execution looks like.

## SCALING UP WITH COMPASSION

This is where most businesses make a critical mistake. They throw bodies at the problem. Revenue's up? Hire more people. Workload's increasing? Add headcount. It feels logical. It's also the most expensive and least effective play you can run.

In a 2X world, as growth happens, people start calling out capacity constraints or limits. I found that my role as a leader is to help them think about capacity limits in a 10X way. We used every one of these four plays to help scale our business without adding too many new people and leveraging our brains and creativity in solving problems. I call it scaling with compassion.

We use a framework I call the **Four Plays**. Think of it as a scaling sequence—and the order matters.

### Play One: Leverage Technology

Before you hire a single person, ask this question: What can technology eliminate?

The answer, in most businesses, is somewhere between fifty and eighty percent of what you're currently doing manually.

I'm not exaggerating. Calendaring. Email automation. Document workflows. Client communication sequences. Data entry. Report generation. Scheduling. Follow-ups.

When we leveraged electronic scheduling tools, my coordinator, Betty, was spending most of her time managing my calendar—and it wasn't working. The technology eliminated ninety percent of her calendar burden. That alone freed up slack and flow for both of us. Small change. Massive impact.

Here's the other thing founders don't always see: your high-end clients expect this. They expect seamless technology. They expect your business to be up to speed with technological advancements. When you're still running on manual processes, you're not just wasting your team's time—you're signaling to your best clients that you're behind.

Strip out everything that can be automated. Then build your execution on top of what's left.

## Play Two: Optimize Right People, Right Seats

Once you've leveraged technology, look at who you already have and where they're sitting.

This is where TUG Cards™ become essential. If someone is operating outside their genius zone—if they're spending eighty percent of their time on work that drains them—you don't have a capacity problem. You have a positioning problem.

Optimize your existing team's workflows. Realign roles based on genius, not just job descriptions. Move people into positions where they don't just perform—they flourish. Sometimes the biggest capacity gain in your business isn't a new hire. It's moving someone from the wrong seat to the right one.

## Play Three: Grow Your People

Your people have far more potential than you give them credit for. Far more. The limiting factor isn't their capacity—it's whether you've created the conditions for them to expand into what they're capable of.

This is where what my team calls "Saša math" comes in.

My TUG Card says I'm an intuitive activator. That means I have the ability to intuitively make a decision based on instinct and move toward it. Most of the time, those decisions take us where we need to go. But the people around me expect precision. They want the full spreadsheet. They want every step mapped out before we move.

During our QL6 last fall, Mark looked at me and said, "Dude, you're fifteen steps ahead of everyone. The problem with you being fifteen steps ahead is that you go and do those steps on your own, and none of us has any idea what you're talking about. You need to show us your work."

He was right. What I discovered is that my intuitive decisions are about eighty percent baked. Like the Marines' eighty-percent-done principle —they train Marines to seek truth and specificity only up to eighty percent, then turn that into action. Saša math is my version of that. I do the thinking through biking, walking, swimming, middle-of-the-night processing—and I arrive at a direction that's eighty percent right. The team needs to move together to figure out the remaining twenty percent.

Growing your people means teaching them to move at eighty percent. Not recklessly—directionally. Show the work. Bring them along. But don't wait for one hundred percent certainty, because it doesn't exist. You develop people by trusting them with eighty-percent-baked decisions and letting them figure out the remaining twenty alongside you.

### Play Four: Add More People

Only after you've exhausted the first three plays do you add headcount.

By this point, you know exactly what you need. You've stripped out the work that technology should handle. You've optimized your existing team's positioning. You've grown their capacity. What's left is a genuine gap—a function that requires a new *who*.

Now you're not hiring out of desperation. You're selecting with precision. You know the seat. You know the genius required. You know the culture fit because your existing team has been refined through the first three plays.

This is scaling with compassion. You're not grinding your people into the ground and then hiring their replacements. You're honoring the team you have, maximizing what they can do, and only adding when the need is real and the role is clear.

## CLEAR ROLES AND OWNERSHIP

The very first thing we learned we needed to do, and redo regularly, is clearly define who owns what.

Most businesses have organizational charts. You've seen them. Boxes and lines. Names and titles. CEO at the top, with layers cascading down like a corporate waterfall.

But org charts are a list of big titles and egos. They show hierarchy. They don't show accountability.

Who's actually responsible for marketing? The org chart might say *"Vice President of Marketing,"* but what does that mean? What specific outcomes does that person own? When something falls through the cracks, whose lap does it land in?

Org charts hide more than they reveal.

We use accountability charts instead. This comes from the EOS, and it's one of the most practical tools we've adopted.

An accountability chart does two things.

First, it pares down to the key accountability functions of the business. Not every role. Not every task. The core functions that have to work for the plane to fly—marketing, business development, finance, operations, advice, visionary, integrator.

Second, it names exactly one person who owns each function. Not a committee. Not "shared responsibility." One human being who will be held accountable for that outcome.

Some people have one role. Some people have multiple roles. That's fine. What matters is that everybody knows who owns what. No ambiguity. No finger-pointing when things go sideways.

Here's the other benefit: Accountability charts create a pathway for G2 and G3 leaders to step into ownership. When you clearly define what each function requires, you can bring emerging leaders into the tent. Let them learn by doing. Give them real responsibility with real consequences. This is how you build the crew that can fly the plane without you in the cockpit.

## What This Looks Like

At ICG, we revisit our accountability chart at least twice a year. Not because people's roles change that often, but because the business evolves. New functions emerge. Old functions get absorbed or eliminated. The chart has to reflect reality, not history.

When someone new joins the leadership team, we walk them through the accountability chart before anything else. Here's what we own collectively. Here's what you own specifically. Here's how your piece connects to everyone else's.

No guessing. No discovering six months in that you were supposed to be responsible for something nobody told you about.

# PRODUCTION MASTERY

Under roles and ownership, there's a deeper question: What business are you actually in?

This sounds obvious. It's not.

When I started in financial planning, the business was straightforward —create financial plans. That was novel. That was valuable. People would pay for the expertise of having someone map out their financial future.

That was 1999.

Today, any AI chatbot can generate a financial plan based on what you tell it. Through Ameriprise, AI does a lot of our financial planning work. The mechanics of creating a plan are no longer the differentiator.

So what business are we actually in?

We're in hospitality.

We help people feel good about being in business with us. We make their financial lives simpler and less stressful. We create an experience they can't get from an algorithm.

This reframe matters because it changes what "production mastery" means.

If you think you're in the financial planning business, you focus on technical excellence. Better models. More sophisticated analysis. Deeper expertise in tax law.

If you know you're in the hospitality business, you focus on human excellence. How does every interaction feel? What's the emotional experience of being our client? Are we making people's lives better, or just checking boxes?

Whatever your business actually is—legal advice, engineering, restaurants, consulting—you have to be excellent at it. Not just competent. Excellent.

And you have to keep it simple.

Simple is scalable. Complex is confusing. And the biggest obstacle to personal agency is confusion.

When your team is confused about what you do and how you do it, everything slows down. Decisions get stuck. Quality gets inconsistent. People spend more time figuring out the system than actually serving clients.

Strip away the complexity. Get radically clear on what business you're in and what excellence looks like in that business. Then, build every system to reinforce that clarity.

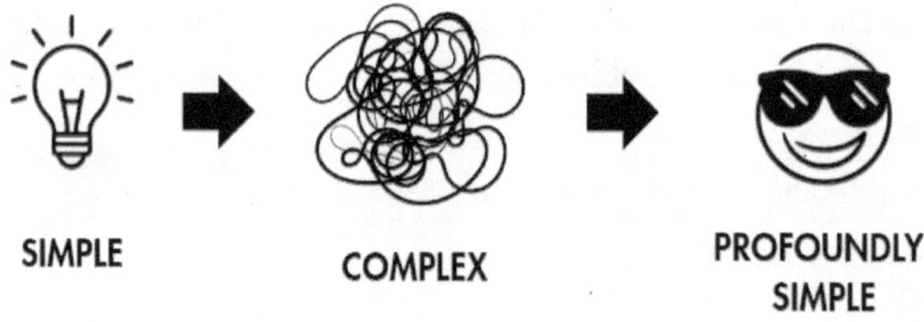

## THE PHYSICS PROBLEM - SAME PROBLEM, DIFFERENT ROOM

You solved the physics problem inside your org chart. Now, let's solve it inside your client map. One body can be in one place at one time.

That's Newton. Or maybe it's not Newton, but the principle is simple and unavoidable all the same.

If your lead advisor is spending time on a client that generates revenue below the profitable threshold for your firm, you're losing money. Not just on that client. On every other client that advisor could have been serving instead.

If your marketing person is chasing prospects who will never become ideal clients, every hour they spend is an hour they're not spending on prospects who would.

This is the physics problem. And every business has it.

I've spent twenty years solving this problem in my own business and fifteen years helping other businesses solve it. Here's what I've learned.

Knowing the problem doesn't fix it. Understanding the solution doesn't fix it. As you now know, you have to direct the rider, motivate the elephant, and shape the path.

Direct the rider: Define who your optimal client actually is.

For us, the optimal client has changed over the past twenty years. It used to be anyone who would pay for financial planning advice. Today, we're moving upmarket. We've created distinct experiences for different types of clients. Think of it like Delta Airlines.

Platinum One is our top tier. Fine dining. White glove. If they live close by, we will take their trash out. These clients get anything they need, however they need it.

Platinum and Gold are our comprehensive financial advisory clients. They want excellent service but don't need or want all the extras. They still get the hospitality of our team. They just don't need the concierge experience.

Financial Wellness is for clients who are building toward the other tiers. Different experience, different level of touch.

Each tier has different expectations, different service models, and different economics. By defining these clearly, we've directed the rider. Everyone on the team knows who we're serving and how.

Motivate the elephant: Your team has to be ready to serve the clients you're targeting.

This is where a lot of businesses get stuck. They define the ideal client, but their team isn't equipped to serve at that level. The elephant—the emotional brain—doesn't feel confident. So it resists. It gravitates back toward the comfortable clients, the easy wins, the people who don't push the team to grow.

You have to develop your people. Help them build the skills to move upmarket. Create wins that build confidence. The elephant needs to feel capable before it will move.

Shape the path: Build systems that make serving the right clients easier than serving the wrong ones.

This might mean adjusting your fee structure so that low-value clients naturally fall away. It might mean creating intake processes that filter for fit. It might mean tracking metrics that highlight when someone's spending too much time in the wrong tier.

The path should make the right behavior the default behavior.

## What This Looks Like

We review our client alignment at least twice a year. Who's in which tier? Are we spending time proportionate to value? Where are the misalignments?

It's like the plane analogy from earlier in the book. Regular maintenance and upgrades. You can't just set the client strategy once and assume it stays calibrated. The market shifts. Your team grows. Your own ambitions evolve. The physics problem requires ongoing attention.

## RADICAL ACCOUNTABILITY–LET MARGO DRIVE

Now let's talk about accountability itself.

I have a car. Her name is Margo. My daughter Stella named her.

Margo is a Lexus LS 500 hybrid with self-driving features. I've been a Lexus guy since 2003—I've used their user experience as a guide for building world-class experience in my own business. So when I heard Lexus was building a car with lane control and self-driving capabilities, I told Pete at Lexus, "I want to be the first one to own it."

Here's what Margo taught me about accountability.

For years, I had lane control indicators on my cars. And for years, I would get annoyed and turn them off. I didn't want the car telling me what to do. I wanted to drive.

Sound familiar?

That's exactly how I used to treat scorecards and accountability systems in my business. I'd reject them. Turn them off. I didn't want the numbers telling me what to do. I wanted to run the business my way.

But Margo changed something. I chose to rely on the lane control features instead of fighting them. The adjustment I had to make? Keep my speed within ten miles of the limit, and the car would drive itself.

Within a couple of trips, something unexpected happened.

I used to drive to our Plattsburgh office—169 miles north—and had to spend the night because I was exhausted. A full day of meetings plus five hours of driving drained my tank completely.

With Margo doing the driving, I arrived four minutes later than my usual speed would have gotten me there. But my energy tank was eighty-five percent full. Maybe ninety percent, depending on whether I was listening to a podcast.

With the tank that full, I was able to do a full day of work, hit my 3 p.m. meditation ritual, and drive home with enough left to spend time with my family.

Correction: Margo drove me home.

Radical accountability is like having Margo drive your business. It's about setting up parameters and giving a clear indication to the leaders of the organization when the team or results are out of alignment so they can realign themselves.

Ninety percent of the time, self-leading teams are driving themselves, like when Margo drives me to Plattsburgh, Kingston, or Bel Air. However, about ten percent of the time, you'll need to step in and take charge.

I used to reject accountability—lane correction, scorecards, scoreboards. By rejecting it, I had to rely on myself to drive everything, and I used up my entire energy tank just keeping the business on the road.

With radical accountability and the technology available today, I can let my team drive the business. We're all watching the lane departure indicators together. When the signals tell us we're off course, we adjust. Together.

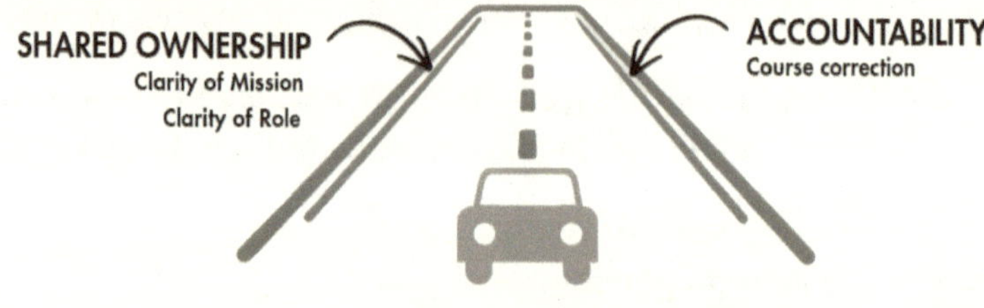


That's the principle underneath the Margo story: Accountability is visibility.

Most people don't fail because they don't care. They fail because they can't see. They're drifting off course, but nothing in their environment shows them the drift. By the time they realize they're lost, they're miles from where they should be.

Radical accountability means building systems that create visibility. Constant, unavoidable visibility into whether you're on track or off.

And here's the trust piece: Visibility is what allows a team to embrace conflict productively. When everyone sees the same numbers, the conversation shifts from politics to problem-solving. You're not arguing about what's happening—you're arguing about what to do about it. That's conflict in service of the mission. That's trust in action.

## HOW WE DO IT

The daily, weekly, monthly, quarterly, and annual rhythms that make execution stick.

Level 10 meetings. Weekly leadership meetings at three levels—business L10, lane L10s for each team, and functional L10s for areas like marketing, finance, and business operations. All run through Bloom Growth with a specific structure—rating the meeting 1–10 at the end to drive continuous improvement. Every week, we're looking at the scorecard, reviewing rocks, and identifying and solving issues. Nothing hides. Nothing festers. Target rating is 8 or above. If it's not, we figure out why.

Effective 1:1s. The purpose of a one-on-one is simple: get and stay in sync. Our leaders have regular 1:1s with their lane leaders. Each lane leader has regular 1:1s with their team members. The objective is to control direction and throw off discouragement. When someone's drifting—in energy, in focus, in confidence—the 1:1 is where you catch it before it becomes a problem the whole team has to solve. It's also where you celebrate the wins that nobody else sees. The quiet victories that keep people going.

Scoreboards. You can't manage what you can't measure. But more importantly, you can't self-correct what you can't see. Our scoreboards show the key metrics for each function—updated regularly and visible to everyone who needs to see them.

90-day sprints. Annual goals are too distant to create urgency. Quarterly rocks break the year into manageable chunks. Every ninety days, we're asking what absolutely has to get done to stay on track. Then we track it. Publicly.

Quarterly business reviews. Remember the airplane? Every quarter, we bring the plane into the hangar. One hundred ninety-four-point inspection. What's working? What's drifting? What needs maintenance? Then we get back in the air.

You'll notice I haven't mentioned ShareCon here—the daily rhythm that is the heartbeat of our team. That's Kayla's story, and we gave it the full treatment in Chapter 10. But I'll say this: if L10s are the weekly pulse and QBRs are the quarterly deep dive, ShareCon is the daily oxygen. Every morning, thirty minutes, the whole team. It's the answer to every founder's question: How do I remove myself from the day-to-day and still know things are happening? If you skipped Chapter 10, go back. ShareCon is where self-leading teams actually become self-leading.

The goal isn't to create a surveillance state. The goal is to create an environment where the right behavior is obvious and the wrong behavior is visible before it becomes catastrophic.

When people know their work is visible, most of them rise to the occasion. They don't need micromanagement. They need clarity. They need to see the scoreboard. Then they self-manage.

That's radical accountability. Not top-down control. Visible systems that enable self-leadership.

## THE FOUR COMPONENTS

Let me pull this all together. Technology-empowered execution has four components:

Integrated technology. The accelerator underneath everything else. Automate what can be automated. Integrate what needs to talk to each other. And if it's not in the CRM, it didn't happen.

Clear roles and ownership. Use accountability charts, not org charts. Every function has one owner. Find your *whos*. No ambiguity about who's responsible for what.

Radical accountability. Build visibility systems—Level 10s, 1:1s, scoreboards, 90-day sprints, quarterly reviews. Create environments where self-correction is possible because people can see whether they're on track. Let Margo drive.

Compassionate scaling. Leverage technology first. Optimize your existing team's positioning second. Grow your people third. Add headcount last. Honor the team you have before you go looking for new ones.

Miss any one of these, and execution breaks down. You might have great technology, but nobody knows who's supposed to be using it for what. You might have clear roles but no visibility into whether people are performing in those roles. You might have great scorecards, but you're burning your people out instead of scaling with intention.

All four, working together. That's how you get traction. That's how you build the fuselage that holds the plane together when turbulence hits.

## BEFORE YOU MOVE ON → SHOULDER TAPS FROM THIS CHAPTER

- Technology comes first, not last. Eliminate fifty to eighty percent of what your team does manually before you even think about adding people. If it's not in the CRM, it didn't happen.
- Find your *whos*. Stop figuring out how to do everything yourself. Delegation isn't dumping—it's transferring trust to elevate performance.
- Scale with compassion. Technology, then optimization, then growth, then headcount. In that order. Your people have more capacity than you think—if you put them in the right seats and give them room to expand.
- Saša math is real. Your intuitive direction is probably eighty percent right. Show the work. Bring your team along. But don't wait for one hundred percent certainty. Move at eighty and figure out the twenty together.

- Solve your physics problem. One body, one place, one time. Define your tiers. Direct the rider, motivate the elephant, shape the path. Review it twice a year—because the market shifts and so do you.
- Let Margo drive. Build visibility systems that let your team self-correct. Accountability isn't surveillance—it's clarity. When people can see the scoreboard, they self-manage.
- Execution is a practice, not an event. Do it this quarter. Then do it again next quarter. And the quarter after that.

That's the traction side of structural capital—the systems, roles, and rhythms that make execution real. But the fuselage has two sides. You've got the engine running. Now let's make sure it stays in the air. Next up: building the financial and entity resilience that lets you play for decades, not quarters.

EIGHTEEN

# Play for Decades, Not Quarters

## STRUCTURAL CAPITAL, PART TWO: THE RESILIENCY ENGINE

### The Other Side of the Fuselage

In the last chapter, we built the operational side of structural capital—the technology, traction, and scaling systems that turn vision into daily execution. That's the engine.

But an engine without a body around it is just a loud machine going nowhere. This chapter is about the other side of the fuselage—the financial health, governance, and entity resilience that keep the plane in the air for decades. Not quarters. Not fiscal years. Decades.

Traction gets things done. Resilience makes sure you're still around to keep doing them.

Before we go further, I want to name something that shapes everything in this chapter.

On our journey to build a resilient business, we found a fork in the road. One path led toward efficiency—a manager-managed business where one person makes the decisions, complexity stays low, and things move fast. The other path was member-managed. Slower. Messier. More voices at the table. More people who need to understand the *why* before you move.

We chose the second path.

Not because we enjoy inefficiency. Because the manager-managed model, as clean as it looks on paper, builds a business that runs at the speed of one person's judgment. The member-managed model builds a business that runs at the speed of trust.

Yes, you have to slow down. You have to bring people along. You have to get everyone on the same page before you move. But here's what I've learned: if you have everyone on the same page, you move a lot faster than you're moving now. Faster than a founder making decisions alone in a room, wondering why nobody's executing with urgency.

Trust over efficiency. That's the mantra for this chapter. Everything that follows—the financial discipline, the compensation philosophy, the road to ownership, the governance, the transition planning—it's all about deepening the trust account with owners and future owners.

I need to take you back to August 2020.

We talked about this moment earlier in the book—the triggering event. The decision to stop commingling business finances with personal finances. The realization that you can't build a business that leads itself if you are the business.

But I didn't tell you how hard that actually was.

For twenty years, I had operated as most founders operate. The business was an extension of me. Revenue came in, I paid expenses, and whatever was left was mine. Simple. Intuitive. And completely unsustainable.

But I didn't understand that the structure was a ceiling. As long as the business and I were financially intertwined, the business could never outgrow me. Every decision ran through my personal risk tolerance. Every investment competed with my personal needs. Every opportunity got filtered through the question of whether or not the business, meaning myself, could personally afford this.

The business didn't have its own lungs. It was breathing through mine.

Separating enterprise and personal assets wasn't just an accounting exercise. It was a psychological transformation. I had to stop thinking of the business as my money and start thinking of it as its own money. Money with a purpose. Money that belonged to the mission, not to me.

That shift made everything else possible.

## HEALTHY BUSINESSES GROW

There's a simple truth that most business owners resist: Healthy businesses grow.

Not businesses with the best marketing. Not businesses with the most charismatic founders. Not even businesses with the best products.

Healthy businesses. Businesses with strong financial foundations. Businesses that can weather storms. Businesses that have the resources to invest in opportunities when they appear.

When your business is financially unhealthy—when you're operating month-to-month, when every unexpected expense creates a crisis, when you can't say yes to opportunities because you don't have the cash—you're playing defense all the time. You can't think strategically because you're too busy surviving tactically.

But when your business is financially healthy, everything changes. You can hire before you're desperate. You can invest in systems before they're broken. You can say yes to the right opportunities and no to the wrong ones without financial pressure distorting your judgment.

Financial health creates optionality. And optionality creates growth.

So how do you build a financially healthy business?

It starts with separation. Then it moves to discipline. Then it becomes culture.

## THE 95/5 RULE

Here's a principle that has shaped how we manage money at ICG: the 95/5 rule.

Manage ninety-five percent of your finances like you don't have any money.

Seriously. Pretend you're broke. Scrutinize every expense. Question every line item. Run lean. Be disciplined. Don't let success make you soft.

Then, take the remaining five percent and splurge unreasonably on things that matter.

This sounds contradictory, but it's not. It's about intentionality.

Most businesses get this wrong. They hemorrhage money on things that don't matter—bloated software subscriptions nobody uses, office perks that don't move the needle, overhead that accumulates like barnacles on a ship. They're not watching ninety-five percent of their spending. Death by a thousand small expenses that nobody's really tracking.

When it comes time to invest in what actually matters, they hesitate. They're stingy about the things that would make a difference—talent development, team compensation, client experience upgrades.

You remove waste in order to prioritize people.

Every dollar you don't spend on things that don't matter is a dollar you can spend on things that do. On your team. On their development. On their quality of life.

The 95/5 rule flips the script. Be ruthlessly disciplined about the bulk of your spending. Then be unreasonably generous about the things that align with your values and drive your mission.

### What This Looks Like

In 2024 and 2025, we managed our balance sheet and cash flow as if we were running out of business. Not because we were in trouble. Because discipline is a practice, not a reaction to a crisis.

We questioned everything. Do we need this subscription? Can we renegotiate this contract? Is this expense actually driving value, or are we just used to paying it?

That discipline created a margin. Margin created options.

Culture eats strategy for breakfast. Compensation eats culture for lunch. I didn't read that somewhere. I lived it. If compensation is aligned with the culture, it exemplifies it. If it is not, it erodes it.

At the end of 2025, we were able to completely upgrade our compensation model for all team members, key players, and partners. We didn't do this because we suddenly had extra money lying around. We did it because we had been disciplined enough to create the resources.

That's the five percent. Unreasonable investment in our people. The kind of investment that would feel reckless if we hadn't been running lean everywhere else.

We hit thirty-plus percent profitability. Not by cutting corners. By being intentional. By managing ninety-five percent like we had nothing so we could invest five percent like we had everything.

## DEFENSE AND OFFENSE

Think of the 95/5 rule as defense and offense.

Defense is protecting what you have. It's the ninety-five. It's managing expenses, maintaining cash reserves, and avoiding unnecessary risk. It's making sure that when—not if—something goes wrong, you have the resilience to absorb the hit.

Defense isn't glamorous. Nobody brags about the expenses they didn't incur or the risks they didn't take. But defense is what keeps you in the game long enough to win.

Offense is investing in growth. It's five percent. It's the unreasonable bets on people, systems, and experiences that differentiate you from everyone else. It's the things that don't show up immediately on the balance sheet but compound over time.

Offense is what makes the game worth playing.

Most founders are naturally offensive players. They see opportunities. They want to invest. They believe in growth. But without defense, offense becomes reckless. You're one bad quarter away from disaster.

The best businesses play both. They're defensively disciplined and offensively bold at the same time.

## THE CFO FUNCTION

To play defense and offense simultaneously, you need someone whose genius is financial stewardship. A fractional or full-time CFO who owns the balance sheet, cash flow, and P&L (profit and loss) statements—and makes strategic decisions on both sides of the ball.

When Derek became our CFO, it was a 10X move. Not because I didn't understand finances. Because financial governance wasn't my genius zone, and the business had grown past the point where a founder's intuition was enough.

A CFO brings discipline to three frameworks that have shaped how we manage money.

The 95/5 Rule—which we just covered. Manage ninety-five percent like you're broke. Invest five percent like you have everything.

The 35/35/30 Rule. Structure your cash flow with intention: approximately thirty-five percent on marketing and operations, thirty-five percent on the cost of human capital, and thirty percent as operating profit. These aren't rigid percentages—they flex with your business stage and model. But they give you a target structure that prevents the two most common mistakes: overspending on overhead while underinvesting in people, or overpaying people while starving the business of operating capital. The 35/35/30 framework forces you to balance all three.

The Forty Percent Rule. Your growth rate plus your profit margin should equal at least forty percent. Growing thirty percent with ten percent margins? You're in good shape. Growing ten percent with thirty percent margins? Also good. But five percent growth with five percent margins? That's a business going nowhere.

And one more metric that keeps us honest: Return on assets. For a fully capitalized business, return on assets close to one percent measures how effectively you're deploying capital. It tells you whether the assets you're holding are actually working—or just sitting there looking impressive on a balance sheet while producing nothing.

These aren't academic exercises. They're the instruments in the cockpit. Without them, you're flying blind. With them, you can make offensive and defensive decisions with confidence, because you know exactly where you stand.

## THE BALANCE THAT MAKES YOU INVESTABLE

Let me share something I learned the hard way.

For years, our business was all growth. I was driving expansion like my hair was on fire. And very few people wanted to invest in that.

Growth without profitability isn't a business people want to be part of. It's a treadmill. Exciting to watch, maybe. But not something you'd bet your future on.

On the flip side, we coach businesses with spectacular margins—but those margins are choking their growth. They're so focused on protecting what they have that they're not building what they could become. That's not investable either. That's a fortress nobody wants to live in.

The magic happens in the balance.

Now here's the real question, and I want you to sit with this one: Would you invest your own money in your business?

I'm not asking whether you'd keep working here or whether you believe in the mission. I'm asking if you would take cash out of your personal account and buy stock in your company.

If you weren't the founder—if you were just an outside investor looking at the numbers—would your business attract you?

Growth-oriented but maintaining margins. Passing value back to the people who contribute. Building something that compounds over time.

That's the business G2s—your next-generation leaders—want to be part of. Not because they want to cash out. Because they want to build something worth owning.

## PROFITABILITY MATTERS BEYOND THE OWNERS

Let me tell you why I was proud to stand in front of our team at our quarterly business review this year.

Thirty percent profit margin. And $500,000 reinvested into compensation increases for the coming year.

Profitability isn't something the owners benefit from alone. When your business is profitable, you can reallocate resources to key contributors. You can further professionalize your operations. You can invest in growth. You can build something people actually want to be part of.

I don't want to be part of something that's dying. I want to be part of something that's growing.

Your best people feel the same way.

When the people in your organization look at your business, you want them to think, *Damn, I wish I could invest in that.* That's the feeling that creates loyalty. That's the feeling that attracts missionaries instead of mercenaries.

A healthy, profitable business isn't just good for the owners. It's good for everyone who contributes to it.

## CULTURE EATS STRATEGY FOR BREAKFAST. COMPENSATION EATS CULTURE FOR LUNCH.

Let's talk about compensation.

Most compensation structures are designed for the past. They're based on what you could afford when you hired someone, adjusted incrementally based on what you can afford now. They're reactive. They reward tenure more than contribution. They create ceilings that frustrate your best people.

We've tried to do something different: design compensation for the future we're building, not the past we're leaving behind.

Here's the philosophy.

Pay people like owners before they're owners. If you want people to think like owners, you can't pay them like employees. Create structures that align their interests with the business's interests. Make their success inseparable from the company's success.

Invest in your people before you have to. Don't wait until someone has one foot out the door to show them they're valued. The best retention strategy is proactive investment—in compensation, in development, in their quality of life.

Be transparent about how it works. Mystery breeds distrust. When people understand how compensation decisions are made—what drives them, what's possible, what the pathway looks like—they can invest in their own growth with clarity.

## What This Looks Like

When we upgraded our compensation model at the end of 2025, it wasn't a surprise announcement. Our team knew we were working toward this. They understood the 95/5 discipline that made it possible. They saw the connection between our financial health and their personal upside.

The upgrade wasn't a gift. It was a logical outcome of everything we'd built together.

That's the difference between compensation designed for the future and compensation designed for the past. One creates *partnership*. The other creates *transaction*.

## THE ROAD TO OWNERSHIP

Now let's talk about the ultimate expression of aligned compensation: ownership.

One of the most important decisions I made was to create a clear and simple road to ownership for every team member.

Not just the star salespeople. Not just the people who negotiate hard. Everyone.

From day one, every person who joins our team can see a pathway. If they want to—and not everyone does—they can become an owner of this company. They can build equity. They can participate in the long-term value they're helping create.

This matters for several reasons.

It attracts the right people. Mercenaries don't want ownership. They want cash now. Missionaries—the people who believe in what you're building—are energized by the possibility of ownership. The road to ownership is a filter that helps you select the right people.

It retains your best people. Your best people have options. They can leave anytime. Ownership creates stickiness, not because people are trapped, but because they're invested. They're not just working for you. They're building something that's partly theirs.

It builds a self-leading business. It all goes back to the plane analogy. A plane that can fly without you in the cockpit. A business that leads itself. That only works if other people have genuine ownership—not just responsibility, but actual skin in the game.

It creates legacy. I didn't build this business to sell it. I built it to last for generations. The road to ownership is how you transfer a business without losing its soul. New owners who grew up in the culture, who understand the values, who earned their stake over time.

## What This Looks Like

At ICG, we've diluted my equity stake intentionally. I went from one hundred percent ownership to thirty-eight percent. Not because I was forced to. Because I invited like-minded leaders who share the vision and values to become partners.

Every percentage point I gave up made the whole thing stronger. More engines on the plane. More people with genuine ownership of the outcome.

The road to ownership isn't one path. It's multiple paths depending on role, contribution, and ambition. But it's visible. It's documented. And it's available to anyone who wants to walk it.

# ENTITY STRUCTURE AND GOVERNANCE

Let me be clear about something: I am not a lawyer, and this section isn't legal advice. But I've learned enough through building, restructuring, and scaling businesses to know that the way you structure your entity either enables or constrains everything else. So I'll give you the principles. Your attorneys and accountants can give you the specifics.

If you're still operating as a sole proprietor with no formal entity, you have no separation between personal and business assets. You have no pathway to bring in partners. You have no vehicle for ownership transfer. You're building on sand.

Get the structure right early. It's much easier to set up correctly from the beginning than to untangle later.

Separate entities for separate purposes. Your operating business should be distinct from your personal assets. As you grow, you may need additional entities for different functions—holding companies, separate LLCs for different business lines, and so on.

Governance that scales. When it's just you, governance is simple—you decide. But as you add partners and owners, you need formal agreements. Operating agreements. Buy-sell provisions. Decision rights. Voting thresholds. When I went from one hundred percent ownership to thirty-eight percent, we didn't do it on a handshake. We documented everything—who decides what, how votes work, what happens if someone wants out, what happens if someone passes away. The stuff that feels like overkill when everyone agrees becomes essential when they don't.

Documentation that outlasts you. If you got hit by a bus tomorrow, could your business continue? Could your partners and team figure out who owns what, who decides what, and how the transition should work? Document everything. Update it regularly.

Annual valuations. A privately owned company doesn't have a stock price updating every ninety seconds. It's imperative for owners to establish a regular ritual of valuations—bringing enterprise value to the forefront, communicating progress, tracking value acceleration. If you don't know what your business is worth, you can't build a plan to make it worth more. And your G2 leaders can't see whether the equity they're building toward is actually growing. Valuations aren't vanity exercises. They're how you make the road to ownership real instead of theoretical.

Pro formas for equity transition. This is a key play in facilitating the handoff between G1 and G2. Forward-looking financial projections that show what the business looks like under different ownership scenarios—how equity dilution affects existing owners, what the revenue and profit picture looks like three to five years out. Pro formas make the road to ownership concrete. When an emerging leader can see the math—not Saša math, but actual projections—they stop hedging and start building.

## TRUST OVER EFFICIENCY

I opened this chapter with the fork in the road—manager-managed versus member-managed. Efficiency versus trust. We chose trust. Let me tell you what that choice actually looks like after you've lived with it for years.

Every section you just read is a trust play.

The 95/5 Rule is a trust play. When we stood in front of our team at QBR and shared the numbers—thirty-plus percent profitability and $500,000 reinvested into compensation—that wasn't a presentation. That was a trust deposit. Our team could see the direct line between disciplined spending and their own upside. They understood why we questioned every subscription, renegotiated every contract, ran lean everywhere else. The discipline wasn't austerity. It was investment in them.

The road to ownership is a trust play. When G2 leaders can see the value they're building, understand the transition pathway, and know the rules are documented and fair, they lean in. They commit. They stop keeping one foot out the door. Without that visibility, your best people hedge their bets. With it, they go all in.

The governance—the operating agreements, the valuations, the pro formas—all of it is trust infrastructure. It takes what could be ambiguous or political and makes it transparent. Documented. Fair.

Financial transparency is one of the most powerful trust-builders a leader has. When your team can see the connection between the financial health of the business and their own future, they stop being employees watching from the outside. They become partners invested in the outcome.

The manager-managed path would have been faster. Simpler. I would have kept one hundred percent ownership and made every decision myself. Some days, if I'm honest, that sounds pretty appealing.

But I wouldn't have Maria, Derek, Brent, Andrea, or any of the partners who now own this business alongside me. I wouldn't have a business that can fly without me in the cockpit.

Trust over efficiency. It's slower at the start. It's unstoppable at scale.

## THE FOUR PILLARS OF RESILIENCE

Let me zoom out and give you the framework we use for thinking about organizational resilience.

Resilience isn't just financial. It's built on four pillars.

- **Financial Resilience:** Cash reserves. Profitability. Diversified revenue. The ability to absorb shocks and invest in opportunities. This is what we've been discussing throughout this chapter.
- **Human Resilience:** Depth of talent. Leadership at every level. Cross-training so no single person is a bottleneck. The ability to lose someone important and continue operating.
- **Market Resilience:** Diversified client base. Multiple service lines. The ability to adapt when markets shift. Not being dependent on any single client, product, or channel.
- **Community Resilience:** Relationships with clients, partners, vendors, and industry peers that create goodwill and support. The network you can draw on when you need help.

A business that's strong in one pillar but weak in others isn't truly resilient. Financial strength means nothing if one key person leaves and everything falls apart. Human depth means nothing if a market shift makes your services obsolete.

Build all four. Balance all four. That's how you play for decades, not quarters.

## TRANSITION PLANNING

I want to end this chapter where we started—with legacy.

Everything in this book—the vision, the culture, the execution, the growth, the resilience—it's all building toward something bigger than any single year or any single person.

I'm entering a stage of life where I believe what I've learned needs to be shared. The dumb tax I've paid. The lessons I've adopted. The principles that actually work. Part of that sharing is this book. Part of it is Inspire Network and the coaching work we do.

But the deepest expression of legacy is what I leave behind at ICG. A business that leads itself. A team full of leaders. Partners who own not just equity, but the vision. Systems that work whether I'm in the building or on a beach in New Zealand.

Transition planning isn't something you do at the end. It's something you build from the beginning. Every partner I've brought in is part of the transition plan. Every leader I've developed is part of the transition plan. Every system I've documented, every process I've delegated, every piece of ownership I've shared—all of it is transition planning.

When you build this way, the transition isn't a crisis. It isn't a fire sale or a desperate search for a buyer. It's a natural evolution. The business doesn't end when you step back. It continues, carrying the values and culture forward into the next generation.

That's the legacy. That's what all of this is for.

## BEFORE YOU MOVE ON → SHOULDER TAPS FROM THIS CHAPTER

- Trust over efficiency. The member-managed path is slower at the start and unstoppable at scale. Everything in this chapter deepens the trust account. Everything runs at the speed of trust.
- Give your business its own lungs. Separate enterprise and personal assets. Psychologically, legally, financially. As long as the business is breathing through you, it can never outgrow you.
- The 95/5 Rule. Manage ninety-five percent like you're broke. Invest five percent like you have everything. Remove waste to prioritize people.
- Know your numbers. The 35/35/30 Rule structures your cash flow. The Forty Percent Rule keeps growth and profitability in balance. Return on assets tells you whether your capital is actually working. These aren't academic—they're the instruments in the cockpit.
- Compensation eats culture for lunch. Design it for the future you're building, not the past you're leaving behind. Pay people like owners before they're owners.
- Build the road to ownership. Make it visible. Make it documented. Make it available. The road to ownership

attracts missionaries, retains your best people, and builds a business that lasts for generations.

- Document everything. Operating agreements. Valuations. Pro formas. Governance. The stuff that feels like overkill when everyone agrees becomes essential when they don't.
- Build all four pillars. Financial, human, market, community. Strong in one but weak in others isn't resilient. It's fragile with good PR.
- Transition planning starts now. Not when you're ready to leave. Every partner, every leader, every system you build is part of the plan.

That completes both sides of the fuselage—the execution engine from the last chapter and the resiliency engine from this one. Together, they're the structural capital that holds everything together when turbulence hits.

We've covered the entire framework, from pressure to turning point to the work. But this isn't just my story. It's an invitation. In the epilogue, we'll come full circle and talk about the garden you're building.

# Tending the Garden You're Building

You made it.

Nineteen chapters. War stories and business frameworks. The engineering brain and the emotional brain, learning to dance together.

Now what?

Here's where most business books fail you. They deliver the insight, close with something inspiring, and leave you nodding your head on a plane somewhere between "That was interesting" and "I should do something about that."

Then you land. Check your email. Put out three fires. And six months later, you can't remember a single thing you read.

Not this time.

Because this book isn't really about me.

It's about you.

Your pressure. Your turning point. Your work.

Let's talk about all three.

## YOUR PRESSURE

I grew up in Bosnia, in an experimental city where ideas collided and anything seemed possible. Theater, rugby, violin, philosophy, engineering—I could try it all. Learn it all. Become whoever I wanted to become.

Then war came and tested every bit of it.

That's Act One. The forging.

Character. Natural ability. Embracing the suck. Finding meaning.

You have your own version.

Maybe yours wasn't artillery fire. Maybe it was a business that failed. A relationship that shattered. A moment when everything you thought you knew got thrown into a furnace, and you had to figure out who you were without the scaffolding.

Or maybe your forging was quieter. The slow pressure of never quite fitting in. The weight of expectations that weren't yours. The grinding work of building something from nothing, while everyone watched and waited for you to fail.

It doesn't matter what it looked like.

What matters is what it made you.

The question Act One asks isn't "What happened to you?" It's "Who did you become because of it?"

And more importantly: Is that who you want to be? Or just who circumstances shaped you into?

Because here's the thing about pressure—it doesn't choose your shape. It only reveals what was possible all along. The decision about who to become is still yours.

## YOUR TURNING POINT

Act Two is where everything shifts.

For me, it was realizing that the same skills that kept me alive during war—adaptability, trust, team, purpose—weren't just survival skills. They were leadership skills. And that the command-and-control style that built my business was now strangling it.

I couldn't force growth. I could only create conditions for it.

That's the gardening revelation. The moment you stop being the hero and start being the cultivator.

Your turning point might look different.

Maybe it's the realization that you've become the bottleneck. That your team can't grow because you won't let go. That your need to be needed is the very thing holding everyone back.

Maybe it's watching someone you trusted walk out the door and recognizing, painfully, that they were right to leave.

Maybe it's simpler. A quiet Tuesday when you look around and think: *There has to be a better way.*

There is.

Purpose worthy of someone's best efforts. People who are leaders. Trust built in a thousand small moments. Conflict embraced, not avoided. Rituals that become culture. Adaptation when the world shifts. Results that create more leaders, not more followers.

That's the framework. Not because I invented it—I just lived it long enough to name it.

The question Act Two asks isn't "Do you know the right principles?" It's "Are you willing to change how you lead?"

Most leaders aren't sitting still. They're spinning. Working harder at the same things that stopped working years ago. Grinding through the same patterns, the same conversations, the same exhausting cycles, and wondering why nothing changes.

Effort isn't the problem. Direction is.

## YOUR WORK

Act Three is where it gets real.

Building your four capitals: human, client, social, and structural.

The practical application of everything that came before.

This is where I tell you I went from owning one hundred percent of a company I was killing myself to run to owning thirty-eight percent of a company that runs without me.

And that thirty-eight percent is worth more than the hundred ever was.

That's not generosity. That's mathematics.

One leader making all the decisions equals one brain solving problems. Ten leaders making decisions equals ten brains. Multiplication beats hoarding. Every time.

But it's not glamorous. It's showing up to the same meetings with the same rhythms and the same accountability conversations week after week. It's having the hard talk you've been avoiding. It's letting go of control when every instinct screams to hold tighter. It's trusting people who haven't earned it yet because that's the only way they ever will.

The work is mundane. The results are magical.

The question Act Three asks isn't "Do you have the right systems?" It's "Will you do the boring work long enough for it to compound?"

Elite teams aren't built in moments of inspiration. They're built on ordinary Tuesdays when nobody's watching, and the right thing to do is also the hard thing to do.

## THE GARDEN

So here you are.

You've walked through pressure, turning points, and work. Mine, and now yours.

You know what to do. You've always known.

The conversation you've been avoiding? You know which one.

The person who isn't right? You know who.

The control you're gripping too tightly? You feel it in your hands right now.

This isn't about becoming me. I don't want you to lead like Saša Mirković—I want you to lead like the best version of yourself with tools that actually work.

Your version will look different than mine. It should. That's the whole point.

I want to leave you with a moment.

It's a random Tuesday. Nothing special about it.

You're driving home, and it hits you.

You didn't solve a single crisis today. Nobody called with an emergency. No fires. No decisions that couldn't be made without you.

For a split second, panic. *Am I still needed?*

Then you realize.

That's not failure. That's the goal.

You built something that doesn't need you to function. Which means you can finally focus on the work only you can do—vision, relationships, the next mountain.

That flutter in your chest? That's not panic.

That's freedom.

The world doesn't need more managers.

The world needs gardeners. People willing to do the patient work of cultivation. People who understand that you can't force growth—you can only create conditions for it. People who measure success not by what they control but by what flourishes without them.

That's the **Inspire** Code. Blue brain and red brain. Engineering and emotion. Logic and heart.

Working together to build something that lasts.

Now close this book and go build your garden.

— *Saša Mirković*

*War survivor. Garden builder. Still learning.*

*Your turn.*

## Thank You For Reading My Book!

Scan here to book a 20-minute intro call and see how our team can help you build a self-leading team.

# Acknowledgments

I am grateful to live in a country where I can be free to be myself. That freedom comes with responsibility to afford the same freedom to others around me. Making a living doing this is a gift that I cannot over-acknowledge. If you lived where I did and saw what I saw, you would know why this is my #1 value.

**Laura.**

Surviving the siege of Sarajevo and leaving everything to start over my life as an immigrant came with a big hole. If you survived a war or left your country or lost everything, you know what I am talking about.

You filled that hole with love. Slowly, completely, permanently. What was a wound became bedrock.

Your humanity. Your humility. You bring the best out of me and quietly neutralize the parts that could go sideways if left unchecked.

We don't just share a marriage. We share a life—fully merged. The household. The kids. The businesses. This book. There is no version of any of it that doesn't have you in it.

You say, "Screw it, let's go," even when you're scared to death.

That's you. That's everything. You are a badass. I love you.

**Oscar. Stella. Kosta.**

Being a father is one of the most important roles in life. Being *your* father is the biggest joy and source of pride I have. Watching you grow into your own people is the greatest reward I could ask for.

Be curious. Be useful. Be courageous.

Everything else will follow. I love you.

**Nataša.**

You are badass in your own way.

Our parents are proud of the contributions we are both making to our family legacy. The sacrifices you have made for your family are what make you the artist, human, and leader that you are.

You are the embodiment of the Inspire Code in your own right.

I love you.

**Maria. Brent. Derek. Jo. Kayla. Andrea. Mark.**

I am grateful for the meaningful relationships we have built doing meaningful work—the exact kind described in this book. Your trust in me as a leader and as a partner is humbling. What we have built together is the second most important self-leading team I have ever been a part of. Right after the one this book is dedicated to.

This book is my point of view. My side of the beach ball. But the work it takes to build a team like ours is never one person's work. I might be the instigator. You are the filter. What emerged as best practice—what made it onto these pages—is joint. Like the Beatles. Like U2. Like Hamilton. It is us, together, that created what this book is actually about.

You trust the leader first, then the mission. I don't take that lightly.

What I am most grateful for is this: we are not afraid to go anywhere to find the best idea. We have a principle—the best interest of the business trumps our own best interests. That's not a policy. That's a sacrifice. And you make it, every time.

That's what self-leading teams actually look like.

**Ray Kelly.**

This book is a testament to the impact you made on me as a person and as a leader. To say I am grateful is an understatement.

Thank you for telling me the truth—no matter how stupid my ideas were. For helping me see it, own it, and change it.

Doug Lennick lit the fire. You helped me keep it burning and turn it into something real.

I am proud to be one of the people with whom you shape cultures and develop leaders. Thank you for being the role model of what a coach can be.

**Maureen Buckley.**

Your integrity is the real thing. You give me tough love when I need it and support when I need it—sometimes in the same conversation. You are my advocate and my truth-teller.

Everyone should have a Maureen.

Thank you.

**Doug Lennick.**

You lit the fire.

You gave me permission to rewrite the script of my life story if I didn't like it. You put enough pressure on me to actually start writing—and when I got stuck, you introduced me to Kathy Jordan. The rest is in your hands right now.

You show me constantly, with the power of your example, that philosophy and business are brother and sister. That winning by doing good is not just possible—it's the point.

**Kathy Jordan.**

You saw it first.

We started with whitepapers. What you were actually doing was teaching me to think out loud—on paper, with precision. You diagnosed me with a "kaleidoscope mind." Thoughts came fast, colorful, pointed in seventeen directions at once.

You didn't slow it down. You helped me find the pattern in it.

I had the commitment. You gave me the courage. Whitepapers became a memoir. A memoir became a leadership book. A leadership book became the Elite Teams Framework.

None of that happens without you asking one more question.

**Christin.**

We met on my first day in upstate New York. The collaborative energy has been growing and finding its form ever since.

You are one of the good people. That's not a small thing. Over time, you became a true rockstar—a leader who puts the team and the mission first. From moving to Albany to help build what is now Inspire Confidence Group, to saying yes when I asked you to join Kathy and me on this project—you showed up every time.

Our collaboration is a living example of the concepts in this book. It helped us name why certain things didn't come as naturally as we expected. It pushed us to embrace conflict with the problem—not each other—and find solutions that wouldn't have existed otherwise.

The book you are reading is one of those solutions.

I am grateful for a partnership that allows us both to be fully ourselves and still create something worth creating. Here's to many more.

Put your mask on first.

**The People of Inspire Teams.**

You are the reason this book exists. Not as inspiration. As evidence.

To the Inspire Holdings Teams—Inspire Confidence Group, the Inspire Network, and Inspire Tax—you are the teaching hospital. Where the best practices are developed, tested, and refined. Where leaders learn by doing.

To the Inspire Network Community—a "team of teams" where coaches are embedded in client businesses, ideas flow in every direction, and the lines between "our team" and "your team" blur in the best possible way. That is not an accident. That is the whole point.

Building self-leading teams takes choosing abundance over scarcity. Every day. It is not easy. It is the right thing to do. The impact on our families and the communities we live in is real. We are making a difference—not just in business, but in the world.

Lead on.

**Jason Ackerman.**

When I hired you as my health coach, I did not dream it would lead to a lifelong friendship.

You nudged me to CrossFit and convinced me I am an athlete—even if I have to age into elite status. Your curiosity showed me that this work transcends my own teams. Your weird sense of humor taught me to take myself less seriously. Everyone needs to have a Jason.

Thank you for being you, brother.

**Game Changer Publishing.**

Cris Cawley and Tracy Shepherd—thank you for the tenacity to land the plane. Six and a half years of work needed a final push. You were it.

# Recommended Reading List

*These are the books that shaped how I think, lead, and build. Some I've read twice. Most I've listened to at 75 miles per hour while I let Margo drive. All of them left a mark.*

---

## LEADERSHIP & TEAM DEVELOPMENT


Brooks, Arthur C. *From Strength to Strength: Finding Success, Happiness, and Deep Purpose in the Second Half of Life.* Portfolio/Penguin, 2022.

Buford, Bob. *Halftime: Moving from Success to Significance.* Zondervan, 1994.

Clear, James. *Atomic Habits: An Easy & Proven Way to Build Good Habits & Break Bad Ones.* Avery, 2018.

Collins, Jim. *Good to Great: Why Some Companies Make the Leap and Others Don't.* HarperBusiness, 2001.

Covey, Stephen R. *The 7 Habits of Highly Effective People: Powerful Lessons in Personal Change.* Free Press, 1989.

Covey, Stephen M.R. *The Speed of Trust: The One Thing That Changes Everything.* Free Press, 2006.

Coyle, Daniel. *The Culture Code: The Secrets of Highly Successful Groups.* Bantam, 2018.

Dalio, Ray. *Principles: Life and Work.* Simon & Schuster, 2017.

Duckworth, Angela. *Grit: The Power of Passion and Perseverance.* Scribner, 2016.

Dweck, Carol S. *Mindset: The New Psychology of Success.* Random House, 2006.

Evans, Ceri. *Perform Under Pressure: Change the Way You Feel, Think and Act Under Pressure.* HarperCollins, 2019.

Gerber, Michael E. *The E-Myth Revisited: Why Most Small Businesses Don't Work and What to Do About It.* HarperBusiness, 1995.

Gordon, Jon. *The Coffee Bean: A Simple Lesson to Create Positive Change.* Wiley, 2019.

Groeschel, Craig. *Lead Like It Matters: 7 Leadership Principles for a Church That Lasts.* Zondervan, 2022.

Guidara, Will. *Unreasonable Hospitality: The Remarkable Power of Giving People More Than They Expect.* Optimism Press, 2022.

Hastings, Reed, and Erin Meyer. *No Rules Rules: Netflix and the Culture of Reinvention.* Penguin Press, 2020.

Kerr, James. *Legacy: What the All Blacks Can Teach Us About the Business of Life.* Constable, 2013.

Kinney, Derrick. *Good Money Revolution: How to Make More Money to Do More Good.* HarperCollins Leadership, 2022.

Krzyzewski, Mike (Coach K), and Donald T. Phillips. *Leading with the Heart: Coach K's Successful Strategies for Basketball, Business, and Life.* Warner Books, 2000.

Krzyzewski, Mike (Coach K). *The Gold Standard: Building a World-Class Team.* Business Plus, 2009.

Lencioni, Patrick. *The Five Dysfunctions of a Team: A Leadership Fable.* Jossey-Bass, 2002.

Lencioni, Patrick. *The 6 Types of Working Genius: A Better Way to Understand Your Gifts, Your Frustrations, and Your Team.* Matt Holt Books, 2022.

Leider, Richard J. *Calling Cards: Uncover Your Calling.* Berrett-Koehler, 2015.

Lennick, Doug, and Fred Kiel. *Moral Intelligence 2.0: Enhancing Business Performance and Leadership Success in Turbulent Times.* Pearson FT Press, 2011.

Lennick, Doug, and Chuck Wachendorfer. *Don't Wait for Someone Else to Fix It: 8 Essentials to Enhance Your Leadership Impact at Work, Home, and Anywhere Else That Needs You.* Wiley, 2023.

Mattis, James, and Bing West. *Call Sign Chaos: Learning to Lead.* Random House, 2019.

Maxwell, John C. *The 5 Levels of Leadership: Proven Steps to Maximize Your Potential.* Center Street, 2011.

McChrystal, Stanley. *Team of Teams: New Rules of Engagement for a Complex World.* Portfolio/Penguin, 2015.

McChrystal, Stanley, and Anna Butrico. *Risk: A User's Guide.* Portfolio/Penguin, 2021.

McRaven, William H. *The Wisdom of the Bullfrog: Leadership Made Simple (But Not Easy).* Grand Central Publishing, 2023.

Michelli, Joseph A. *The New Gold Standard: 5 Leadership Principles for Creating a Legendary*

*Customer Experience Courtesy of the Ritz-Carlton Hotel Company.* McGraw-Hill, 2008.

Palaveev, Philip. *The Ensemble Practice: A Team-Based Approach to Building a Superior Wealth Management Firm.* Bloomberg Press, 2012.

Palaveev, Philip. *G2: Building the Next Generation.* Bloomberg Financial, 2017.

Scott, Susan. *Fierce Conversations: Achieving Success at Work and in Life One Conversation at a Time.* Viking, 2002.

Sinek, Simon. *Leaders Eat Last: Why Some Teams Pull Together and Others Don't.* Portfolio/Penguin, 2014.

Sinek, Simon. *Start with Why: How Great Leaders Inspire Everyone to Take Action.* Portfolio/Penguin, 2009.

Sinek, Simon. *The Infinite Game.* Portfolio/Penguin, 2019.

Sullivan, Dan, and Dr. Benjamin Hardy. *10x Is Easier Than 2x: How World-Class Entrepreneurs Achieve More by Doing Less.* Hay House Business, 2023.

Sullivan, Dan, and Dr. Benjamin Hardy. *The Gap and the Gain: The High Achievers' Guide to Happiness, Confidence, and Success.* Hay House Business, 2021.

Sullivan, Dan. *The 4 C's Formula: Your Building Blocks of Growth: Commitment, Courage, Capability and Confidence.* Ethos Collective, audiobook.

Sullivan, Dan. *My Plan for Living to 156: Imaginatively Extend Your Lifetime to Transform How You Live in the Present.* 2018.

Tjan, Anthony K. *Good People: The Only Leadership Decision That Really Matters.* Portfolio/Penguin, 2017.

Wickman, Gino. *Traction: Get a Grip on Your Business.* BenBella Books, 2011.

Wickman, Gino, and Mark C. Winters. *Rocket Fuel: The One Essential Combination That Will Get You More of What You Want from Your Business.* BenBella Books, 2015.

Willink, Jocko, and Leif Babin. *Extreme Ownership: How U.S. Navy SEALs Lead and Win.* St. Martin's Press, 2015.

---

## EXECUTION & OPERATIONS

Covey, Stephen R., Chris McChesney, and Jim Huling. *The 4 Disciplines of Execution: Achieving Your Wildly Important Goals.* Free Press, 2012.

Cunningham, Keith J. *The Road Less Stupid: Advice from the Chairman of the Board.* Keys to the Vault, 2017.

Heath, Dan. *Upstream: The Quest to Solve Problems Before They Happen.* Avid Reader Press, 2020.

---

## PSYCHOLOGY, BEHAVIOR & PERFORMANCE

Bridges, William. *Transitions: Making Sense of Life's Changes.* Addison-Wesley, 1980.

Chapman, Gary, and Paul White. *The Five Languages of Appreciation in the Workplace: Empowering Organizations by Encouraging People.* Northfield Publishing, 2011.

Csikszentmihalyi, Mihaly. *Flow: The Psychology of Optimal Experience.* Harper & Row, 1990.

Epstein, David. *Range: Why Generalists Triumph in a Specialized World.* Riverhead Books, 2019.

Frankl, Viktor E. *Man's Search for Meaning.* Beacon Press, 1959.

Gallwey, W. Timothy. *The Inner Game of Work: Focus, Learning, Pleasure, and Mobility in the Workplace.* Random House, 2000.

Grant, Adam. *Originals: How Non-Conformists Move the World.* Viking, 2016.

Grant, Adam. *Think Again: The Power of Knowing What You Don't Know.* Viking, 2021.

Grant, Adam. *Hidden Potential: The Science of Achieving Greater Things.* Viking, 2023.

Haidt, Jonathan. *The Happiness Hypothesis: Finding Modern Truth in Ancient Wisdom.* Basic Books, 2006.

Heath, Chip, and Dan Heath. *Made to Stick: Why Some Ideas Survive and Others Die.* Random House, 2007.

Heath, Chip, and Dan Heath. *Switch: How to Change Things When Change Is Hard.* Crown Business, 2010.

Housel, Morgan. *The Psychology of Money: Timeless Lessons on Wealth, Greed, and Happiness.* Harriman House, 2020.

Housel, Morgan. *Same as Ever: A Guide to What Never Changes.* Portfolio/Penguin, 2023.

Leonard, George. *Mastery: The Keys to Success and Long-Term Fulfillment.* Dutton, 1991.

Marcus Aurelius. *Meditations.* c. 161–180 CE. Trans. Gregory Hays. Modern Library, 2002.

Roth, Bob. *Strength in Stillness: The Power of Transcendental Meditation.* Simon & Schuster, 2018.

Sandberg, Sheryl. *Lean In: Women, Work, and the Will to Lead.* Knopf, 2013.

---

## COMMUNICATION, STORYTELLING & IDEAS

Allen, Mike, Jim VandeHei, and Roy Schwartz. *Smart Brevity: The Power of Saying More with Less.* Workman Publishing, 2022.

Chouinard, Yvon, and Vincent Stanley. *The Responsible Company: What We've Learned from Patagonia's First 40 Years.* Patagonia Books, 2012.

Coelho, Paulo. *The Alchemist.* HarperOne, 1988. Trans. Alan R. Clarke, 1993.

Ferriss, Tim. *Tools of Titans: The Tactics, Routines, and Habits of Billionaires, Icons, and World-Class Performers.* Houghton Mifflin Harcourt, 2016.

Gladwell, Malcolm. *The Tipping Point: How Little Things Can Make a Big Difference.* Little, Brown and Company, 2000.

Gladwell, Malcolm. *Outliers: The Story of Success.* Little, Brown and Company, 2008.

Gladwell, Malcolm. *Talking to Strangers: What We Should Know About the People We Don't Know.* Little, Brown and Company, 2019.

Junger, Sebastian. *Tribe: On Homecoming and Belonging.* Twelve, 2016.

Koch, Richard. *The 80/20 Principle: The Secret to Achieving More with Less.* Currency/Doubleday, 1997.

Koch, Richard. *Unreasonable Success and How to Achieve It.* Piatkus, 2020.

Koch, Richard, and Greg Lockwood. *Simplify: How the Best Businesses in the World Succeed.* Piatkus, 2016.

Leslie, Ian. *John & Paul: A Love Story in Songs.* Celadon Books, 2025.

Rubin, Rick. *The Creative Act: A Way of Being.* Penguin Press, 2023.

Seinfeld, Jerry. *Is This Anything?* Simon & Schuster, 2020.

---

## BUSINESS STRATEGY, FINANCE & SCALING

Cagan, Marty. *Inspired: How to Create Tech Products Customers Love.* 2nd ed. Wiley, 2018.

Hardy, Dr. Benjamin. *The Science of Scaling: Grow Your Business Bigger and Faster Than You Think Possible.* 2024.

Lee, Kai-Fu, and Chen Qiufan. *AI 2041: Ten Visions for Our Future.* Currency, 2021.

Lennick, Doug, and Kathleen Jordan. *Leveraging Your Financial Intelligence: At the Intersection of Money, Health and Happiness.* Wiley, 2020.

Perkins, Bill. *Die with Zero: Getting All You Can from Your Money and Your Life.* Houghton Mifflin Harcourt, 2020.

---

## MEMOIR, BIOGRAPHY & HISTORY

Bills, Peter. *The Jersey: The Secret Behind New Zealand's All Blacks, the World's Most Successful Sports Team.* Macmillan, 2017.

Castoro, Amy A., and Roy O. Williams. *Bridging Generations: Transitioning Family Wealth and Values for a Sustainable Legacy.* 2017.

Chernow, Ron. *Alexander Hamilton.* Penguin Press, 2004.

Harari, Yuval Noah. *Sapiens: A Brief History of Humankind.* Harper, 2015.

Isaacson, Walter. *Steve Jobs.* Simon & Schuster, 2011.

McConaughey, Matthew. *Greenlights.* Crown, 2020.

Paul, Gregor. *The Captain's Run.* Upstart Press, 2019.

---

## EXIT PLANNING & BUSINESS VALUE (CEPA)

Goodbread, Justin. *Your Baby's Ugly: Maximize the Value of Your Business or You Will Have Nothing to Sell.* Financially Simple Publishing, 2020.

Snider, Christopher M., and Scott Snider. *Walking to Destiny: 11 Actions An Owner Must Take to Rapidly Grow Value & Unlock Wealth.* 2nd ed. Exit Planning Institute, 2017.

www.ingramcontent.com/pod-product-compliance
Lightning Source LLC
LaVergne TN
LVHW100510110826
845146LV00002B/583

* 9 7 9 8 9 0 1 5 8 2 0 9 1 *